Celine Whitfield
3324 Tulip Dr.
Hazel Crest, Illinois
60429

Whatever Became Of . . . ?

EIGHTH SERIES

Also by the Author

Lamparski's Hidden Hollywood: Where the Stars Lived, Loved, and Died

Whatever Became Of . . . ?

EIGHTH SERIES

The best (updated) and newest of the famous Lamparski profiles of personalities of yesteryear

Richard Lamparski

CROWN PUBLISHERS, INC.
NEW YORK

Published by Crown Publishers, Inc., One Park Avenue,
New York, New York 10016, and simultaneously in
Canada by General Publishing Company Limited
Portions of the material contained in this book have been
previously published in *Whatever Became Of . . . ?*,
Volumes I–V, by Richard Lamparski
Library of Congress Cataloging in Publication Data
Lamparski, Richard.
Whatever became of . . . ?
1. United States—Biography. 2. Performing arts—
United States—Biography. I. Title.
CT220.L285 1982 790.2'092'2 [B] 82-5039
ISBN: 0-517-54346-X (hardcover) AACR2
0-517-54855-0 (paperback)
Book design by Camilla Filancia
10 9 8 7 6 5 4 3 2 1
First Edition

For *George Eells*

and

Don Miller—

colleagues whose humor

and encouragement

have so often nourished me

Contents

Acknowledgments

The author gratefully acknowledges those who have helped to make this book possible:

Bobby Downey
Dick Lynch
Shelly Davis
Jay Loft-Lynn
Eddie Brandt's Saturday Matinee
De Witt Bodeen
Mike Marx
Roy Bishop
Metro-Goldwyn-Mayer
Paramount Pictures
Columbia Pictures
Universal Pictures
Beverly Hills Public Library
Don Miller
Warner Brothers
National Screen Service
Michael Back
Sloan Nibley
Howard W. Hays
Charles Higham
R. C. Perry
Michael Knowles
Don Koll
Anton La Vey
Donna Schaeffer
Paul Schaeffer
Peter Schaeffer
Richard Schaeffer
Schaeffer Photo Lab
Tony Slide
Jon Virzi
Virginia I. Reidy
Sarah Richardson
Art Ronnie
Terry T. Roach and the Staff of the Library of the Academy of Motion Pictures Arts and Sciences
William Bass
Roy Bishop
Jimmy Jeneji
Jim Janisch
James Brennan
Peter Machiaverna
Jeff Lenburg
Greg Lenburg
Bob Cushman
Don Schneider of the Electric Theatre Museum
Mathew Tombers
Richard Fletcher
Tim Doherty
Samson De Brier
George Eells
Michael R. Hawks
Doug Hart's Back Lot
Diana Serra Cary
Chapman's Picture Palace
Bill Chapman
Wayne Parks
Marc Wanamaker of the Bison Archives
Tom Fulbright

Whatever Became Of . . . ?

EIGHTH SERIES

The late Fuzzy Knight and Iris were a romantic duo in The Singing Sheriff (1944).

Iris Adrian

The sharp-tongued, brassy blonde was born Iris Adrian Hofstadter in Los Angeles on May 29, 1912. "I tell my age," she says, "because I want credit for all the time I've done."

Her father died during the flu epidemic at the end of World War I. Iris left the eighth grade to go to work. "I never dug school anyway, so that was fine with me," she recalls.

The teenager won a "perfect back" contest and was hired as a chorine in a revue at Hollywood's Paramount Theatre. From that show she went into Fred Waring's *Rah Rah Days,* where she danced and sometimes took over the lead from Dorothy Lee.

In New York City Iris played in *The New Yorkers* (1930), another Fred Waring show. Waring liked her so much he used her in his next production, where she was spotted by Flo Ziegfeld, who signed her for his *Ziegfeld Follies of 1931.* It was in that show that she met another memorable blonde, the flashy Marion Martin (married and living in Santa Monica, California). The two became close friends and worked together later at Nils T. Granlund's Hollywood Restaurant on Broadway. It was there that Iris Adrian began to develop her skill at comedy by working in skits.

Her flawless timing and delivery of lines led many to believe she often wrote her own dialogue in movies. Recently, with no script in front of her, she made the following remarks:

"I never went with actors. Basically they're

bums who got lucky in the looks department. Very vain. It would be like dating another dame."

"I feel great, but every time my Social Security check comes in it reminds me of my age. Believe me, a dame over forty is in big trouble."

"Iris is not quite a millionaire, but don't worry about her. I socked all the money I made into real estate years ago and made a bundle when I sold out a while back. I got rid of everything, including the damn tenants. No more aggravation for this broad!"

"I've been married to the same guy for over twenty-five years. The others—yes, honey, Iris has been wed before—only lasted about two years each. Let's face it, that's as long as the romance lasts anyway. Then guys start looking around, and frankly, I hadn't gone blind either. I always liked cute guys."

On the screen she played walk-ons, bit parts, featured roles, and once was costarred with the late Frank Jenks in a B feature, *Shake Hands with Murder* (1944). Two of her best parts were as the murderess "Two-Gun Gertie" in *Roxie Hart* (1942) and as the loud-mouth cutie in *Lady of Burlesque* (1943). Playing another stripper in *The Trouble with Women* (1947), she sang a song, "Trap That Wolf," that had a line in defense of her honor: "I have, too, been a good wife—five times!" She was usually tough but never really mean.

Some of her other screen credits are *Paramount on Parade* (1930), *Gay Deception* (1935), *Stage Struck* (1936), *Road to Zanzibar* (1941), *The Paleface* (1948), *My Favorite Spy* (1951), *That Darn Cat* (1964), and *Paternity* (1981).

Iris guested frequently with Jack Benny, for more than twenty years, on his television programs and in the shows he took on the road. She is still close friends with Giselle MacKenzie (married and living in Encino, California) from those tours. Her other longtime chum is silent and early talkie star Alice White (single and living in the Hollywood Hills).

Iris Adrian is the wife of "Fido" Murphy, a former professional football player. They live in a hillside home near Warner Brothers and Columbia Pictures. Although she does not own any animals, she feeds many of the dogs and cats in the area. Says Ms. Adrian: "I never had any kids, and the older I get the gladder I am. But animals are God's kids and we damn well better be good to all of them. They're nicer than most of us."

Iris Adrian holding a copy of Dime-Store Days, a recent book that featured many of her photos.

Richard Lamparski

Shirley Temple and John Agar were one of the most publicized and popular couples in the world in 1946.

John Agar

The actor who became famous as Shirley Temple's husband (her first) was born in Chicago on January 21, 1921. His father headed the family-owned meat-packing company. While John was in the army (an air force sergeant) he was visiting his mother's friend ZaSu Pitts. The former star's next-door neighbor, Shirley Temple, asked John to take her to a party hosted by her boss, David O. Selznick. At the party, the producer felt Agar out about an acting career, and after John's army discharge he was put under contract.

When Shirley Temple became Mrs. John Agar in 1946 they announced that they would manage on his earnings—then $150 a week—and save all of hers, and moved into what had been her dollhouse on her parents' property. The Agars were surely the most popular newlywed couple in the United States.

John made his debut in *Fort Apache* (1948) with his wife, and they were teamed again in *Adventure in Baltimore* (1949). But almost from the beginning of their marriage, rumors of discord filtered through Hollywood and into the press. The overnight success and the inevitable title of "Mr. Shirley Temple" set Agar off on a drinking spree that brought them to a bitter divorce in 1949.

John stayed with Selznick for five years, although all of his films, such as *She Wore a Yellow Ribbon* (1949) and *Breakthrough* (1949), were made on loan-out. His divorce didn't stop his career, but neither did it slow his drinking. By 1951 his numerous arrests for drunk driving had brought him sixty days on a prison farm. In May 1951 a judge refused to marry him to the woman who is his present wife until he drank enough black coffee to be sober for the ceremony. Two years later he was arrested twice in one day and drew a four-month sentence.

In 1954 John made three features, including *Shield for Murder.* He then began making low-budget science-fiction and horror movies, almost an irreversible course to oblivion in Hollywood. *Revenge of the Creature* (1955) helped. There was also the cheapie *Young Fury* (1965) and a bit part in *Chisum* (1970).

John tried a number of business ventures, without much success. He attempted to form a lecture bureau that offered movie stars, and briefly operated a chain of cotton-candy concessions. He has also sold real estate and insurance.

Of his acting career he has said: "I never made a movie that pleased me, but living has given me more dimension than I had then. I simply wasn't ready when it was handed to me. Yes, I'd really like another shot at it."

His mentions of Shirley Temple are infrequent and always gracious, but he has not heard from his ex-wife or their daughter since the divorce. "I know that Shirley and I are now grandparents," he said recently. "That is because it was in the news. I was not invited to her wedding. We are not in touch."

Agar has been sober now for over a decade. He has two grown sons by his second wife. John and his family live only a few blocks away from three major studios in Burbank, but he has not had an acting role since *King Kong* (1976), in which he played a public official and was billed fourteenth.

Asked what he is doing at present, he replied: "I'm attempting to reactivate an acting career."

John Agar today, posed in the den of his home beside a poster of a picture he made in 1956.

Brian Aherne in the early forties.

Brian Aherne

The dapper English leading man of the stage and screen was born on May 2, 1902, in King's Norton, Worcestershire. At the age of three he began acting with an amateur group led by his mother. As a young boy he trained for several years with the Italia Conti, a noted acting school. He became a serious student of architecture, which he intended to make his career. When he couldn't find a job in that profession, Brian decided to try acting, "until something better comes along."

By the time Guthrie McClintic brought him to the U.S. to play on Broadway with Katharine Cornell in *The Barretts of Wimpole Street* (1931), Aherne had established himself in England as one of the most promising young thespians of the day. He had had success in England in both plays and films. *Romeo and Juliet* (1934) and *The Constant Wife* (1951) were among the other plays he did with the late Ms. Cornell.

Aherne was never under contract, so he could pick and choose what he did in pictures. His first Hollywood film, *Song of Songs* (1933) with Marlene Dietrich, was a dismal failure. Although he made many movies during the next thirty years, he never became a box-office draw. He was often cast in roles that had been patented by some other, more magnetic personality. In *The Fountain* (1934) he played a Ronald Colman part. *Captain Fury* (1939) cried out for Erroll Flynn. *A Night to Remember* (1958) was meant for Cary Grant. He did them all capably, but in none of his screen appearances did he radiate real star quality.

He was a handsome foil for such stars as Constance Bennett, Joan Crawford, Helen Hayes, Katharine Hepburn, Rosalind Russell (his favorite), Merle Oberon, and Loretta Young. Bette Davis, however, once said that during a scene of great intensity she found him looking not at her but at himself in a mirror behind her.

Brian brought a great dignity to the role of Emperor Maxmilian in *Juarez* (1939) and engendered a real sympathy for the character. It won him an Oscar nomination. He more than held his own with a very well thought-out performance amid strong competition in *My Son, My Son* (1940). Whenever chance presented itself Aherne showed himself to be a most engaging light comedian, as in *Merrily We Live* (1938), *A Night to Remember* (1942), and *My Sister Eileen* (1942).

He was reunited in 1960 with Katharine Cornell in *Dear Liar,* which they did on Broadway and on tour. He had great success as "Professor Higgins" in *My Fair Lady* on stage in the sixties. He was last seen on Broadway in *The Chinese Prime Minister* in 1965.

In his private life Brian Aherne seems more glamorous than he was on stage or screen. He was married for four years to Joan Fontaine, at the peak of her fame and beauty. They lived part of the time on a ranch. When in Hollywood, they held forth in the palatial beach house that had been built for silent star Norma Talmadge. He and his second wife lived there until recently, entertaining longtime friends such as Greta Garbo, Olivia de Havilland, Lillian Gish, and Marlene Dietrich. They sold the property in the late seventies for several million dollars. Most of the time now the Ahernes live in part of an ancient châlet overlooking a lake in Switzerland.

His autobiography, *A Proper Job,* was published in 1969. Aherne also wrote *A Dreadful Man* in 1979, a collection of letters and recollections concerning his friend George Sanders.

There are two big roles for which he was seriously considered, in *A Tale of Two Cities* and *Lost Horizon.* Either would have given his career a big boost. Both parts went to his close friend Ronald Colman. Asked if the loss of these assignments and the Academy Award had been severe disappointments, he replied with his familiar suavity, "No, not really. You see, I never have taken acting very seriously."

Jon Virzi

Brian Aherne today.

Lola Albright is best known as the sultry night-club singer and girlfriend of "Peter Gunn" on the TV series of the same name.

Lola Albright

"Peter Gunn's" lady was born on July 20, 1924, in Akron, Ohio.

Lola's original goal was to act on radio. She got her first job at Cleveland's WTAM as a receptionist and typist. Then she moved to WJW in the same capacity. She was only nineteen years old when she married a radio executive and moved with him to Chicago.

An advertising executive in Chicago spotted her and offered a job as a model. "I modeled in shampoo and toothpaste ads," she has said. "I hated all of it, but my husband had children and we needed the extra money."

The glamour photographer Paul Hesse suggested she come to Hollywood and try for a career in movies. Lola was screen-tested by Metro-Goldwyn-Mayer. "I had no desire to be in pictures," she admitted recently. "But the money was just too tempting." When the studio offered her a contract, she accepted.

During her year under contract to the Culver City lot and another as a Columbia contractee, Lola appeared in films she has described as "humiliating." She didn't refuse any of the parts she was given, because "I just couldn't afford to take a suspension." She resented the restrictions of being under contract: "Having to ask permission to do such things as go horseback riding was part of the agreement. I'm sure they had what they felt were good reasons, but it was not my idea of living."

Her first real break was being cast in *The Champion* (1949). Even among the strong competition in that popular film Lola's work stood out. It got her out of bit parts and into a string of romantic leads in some rather mediocre features. She developed a reputation for stealing any scene she was in, not by tricks but by sheer screen presence.

After her first marriage ended in divorce she married the late Jack Carson. They had appeared together in the successful comedy *The Good Humor Man* (1950). They were divorced in 1958.

The part that could really have put her over was in the low-budget classic *A Cold Wind in August* (1961). Had it gotten the attention it deserved and been released by a major studio, Lola would almost certainly have been nominated for an Oscar. She played a stripper who becomes romantically involved with a teenage boy—very steamy for the time. Although the role is one of her two favorites, she says she is not attracted to younger men.

Lola thinks her best work was in *Lord Love a Duck* (1966), in which she played a cocktail waitress and the mother of Tuesday Weld. "She was funny and poignant simultaneously, a hellava performance!" wrote filmologist Don Miller.

Some of her other screen appearances were in *The Killer that Stalked New York* (1951), *The Tender Trap* (1955), *Kid Galahad* (1963), and *Where Were You When the Lights Went Out?* (1968).

The closest Lola Albright came to becoming the star that many felt she should be was on *Peter Gunn.* She was Craig Stevens's sultry girlfriend on the series, which ran from 1958 to 1961. She played a nightclub singer, and her throaty delivery went over so well that she cut several albums, which still stand up.

After making *The Impossible Years* (1968) Lola announced her retirement. By then she was married to a restaurateur, who objected to her working long hours in the studios. "I've always put the man in my life ahead of my career," she said recently. "I sang in one of his places, which took care of what little need I have to perform."

Ms. Albright is now divorced and has made herself again available for acting. She has turned down several Broadway offers because she does not want to live in New York.

Lola and her toy poodle, "Betsy," live in an apartment in Toluka Lake, California. Asked how she spends her days, she replied, "Asleep. I am nocturnal by nature. I love to read all through the night."

Richard Lamparski

Lola Albright today, wearing what she calls "my aging-actress hat."

One of Leon Ames's many screen appearances was in Let's Do It Again (1953).

Leon Ames

The durable character actor was born in Portland, Indiana, on January 20, 1902. His original name was Leon Wycoff. Educated in Delphi, Indiana, Leon received much of his early training as an actor with the Champlin Players, a repertory company in Langsford, Pennsylvania.

Almost from the beginning Ames was kept busy as an actor. He did summer stock, went on the road with plays, and acted on Broadway.

As early as 1931 he was tested for movies. That year he made a screen test for Universal with a Broadway ingenue named Bette Davis. The following year he was in *Murders in the Rue Morgue* with Arlene Francis and *That's My Boy* with Dorothy Jordan (widowed and living in Coronado, California). He returned to the stage and was seen on Broadway in *Bright Honor* (1936) and *A House in the Country* (1937).

Leon began working steadily in Hollywood in the late thirties. Among his more than one hundred features were *Dangerously Yours* (1937) with Phyllis Brooks (widowed and living in Ogunquit, Maine), *Island in the Sky* (1938) with the late Michael Whalen, *Calling All Marines* (1939) with Helen Mack (widowed and living in the former Marion Davies mansion in Beverly Hills), *East Side Kids* (1940), *Thirty Seconds over Tokyo* (1944), *Son of Lassie* (1945), *The Postman Always Rings Twice* (1946), *Lady in the Lake* (1947), *Little Women* (1949, *On Moonlight Bay* (1951), *By the Light of the Silvery Moon* (1953), *Peyton Place* (1957) with Diane Varsi (married and living in Larkspur, California), *The Absent-Minded Professor* (1961), *Son of Flubber* (1963), *The Monkey's Uncle* (1965), *Tora! Tora! Tora!* (1970), *Claws* (1978), and *Timber Tramp* (1978).

Ames feels that nothing he did in movies was really worthwhile. If he has a favorite screen role, it was as the father in *Meet Me in St. Louis* (1944). His real love is the New York theatre. He is especially proud of playing with Henry Hull in *Tobacco Road.* Leon's big Broadway hit was *The Male Animal* (1940), in which he originated the role of the football hero. It brought him several awards. *Guest in the House* in 1942 was another of his Broadway successes. The only real disappointment of his career was having to turn down the role of "Doc" in *Come Back, Little Sheba* when his studio, M-G-M, refused to release him.

For all his appearances in films and on the stage, Leon Ames is known by most people for his work on TV. He played the pompous title role in *Life With Father,* a charming adaptation of the immensely successful Broadway play; it ran on CBS from 1954 through 1955. He had a running part in *Mr. Ed,* which was on the network for six seasons and is still in syndication.

Ames and Bradley Page (a realtor in Northern California) are the only two living founders of the Screen Actors Guild. Ames was its president for two terms and is its president emeritus.

In 1945, when Leon filled out a form for the Metro publicity department he listed "loafing" as his favorite recreation. Now that he has retired, however, he finds it very difficult to do nothing. "When I was younger I never had time for a hobby," he said recently. "I've tried golf but it bores me. I enjoy reading but you can't do it all day and evening. I traveled all over the world and want to stay put now. But I'm not complaining. I have splendid health, a wonderful family, and good friends. I've been very lucky."

Leon married starlet Christine Gossett shortly after they met while he was playing Napoleon in *Suez* (1938). They have a son, who owns an auto agency in Abilene, Texas, and a daughter, who is an executive with Walt Disney studios. Faith healer Kathryn Kuhlman once lived in the home Ames bought a few years ago in Corona Del Mar, California. He often drives into Santa Monica to visit his close friend Lloyd Nolan, and attend meetings of the board of SAG and the Motion Picture and Television Country House.

Ames doesn't rule out acting again in movies, but he refuses to come in to Hollywood for interviews or tests. "I wouldn't test for M-G-M and they still signed me," he says proudly. "I refused again when CBS wanted a test for *Life With Father,* but I got the part. I'll be damned if I'm going to audition at this point in my life. Anyway, I don't need to work." Then with a laugh he said, "And you know, the entire movie and TV industry seems to be getting along just fine without me."

Leon Ames recently in his home in Corona Del Mar, California.

Sarah Richardson

Freeman Gosden as "Amos Jones" and Charles Correll as "Andy H. Brown," the Kings of Radio, Amos 'n' Andy in 1951.

"Amos 'n' Andy" (Radio)

The popularity of *Amos 'n' Andy* has no counterpart in television, movies, or the stage. Their tenure on radio was the longest, their salaries were the highest, and their impact on life in the United States from the late twenties through the forties was the greatest. Throughout their careers they were the undisputed Kings of Radio.

The original names of the couple were "Sam 'n' Henry," one of the many blackface acts playing amateur shows from the time they met in 1919 until they went on the air over station WGN in Chicago in 1926. The program was only mildly successful at first, but began to pick up listeners as they started to add some of their famous characters. When they moved to another Chicago station, WMAQ, they changed their names to "Amos 'n' Andy." On August 19, 1929, the National Broadcasting Company put them on from coast to coast. Their appeal was immediate and seemingly universal—they were popular on Park Avenue as well as Harlem. They were referred to in speeches on the floor of the United States Senate, and "Silent Cal" Coolidge spoke out long enough to advise his presidential staff that he was not to be disturbed while the show was on the air.

Amos, the working member of the team, was played by Freeman F. Gosden. He was supposed to run the Fresh Air Taxicab Company, which consisted of one old car. His wife was Ruby. They had a little girl, Arbadella (who was played by a Chinese actress). Andy, who had no job or business, was portrayed by Charles Correll. In spite of his lack of ambition, he maintained an office and a secretary, Miss Blue.

Sponsored by Pepsodent Toothpaste for the first eight years and by Campbell Soups for the next eight years, *Amos 'n' Andy* was heard Monday through Friday from 7:00 P.M. to 7:15 P.M. EST in every state in the Union, plus Canada. In some sections of the country theatre marquees announced that the feature film ended before 7:00 P.M. and the next show did not begin before 7:15. Department stores that stayed open late some evenings broadcast the shows on every floor, lest the patrons stay home for fear of missing an episode. When Andy was about to marry Madame Queen (which he never did) and when she brought a breach-of-promise suit against him, streets were all but deserted while America listened to the testimony of "Brother Crawford," "Lightnin'," the "Kingfish," and "Henry Van Porter."

Much of the show's activity centered around the Hall of the Mystic Knights of the Sea, the lodge to which all male members of the cast belonged. Characters included Lawyer Calhoon, who conferred with his clients in the alley behind the jail, Needlenose Fletcher, and Sapphire Stevens, the Kingfish's wife. The show's expressions became a part of the American idiom: "Buzz me, Miss Blue," "Check and double-check," "I'se regusted!" and the famous lament "Oh wah! Oh wah!" A foreigner walking down a typical American street on a warm evening during those years could have heard the show's theme, "The Perfect Song," coming from almost every window on the block.

In 1948 Gosden and Correll sold *Amos 'n' Andy* to CBS lock, stock, and barrel, giving them an enormous tax break through capital gains. They continued to do the show as employees of the network.

There was, however, a segment of the country that never found the characters amusing. After the war the rumblings of discontent among civil rights organizations protesting the stereotypes of blacks the show created became more and more vocal. In the fifties the format was changed to permit guest stars, and the racial humor was toned down considerably. They were now on only once a week for thirty minutes in a program they called *The Amos 'n' Andy Musical Hall,* and when black actors played the parts in the TV series (with Gosden and Correll keeping a hand in behind the scenes) it was hoped the complaints would cease, but if anything, the pressure grew.

Gosden and Correll discontinued the radio show in 1958, and in 1965 CBS announced that the television series was being withdrawn from circulation, although the network denied the reason was protests from civil rights groups.

In an interview held shortly before he died Charles Correll spoke of "the luckiest day of my life," the day on which he met his partner at an amateur show in Durham, North Carolina. He said he always portrayed the characters with lower voices, leaving Gosden the higher ones, but that their real voices were very similar (he was from Peoria, Illinois, and Gosden was from Richmond, Virginia). In spite of their huge popularity the duo were very worried about their only real competition, *Myrt and Marge* on a rival network, and they expected every season to be their last. He did not feel that he and his partner had any negative influence on the image of black Americans: "My wife and I have a maid who has been with us for many years. She's a Negro and we think of her as one of the family."

Freeman Gosden maintains residences in Beverly Hills and Palm Springs. He is a familiar face on the golf courses in both. His personal friend and sometimes golfing partner is Richard M. Nixon.

Gosden and Correll remained close friends until the latter's death in 1972 and shared many interests aside from the characters that became part of Americana. One was fishing. In fact, the only time they ever missed a show was once in the thirties when they got so engrossed in a big catch that they forgot the time, disappointing more Americans than had ever voted for a presidential candidate.

Charles Correll photographed shortly before his death in 1972.

Richard Lamparski

Freeman Gosden at a recent social function in Beverly Hills.

John Virzi

Ernestine Wade played "Sapphire Stevens," the wife of the "Kingfish."

Alvin Childress had been on Broadway in Anna Lucasta and Brown Sugar before becoming "Amos" on television.

"Amos 'n' Andy" (Television)

The television version of the famed radio series debuted in 1951. By the time it went off the network in 1953 it was rated by viewers as either the funniest or the most offensive show they had ever seen.

It was produced by Freeman F. Gosden and the late Charles Correll, who played the title roles on radio. They took great care with the casting.

Alvin Childress had a background of Broadway shows and films, but he suspected he might not look right for any of the parts. So he spent months listening to air checks of the radio programs and mimicking all the voices. He was hired first, in 1949, and spent a year helping to scout other actors. The role he won was Amos, owner of the Fresh Air Taxi Company (one cab) and father of Arbadella.

Ernestine Wade, who played the battle-ax Sapphire, had been on the radio show since 1939 playing Mrs. Henry Van Porter and the old maid Sara "Needlenose" Fletcher.

Spencer Williams, who played Andy, died in 1969, and Johnny Lee, who was Lawyer Calhoon, has been dead since 1965. The part of the slothful Lightnin', a character particularly criticized by civil rights groups, was taken by Nick Stuart. He now owns and operates the all-black Ebony Showcase Theatre in Los Angeles.

Harry R. Tim Moore, who had long been a star in black theatre, took the part of the "Kingfish." He died in 1958.

But it was Amanda Randolph as Mama, the Kingfish's mother-in-law and mother of Sapphire and Opalescent, who stole the show. Her rages were overshadowed only by her huge hats, which resembled a child's grave. She has been dead since 1967.

Amos and Sapphire were very sorry to see

the show end and regret that it has been withdrawn from both domestic and international syndication, even though they were never paid residuals. Says Childress: "What its detractors fail to mention is that it was the very first time that we saw blacks playing professionals—judges, lawyers, and doctors." He retired a few years ago from a position as employment interviewer for the County of Los Angeles.

In the last few years Ms. Wade has been seen on TV commercials for Bell Telephone Company, McDonald's restaurants, and Greyhound Bus. She is single and lives in Los Angeles.

Alvin Childress says, "I seem to have shaken the Amos image completely. I've played a preacher on *Sanford and Son, Fish,* and *Good Times.* And I've been a drunk several times, mostly recently in *The Main Event* (1979).

Ernestine Wade has stated that she is very proud to have been on the series. "It was a happy experience. I know there were those who felt offended by it, but I still have people stop me on the street and tell me how much they enjoyed it. And many of those people are black members of the NAACP."

However, the show is not coming back, and CBS, which owns all rights, has said that although the films do exist, they are not for sale or loan. In a nationwide survey of regular television viewers *Amos 'n' Andy* rated among the very top of the list of those most wanted to be repeated.

"Sapphire" and "Amos" together again recently.

Richard Lamparski

Russell Arms's hit "Cinco Robles" was on Billboard's chart for fifteen straight weeks in 1957.

Russell Arms

The star of TV's *Your Hit Parade* was born in Berkeley, California, on February 3. His parents were much against his going into show business at first, but finally relented and helped with his tuition at the Pasadena Playhouse.

Arms was given a stock contract at Warner Brothers, where he made brief appearances in *The Man Who Came to Dinner* (1942) and *Always in My Heart* (1942). He was also in several Gene Autry westerns. The late Marilyn Maxwell, Russell's frequent date during this period, was the first person to suggest that he try singing.

Arms became the vocalist on *School Days,* a radio show that featured Kenny Delmar and Buddy Hackett. From that program he got a spot on *The 54th Street Review,* a television show of 1949–50.

During *Your Hit Parade*'s first season on TV, 1950–51, Arms sang the famous Lucky Strike jingle, "Be Happy, Go Lucky." The second year he did the commercial pitches and was general understudy. Snooky Lanson, Dorothy Collins, and Eileen Wilson were the featured singers. On the last show of the season he was allowed to sing one of that week's hits, "My Truly, Truly Fair." During the program's summer hiatus the sponsor received quite a bit of mail asking who he was and if he would be back in the fall.

When *Your Hit Parade* resumed, Russell Arms and Gisêle Mackenzie were added as regulars. He continued with the show until he and all other on-camera personnel were let go at the end of the 1958 season.

While Arms was well paid and became a household name as a "Hit Parader," he has mixed feelings about the experience. The sponsor allowed him to appear in a movie, *By the Light of the Silvery Moon* (1957) with Doris Day, but vetoed a lucrative offer from NBC's New York City radio station that would have given him his own show. But it was the politics of the show that irked him the most. "I liked Snooky personally," he said recently, "and we still have a good time when we run into each other, but he was very threatened by me. If I got to sing the number-one song one week he'd go straight to the agency or sponsor and raise hell. Every advancement in my career came from the public, not because I kissed up to anyone. I take great pride in that. I'm a professional."

Russell and Dorothy Collins dated after they were off the show. "We got quite serious for a while," he says "but somehow we ended up marrying other people." Arms has been married and divorced twice. Both wives were dancers.

Russell has not yet made it to Broadway, which is his goal, but he works much of the time acting on television and in road shows and as a narrator for industrial films. For several years he has been emceeing the Our Little Miss and Ideal Miss shows, a kind of junior Miss America pageant for girls between three and seventeen years old. He directed and emceed the Miss World—U.S.A. competition in 1976, 1977, and 1978.

When he isn't on the road Russell Arms lives by himself in an apartment in North Hollywood. He is still recognized almost daily as a "Hit Parader."

John Schoefield

Russell Arms is single and lives in North Hollywood.

Gene Autry was named one of the world's top ten money-making stars three times.

Gene Autry

Gene Autry is one movie cowboy who really was a westerner by birth and upbringing. Born in Tioga, Texas, on September 29, 1907, he later moved to Sapulpa, Oklahoma, where he worked as a telegrapher at the local railroad junction. When he was in his late teens he got an additional job singing on the local radio station. One of his admirers was another Oklahoman, Will Rogers, who encouraged him to continue as an entertainer.

Gene became so popular in Oklahoma that within three years the radio show was his own and was being heard in several adjoining states. Columbia Records gave him a contract, and he was off to the races with his first hit, which he also coauthored, "That Silver-Haired Daddy of Mine." It sold 5 million copies.

In 1933 he left radio for a while to make movies. His first was *In Old Santa Fe* (1934) with the late Ken Maynard. His thirteen-chapter serial *The Phantom Empire* (1934) is a classic of its type, and is still shown among devotees of the bizarre in early sound films. He made more than sixty-four features films for Republic Pictures, beginning with *Tumblin' Tumbleweeds* (1935). The studio was then called Mascot Pictures.

Gene was the first western star to show up among the top ten money-makers in Hollywood. His name appeared on the list three times. He was also the first western star to allow his name to be associated with merchandising, and has had as many as a hundred different products on the market at one time bearing his name and likeness. Another first in Autry's career was in 1950, when he became the first cowboy to be named as one of the ten best-dressed men in America.

His coast-to-coast radio shows for Wrigley Gum enjoyed great popularity, beginning in 1940. Listeners were always told that Gene was speaking to them right from Melody Ranch, and that his horse, Champion, was right there with him. Melody Ranch, which Gene still owns, is in Newhall, California. *Annie Oakley, Range Rider,* and *Buffalo Bill, Jr.*, the TV series that Gene's firm produced in the fifties, were all made there. CBS Radio carried the Autry shows for seventeen years.

From 1942 to 1945 he served in the United States Air Force, from which he emerged a flight officer. After the war he formed his own independent film company, for which he made forty-six features.

During the years Gene reigned supreme as the screen's top cowboy, his formula set the pace for many other westerns. The late Smiley Burnette was his sidekick and provided the comic relief. Gene is credited with popularizing songs in westerns, and had some of the best ones in his pictures. "South of the Border" is one he introduced in his 1939 feature of the same title.

There was very little dalliance with the ladies in his films. If he found it absolutely necessary to kiss the young woman, it would usually come in the last scene, and even then, during the clinch, the camera would pan to Champion, who looked about as uncomfortable as Gene wiping off the lipstick at the fade-out.

"The Sons of the Pioneers" supplied the backing for Gene's numbers in many of his pictures. One young man appearing as a member of the group was Roy Rogers, who later became "The King of the Cowboys."

In 1932 he married Ina Mae Spivey, the niece of his song-writing collaborator. He was widowed in 1980 and remarried the next year to a thirty-nine-year-old bank executive.

Some of the songs he introduced or popularized are "Mexicali Rose," "Here Comes Santa Claus," and "Rudolph the Red-Nosed Reindeer." The last brought him a platinum copy after sales went to two and a half million records. Both of the others have sold well over one million copies each.

Autry's other interests include his two TV stations, a ten-acre movie and TV production center, five radio stations, a subscription-TV company, a collection of vintage autos and locomotives, recording and music-publishing companies, and the Los Angeles Angels baseball team.

He commutes between the Gene Autry Hotel in Palm Springs, which he owns, and his palatial home in Los Angeles in a limousine complete with chauffeur-bodyguard.

Fortune magazine has called Gene Autry "Hollywood's Number One Businessman." In 1980 the *Los Angeles Times* named him the eighth richest man in the state of California.

Seventy-two hours after his election to the presidency, Ronald Reagan was Gene Autry's guest for lunch.

Jon Virzi

Gene Autry was grand marshal of the Hollywood Christmas Parade in 1980.

By the late thirties Lew Ayres was under contract to Metro-Goldwyn-Mayer.

Lew Ayres

The movie star who became America's first well-known conscientious objector was born Lewis Frederick Ayres on December 28, 1908, in Minneapolis, Minnesota. Both of his parents were accomplished musicians, as was his paternal grandmother. In 1923 Lew's mother, who had separated from his father, took him to live in San Diego. Upon graduation from high school Ayres formed a band and toured briefly before joining the Henry Halstead aggregation.

It was at a tea dance at the Hollywood Roosevelt Hotel that a movie executive spotted him gliding across the floor with a girl and signed him to a six-month contract with Pathé. He made one film for them, *The Sophomore* (1929), and then went to M-G-M, where he made the silent *The Kiss* (1929) opposite Greta Garbo.

Carl Laemmle, Jr., was producing *All Quiet on the Western Front* (1930) when Lew's agent suggested him for the lead. In his interview with the director Lew seemed "like a young king. Sensitive, but like steel." With some misgivings about his self-assurance, which bordered on arrogance, he was cast in the part. Most agree that it was the greatest antiwar picture ever made. Ayres read the book and developed strong feelings not only about the role but also about the character's pacifist sentiments.

After that film Ayres was one of Hollywood's most popular leading men. Some of his leading ladies were the late Constance Bennett in *Common Clay* (1930), the late Lillian Harvey in *My Weakness* (1933), Alice Faye in *She Learned About Sailors* (1934), Alice White in *Cross Country Cruise* (1934), and Joan Perry (who later became Mrs. Harry Cohn) in *Panic in the Air* (1936).

Then he made the delicious comedy *Holiday* (1938), from which he got an M-G-M contract. At Metro Lew was cast as the young intern Dr. Kildare in a series of nine features. Although the films were low-budget programmers, they were well acted, and the series became one of the studio's top moneymakers.

With the outbreak of World War II, Ayres was among the first of the stars to be called into service. Few in Hollywood had as clean an image, but when induction time came, he put his convictions—and career—on the line and declared himself a conscientious objector. Most of the press damned him. Thousands of fans wrote to his studio telling how he had been their favorite star but now seemed a coward and a traitor. Many theatres around the country refused to show his pictures.

Lew spent the war years as a medic's and chaplain's aide and was discharged as a sergeant with three battle stars, for the Luzon, Hollandia (Kotabaru), and Leyte invasions.

On his return to Hollywood, Ayres was not generally warmly received, but with the war over, some of the press and fellow actors did extend themselves to welcome him. He got off to a good start, resuming his career with parts in two hits of the era, *The Dark Mirror* (1946) and *Johnny Belinda* (1948). For the latter he received an Oscar nomination as Best Actor of the year. But he was getting a bit mature for his former image, and began to be seen doing some fine character work.

In 1955 he got excellent notices for a documentary he put together called *Altars of the East,* a film about the world's great religions. In 1957 Secretary of State Dulles appointed him to a three-year term on the United States National Committee for UNESCO, and the following year Lew was hosting *Frontier Justice* on television.

Two of his better features of the latter part of his career were *Advise and Consent* (1962) and *The Carpetbaggers* (1964). Occasionally he can be seen guesting on a television show.

His first wife was the late Lola Lane. They were divorced after three years in 1933. In 1934, when he married Ginger Rogers, Mary Brian and Janet Gaynor were the bridesmaids. He and Ginger were divorced in 1936. In 1964 Lew married his present wife, a former stewardess. His only child, Justin, was born two days before Ayres's sixtieth birthday.

The Ayres live in the Brentwood section of Los Angeles. He sees very few people connected with the movie industry. Lew is interested in peace, social justice, and astronomy, in that order. He answers yes to whether he would again declare himself against any military conflict. Recently he volunteered the fact that if he had it to do all over again he would not become an actor. He does not like to talk about his screen career, stating, "There are so many important things to be thinking and talking about. I really don't see how people can waste precious time on such irrelevancies."

Lew Ayres in 1977, holding his Golden Globe award.

Jon Virzi

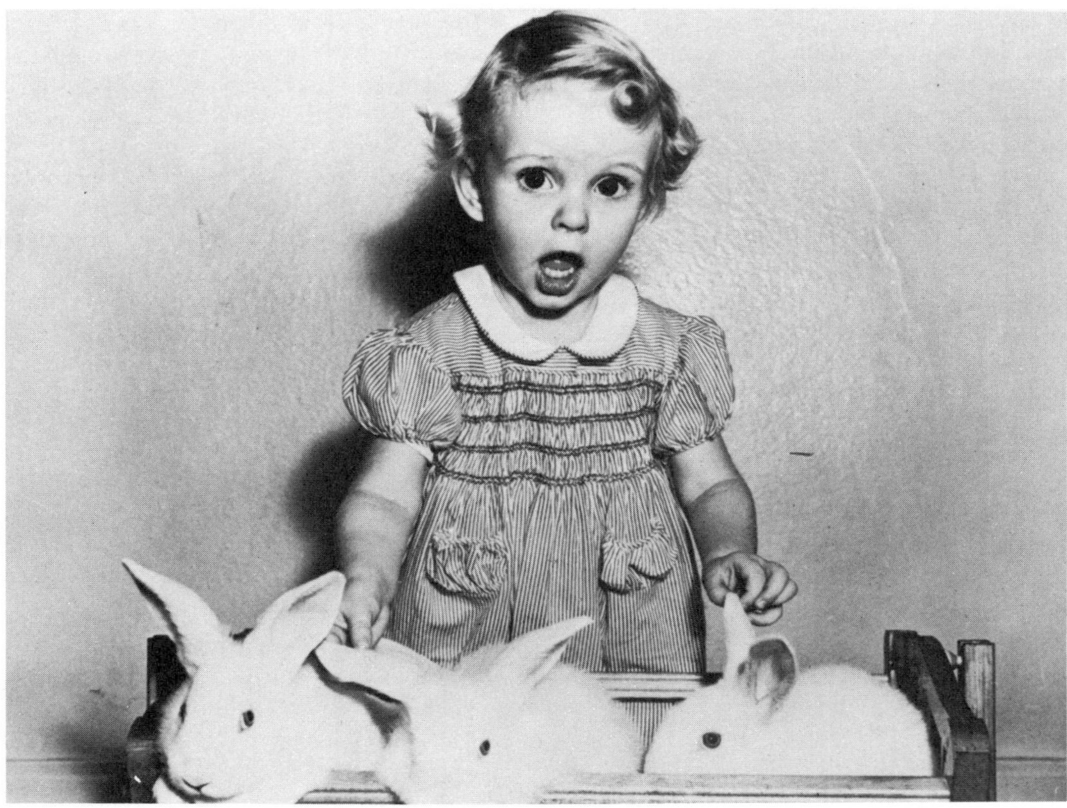

Baby Sandy wishes her fans a happy Easter, 1940.

Baby Sandy

The star who became a has-been when she was four years old was born Sandra Lea Henville two months prematurely on January 14, 1938, in Los Angeles.

Her father, who was a milkman, read in the paper that Universal Pictures was looking for a ten-month-old baby to play with Bing Crosby in *East Side of Heaven* (1939). When he left milk that morning on the doorstep of Charles Previn, the studio's musical director (and the father of André Previn), he included some snaps of Sandy. Previn showed the pictures to the film's director, David Butler, who hired her.

Sandy was on the picture two days before someone discovered that she was a girl. Although the script called for a boy, by that time she had done so well there was no thought of replacing her. Sandy's chief virtue was in how she would look from one adult to the other as they spoke while she was between them. Graham crackers were used to bribe her for special scenes, such as climbing on ledges and in front of automobiles. Audiences loved it, and Universal signed her to a contract that began at $50 a week. Her mother was paid another $100 to be with her at all times. She was the first baby star since Baby Le Roy (Leroy Overacker, now the skipper of a merchant marine ship), and the studio's publicists made the most of it. She rated two pages in *Life,* and *Look* spread the story of Sandy over four pages. There was a Baby Sandy mug, a doll, diapers, a pull-toy, the Baby Sandy story book, and a coloring book. All this provided the Henvilles with much more money than their salaries. The little star was represented by Deanna Durbin's agent.

She starred in *Unexpected Father* (1939) with Donald Woods (a real estate agent in Palm Springs) and *Little Accident* (1939). She developed such a following that her name became part of the title in *Sandy Is a Lady* (1940) with Fritz Feld (living in Los Angeles) and *Sandy Gets Her Man* (1940).

Today her single recollection of her career is the line "I'd rather be in kindergarten," which she delivered in her last movie, *Johnny Doughboy* (1942).

Sandy is now the twice-divorced Mrs. Sandra Magee of Highland Park, California. When she gave her first and only interview a few years ago she said that her parents almost never referred to her career after it ended. Nor does she discuss it now with her two sons. Sandy is a legal secretary for the County of Los Angeles.

Occasionally she watches herself on the late show, but thinks the plots of her films are hopelessly corny and that she was a "hammy brat."

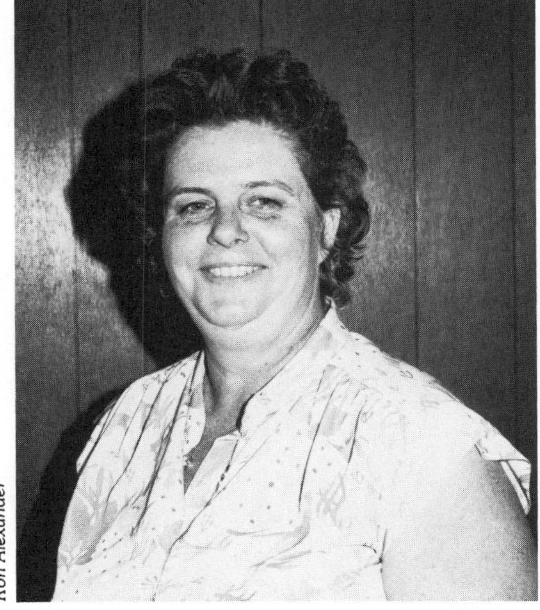

Ron Alexander

Today Baby Sandy is a legal secretary living in Highland Park, California.

"When I was about thirteen," she says, "I was going to take drama lessons and become a big star again, but my mother thought that was ridiculous. I suppose she was right. The thought of even being in a play terrified me. It still does."

She has no memory of ever having even met a movie star and has no idea of what the inside of a studio looks like. Most of the money she made is still in the bank.

Lynn Bari was under contract to Twentieth Century–Fox for fourteen years.

Lynn Bari

The star of early TV and the "other woman" of feature films was born Marjorie Schuyler Fisher on December 18, 1919, in Roanoke, Virginia. When she was seven years old her stepfather, a Religious Science minister, was transferred to Boston. The family moved to Hollywood when she was ten.

Answering a newspaper ad for tall chorus girls (she is 5 feet 7 inches), Lynn landed an $8.43-a-day job dancing in the Joan Crawford movie *Dancing Lady* (1933). She remembers swooning over the costar, Clark Gable, who used to drive her home. His name for her was "jail bait." The picture's choreographer, Sammy Lee, got her a stock contract at Twentieth Century–Fox. There she labored in such B pictures as *Spring Tonic* (1935), *Lancer Spy* (1937), and *Charter Pilot* (1940), until she did *Blood and Sand* (1941); its star, Tyrone Power, was one of her great crushes. "That film was supposed to be my punishment for refusing a perfectly dreadful script," says Ms. Bari. "It was a vile experience except that it got me my first part in an A."

Lynn did another A, *The Magnificent Dope* (1942), but was returned to the back lot for more low-budget features. She was often the woman with a gun in her purse. She loathes guns. The only time she caused a delay on a set was when she had to fire one. She would close her eyes tight. "I made as many as three pictures at a time," says Lynn. "I'd go from one set to another shooting people and stealing husbands." Of the pace, she says it was "so fast I never knew what the hell the plots were." She was disappointed in the quality of *The Bridge of San Luis Rey* (1944), which had a rushed production schedule. Her studio requested a unique fee for loaning her to appear with the late Akim Tamiroff and Joan Loring (married to a physician and living in Manhattan): a piece of equipment, still referred to on the Fox lot as "the Bari boom." Some of her other movies were *Hotel For Women* (1939), *Sun Valley Serenade* (1941), *Orchestra Wives* (1942), *Hello Frisco Hello* (1943), *Margie* (1946), *The Kid from Cleveland* (1949), *Francis Joins the Wacs* (1954) and *The Young Runaways* (1968).

She was a great favorite at Fox during her fourteen years under contract, due to her unpretentious, direct manner.

Entering TV early, Lynn starred on the live series *The Detective's Wife* in 1950 and followed it with *Boss Lady*, a widely syndicated series.

Her marriages earned her as much newspaper space as her film roles. In 1943 she divorced her first husband, Walter Kane, after two and a half years. Asked what his job was with Howard Hughes, the former Mrs. Kane referred to him as a "sort of talent scout." Next she wed Sid Luft (who later was married to Judy Garland). The five-year union produced a son, a great deal of publicity over his custody during the divorce proceedings, and much bitterness. She now recalls that experience cost her $1 million. Finally, a divorce from a Beverly Hills psychiatrist in 1972 was without fanfare.

Lynn's fans recognized a quality in her work that is very evident on the stage but was never really developed in films. On her 111-city tour with *Barefoot in the Park* in 1965 and again in *Follies* in 1973 she got star billing and excellent notices. Her last play was *The Gingerbread Lady*, which she did in dinner theatres in 1974.

Lynn's son is an artist. He and his mother share a pretty apartment overlooking the Pacific Ocean in Marina Del Rey, California. She considers herself a liberal politically.

Asked whom she sees from her heyday in Hollywood, she responded, "They all seem to be dead except for Jean Rogers. We're great friends. Jean and all the fan mail that comes in from all over the world are my only links to the past."

Richard Lamparski

Lynn Bari and her son by Sid Luft share an apartment in Marina Del Rey, California.

Binnie Barnes in 1938.

Binnie Barnes

No one ever shot a furtive glance or delivered a caustic comment better than the actress who was born in London on March 25, 1908, with the name Gertrude Maude Barnes. She is of English-Italian descent. Her father was a bobby, and one of her mother's three husbands. Binnie was one of seventeen children in the family.

Her first job was as a milkmaid. She soon left it to learn nursing at London's Great Northern Hospital. She then became an assistant in a draper's shop. When she saw "Tex" McLeod doing a rope-spinning act at the Cosmos Club, Binnie got a job working with him. Together they toured South America for a year. By 1928 Binnie had gone out on her own, billed as "Texas Binnie" Barnes. She twirled a rope and spun tales about the great cattle ranges of the West she had never seen.

In 1929 she began her stage career with Una O'Connor and Charles Laughton in Sean O'Casey's *Silver Tassie*. Her big break came when she got the part of "Fanny," the cabaret singer, in Noel Coward's *Cavalcade*. Binnie was brought to the U.S. on the *Queen Mary* to repeat her performance in the film version, but after a brief glimpse of New York City she returned to England on the same ship that had brought her.

Ms. Barnes played Catherine Howard in *The Private Lives of Henry VIII* (1933). Charles Laughton won an Academy Award for his portrayal of the title role, and Binnie was seen for the first time by American audiences. Then she made *The Private Life of Don Juan* (1934) with Douglas Fairbanks, Sr., and twenty-six two-reel comedies with Stanley Lupino, father of Ida Lupino and a top comedian of his day. She was then brought back to fulfill the contract she had walked out on in the United States.

Whether menacing the hero or trying to break up a marriage, Binnie excelled at both brittle dialogue and withering looks. She managed to bring subtlety to some very heavy-handed scripts. During the thirties and forties she made *The Lady Is Willing* (1934) with Leslie Howard; *Diamond Jim* (1935), in which she played Lillian Russell; *Sutter's Gold* (1936); *The Adventures of Marco Polo* (1938) with Lawrence Olivier; *Daytime Wife* (1939) with Linda Darnell and Tyrone Power; *Til We Meet Again* (1940); *The Man from Down Under* (1943); *The Hour Before the Dawn* (1944) with Veronica Lake; *It's in the Bag* (1945) with Fred Allen and Jack Benny; and *If Winter Comes* (1948). Her last pictures during this period were *Fugitive Lady* (1951) and *The Decameron Nights* (1952).

From 1931 until 1936 she was the wife of

Samuel Joseph, an art dealer and publisher. In 1940 she married former UCLA all-American football hero Mike Frankovitch, who at the time was a sportscaster. The next year Binnie made the papers when she threatened to sue Columbia Pictures after being duped by director Alexander Hall into doing a scene in black lace bra and panties for *This Thing Called Love*. According to Binnie, she had been assured that she would be seen on the screen in silhouette. Her new husband was most annoyed, but they both wished that Binnie had let the whole thing drop when newspapers around the country printed a still from the scene showing Binnie in her unmentionables. Thirty years later Mike Frankovitch was one of the production heads of Columbia Pictures.

The couple live in a penthouse near their offices. Their twin sons and daughter are adopted. Binnie says she likes to work only once in a great while and hasn't the time to miss acting because of all her duties as wife of a producer. "I raise orchids," she says, "work closely with my husband on all his projects, and contribute a good deal of time to my church [Roman Catholic] and the Variety Clubs. Then too, acting came very easily to me, so I never felt it was much of an accomplishment. The last thing I did was *Forty Carats* [1973], and I only took that part because Mike, who produced it, couldn't find anyone else who pleased him."

Richard Lamparski

Binnie Barnes in the office of her husband, producer Mike Frankovitch.

Barbara Billingsley, Jerry Mathers, and Hugh Beaumont in a publicity still for Leave It to Beaver, circa 1960.

Hugh Beaumont and Barbara Billingsley

Hugh Beaumont and Barbara Billingsley played the parents of "Beaver Cleaver" on all 234 of the *Leave It to Beaver* TV shows. The half-hour series was filmed in black-and-white between 1957 and 1963 by George Gobel's production company.

Set in Shaker Heights, Ohio, the program extolled the virtues of growing up in Middle-America under the guidance of a strong father figure and a mother who seemed to have no interests other than her family and her home. The plots had a gentle sweetness to them, and the writing was never condescending. The focus of the scripts was always on the two "Cleaver" boys: "Wally," played by Tony Dow, and his younger brother "Beaver," played by Jerry Mathers.

Hugh Beaumont was a familiar face on television before he was cast as "Ward Cleaver." When he got the part he was about to move to New York City to pursue a career on Broadway. He is somewhat disappointed that the role typecast him and that the work he did on the stage is unknown. Although he was well paid for *Beaver* and was permitted to direct twenty-five of the episodes, Hugh was not unhappy when the program ceased production. He never watches the show's reruns.

Beaumont was born in Lawrence, Kansas, on February 16, 1910, and is the divorced father of two sons and a daughter. During World War II he was a conscientious objector. Until he suffered a stroke in 1972 Hugh spent most of his time fishing or playing golf. His summers are spent on Balgillo Island, which he owns, in northern Minnesota. In the winter he lives with one of his sons in South Carolina. Hugh Beaumont is a devout Methodist.

Barbara Billingsley was born Barbara Combs in Los Angeles on December 22. She was a regular on the TV series *Professional Father* before becoming "June Cleaver." She still acts occasionally and had a prominent role in *Airplane* (1980).

The mother of two sons, Barbara lives in a house built right on the beach in Malibu, California. When she and her physician husband are not traveling Billingsley volunteers her time to work with emotionally disturbed children. "I lead a very happy life these days," she says.

She has seen *Leave It to Beaver* only about half a dozen times since it was canceled, once in Singapore, where it was shown with Chinese subtitles. Often recognized, Barbara says most of her fans are college students and young married couples who tell her how much the shows meant to them while they were growing up.

Hugh and Barbara have always kept in touch and see other members of the cast from time to time. Both speak fondly of the other actors and their experiences of being part of the show.

Jerry Mathers and Tony Dow have both been married, divorced, and remarried. They appear together now and then in plays that tour the country. "Beaver" and "Wally" are residents of the San Fernando Valley, as is Ken Osmond, who played the troublemaking next-door neighbor, "Eddie Haskell." Osmond is a member of the Los Angeles police department. Frank Banks, who played "Lumpy Rutherford," works in an insurance firm in Century City, California.

(Hugh Beaumont died on May 14, 1982.)

Barbara Billingsley lives in an oceanfront house in Malibu, California.

Richard Schaeffer

Hugh Beaumont divides his time between Minnesota and South Carolina.

Peter Schaeffer

Sally Blane in the late twenties.

Sally Blane

The leading lady best known for being Loretta Young's sister was born Elizabeth Jane Young in Salida, Colorado, on July 11, 1910, after the onset of labor forced her mother to disembark from a train. In 1915, when Sally was five years old, Mrs. Young separated from her husband and took the family of five to Hollywood. Eventually all of the Young children worked as extras; Sally was the first to get featured parts. Her first extra work came when the late Ben Alexander's mother took him home from film location when food had become scarce: Sally got the part as a sea nymph in *Sirens of the Sea* (1917), which starred the late Jack Mulhall.

When she was fourteen, director Wesley Ruggles spotted her dancing at the Café Montmartre and asked her to test for the part of Dorothy Gulliver's (widowed and living in Los Angeles) friend in the *Collegian* series. She got the role and shortly afterward signed a contract with Paramount. At the same time her younger sister Loretta signed with First National. Sally's first big part for that studio was in *Rolled Stockings* (1927). Even after Sally had become a leading lady, she remembers, she bummed a ride on many occasions from an extra named Dennis O'Keefe because her mother, who had a strong influence on her children's professional and personal lives, would not allow her to buy a car.

Sally then made such films as *Horseman of the Plains* (1928) with Tom Mix, *Vagabond Lover* (1929) with Rudy Vallee, and *Little Accident* (1930) with Anita Page (Mrs. Herschel A. House of Coronado, California). She then went to work for such low-budget studios as Chesterfield and Artclass. She appeared in *Trick for Trick* (1933) and *No More Women* (1934) with Edmund Lowe. There was also a series of B pictures in the mid-thirties with the late Frankie Darro.

In 1937 Sally married director and former actor Norman Foster, on whom she had had a crush ever since he had dated Loretta a few years before. In 1935 Sally had gone to work for a year in England, where she and Foster became reacquainted at a dinner party given by Coleen Moore. She worked occasionally until 1948, when one of her children became ill just as she was scheduled to do a television show. It was then that she decided she would devote all her time to her family.

During World War II the Fosters lived in Mexico, where her husband made Spanish-language pictures.

Sally says of her career and the inevitable comparison people made of her with Loretta Young: "She had more drive than the rest of us. Loretta was always really ambitious. She would turn down parts that I would have given anything to have played, but she never realized how much I wanted them. But while Loretta was concentrating on her career, I had all the beaus." Asked about her own ambitions, she said, "There were two things against me. I was never resilient enough. I've always felt rejection deeply and took it personally. Then, too, I wasn't as slim as Loretta. The late director Dorothy Arzner once said I had the body of a peasant." The part she most wanted was played by Helen Vinson (a widowed Philadelphia socialite) in *I Am a Fugitive from a Chain Gang* (1932). Mrs. Paul Muni had vetoed Sally, and she was cast instead in a lesser part.

Norman Foster died in 1976. He and Sally had a son, who is a writer, and a daughter, who is a photographer and the mother of their granddaughter. Her other sisters and one brother had brief careers in films also. Pollyanne, the eldest, is a widow. Georgianna, the youngest, is married to Ricardo Montalban, and Jack is an attorney and the father of five.

Jon Virzi

Sally Blane is a widow and a grandmother. She lives by herself in a Beverly Hills apartment.

Asked if she would do it all over again, Sally said, "No, I think I'd try for the stage. I never felt I was photogenic. People ask if I watch my old movies on television. I don't. I never liked a single thing I did."

Beulah Bondi in Of Human Hearts (1938).

Beulah Bondi

The distinguished character actress, who was born Beulah Bondy on May 3, 1888, in Chicago, debuted at the age of seven in the title role of *Little Lord Fauntleroy*. By the time she was ten, her acting had won a gold medal.

Stuart Walker, then head of one of the country's leading repertory companies, signed her at $25 a week. After two years she left to tour with various stock productions. In 1925 she debuted on Broadway in *One in the Family*. After several more plays she won the part of the landlady in the original company of *Street Scene* (1929) and was signed by Samuel Goldwyn to repeat the part in his film version (1931). She returned to Broadway only four more times: for *The Late Christopher Bean* (1932), *Mother Lode* (1934), *Hilda Crane* (1950), and *On Borrowed Time* (1953), which she had done in the 1939 film version.

Beulah Bondi differed from other character actresses in several respects. She was never under contract and therefore was not forced to accept parts she felt were unsuitable. This also worked well for her financially: when producers wanted her they had to pay her price, which was $500 a week even in 1931. Her art was not in tricks, scene stealing, or a flamboyant personality indigenous to her every role. She was quite different in every one of her sixty-three feature films. When people recognized her in public as one of the warm, cruel, or eccentric women she had protrayed in movies and not as an actress, she felt that she was being paid the ultimate compliment.

Her more important films were *Arrowsmith* (1931), *Rain* (1932), *The Sisters* (1938), *Mr. Smith Goes to Washington* (1939) with Jean Arthur (single and living in Carmel Highlands, California), *Our Hearts Were Young and Gay* (1944), *The Southerner* (1945) with the late J. Carrol Naish, *The Snake Pit* (1948), and *Our Town* (1940). She made mediocre as well as bad pictures, but her work in them was always of top quality. A few that appeared on television are *Two Alone* (1934), *The Buccaneer* (1938) with the late Franceska Gaal, *The Under-Pup* (1939) with the late Virginia Weidler, *High Conquest* (1947) with Anna Lee (married to novelist Robert Nathan and living in Los Angeles), *So Dear to My Heart* (1948) with the late Bobby Driscoll, and *Latin Lovers* (1953). Her last screen appearance was in *Tammy and the Doctor* (1963) with the late Margaret Lindsay.

Beulah had no regrets about not winning an Oscar for *The Gorgeous Hussy* (1936) or *Of Human Hearts* (1938). She received a Best Supporting Actress nomination for each. She was, however, deeply disappointed when after several days of shooting she was replaced by May Robson in *The Adventures of Tom Sawyer* (1938). (Ms. Robson, who was the original choice, recovered from an illness sooner than expected.) The real hurt came when the role of Ma Joad in *The Grapes of*

Wrath (1940) was awarded to Jane Darwell after Beulah had been told it was hers.

Ms. Bondi had never been married. She lived by herself in a beautiful old three-story house built into the face of the Hollywood Hills. Her home was filled with mementos not of her screen career but of the many countries she had visited during her two trips around the world. Much of her retirement was spent in travel. She was so fascinated by Africa that she visited the continent four times.

Beulah Bondi appeared infrequently on television. When she did it was always an occasion not only for the viewers but for her fellow actors as well. She received the kind of attention on a set usually afforded a major star. It was not at all unusual for several stars to request permission to stand on the sidelines when Ms. Bondi was doing a scene, to "watch Bondi work." Her performance in an episode of *The Waltons* won her an Emmy in 1977.

Although Beulah played with such stars as Bette Davis, Claudette Colbert, Barbara Stanwyck, Clark Gable, and Joan Crawford, she was never part of the Hollywood scene. She was more interested in good books, metaphysics, and world politics than Hollywood.

She attributed her excellent health and open-mindedness to her mother: "She believed in raising and expanding consciousness—in letting go of the past, planning for the future, and living in the now."

After her death on January 12, 1981, her friend Ann Doran said of her: "Beulah played all those old-woman roles, without ever being old herself."

Jon Virzi

Beulah Bondi in 1980, only a few months before her death.

When Cammie King made Gone With the Wind (1939) her parents had just been divorced. "Clark Gable was very much of a father figure to me during the filming," she said recently. "I'll never forget the loving attention he gave me."

"Bonnie Blue Butler": Cammie King

The little girl who played "Rhett and Scarlett Butler's" daughter was born Eleanore Cammack King in Los Angeles on August 5, 1934. Her mother was Eleanore King, the lecturer and Hearst newspaper columnist.

Cammie's older sister was first chosen to play "Bonnie Blue Butler," at the suggestion of a friend of their mother. The woman, who worked for *Gone With the Wind*'s producer, David O. Selznick, thought the older King girl bore a striking resemblance to both Clark Gable and Vivien Leigh. The film, however, was so long in preproduction that the little girl had outgrown the role by the time shooting started. Cammie replaced her.

"I was so young I didn't fully understand what was happening," she said recently. "I'm not even sure I'd ever seen a movie before I made *Gone With the Wind*. My few memories of the picture are very happy ones. Everyone was wonderful to me, but Hattie McDaniel was my favorite. I just loved all the attention. In fact, my mother asked the director, Victor Fleming, to tell his crew that they were making too much of a fuss over me. She didn't want me spoiled by the experience."

Cammie remembers Clark Gable as "a very warm, friendly man. When he kissed me his mustache used to tickle. I'd tell that to my mother's friends and they'd swoon."

Later Cammie was given a part in a *Dr. Kildare* feature, but came down with chicken pox and was replaced. Shortly after *Gone With the Wind* (1939), her parents were divorced and her mother decided Cammie should have a normal childhood away from movie-making. Eventually Mrs. King married Dr. Kalmus, the founder and inventor of Technicolor.

Cammie, however, longed to return to movies and become a star. "But," she says, "by the time I was twelve years old I was five feet ten inches. I sensed that I had a problem from the way boys were reacting to me. That ended my ambitions for an acting career. I'm awfully glad, though, I played 'Bonnie.' The role really didn't change my life, but I don't recall ever meeting people, either in business or socially, where it doesn't come up."

Cammie King was widowed by her first husband and is divorced from her second. Her son is away at college, and her daughter lives with Cammie in Mendecino, California. Until she moved there from Los Angeles in 1980 Ms. King worked in fund raising. She is still a consultant with several large charities and schools.

Cammie's sole contact with Hollywood is her longtime friendship with the actress Judy Lewis. It has been stated in several books that Ms. Lewis, who is the daughter of Loretta Young, was conceived during the filming of *Call of the Wild*. According to these reports, which have never been denied, Judy Lewis's father was her mother's costar in that 1935 film—Clark Gable.

Cammie King has a son and a daughter. She lives in Mendecino, California.

Amaryllis Beirne-Keyt

The Boswell Sisters in the early 1930s. **From left to right:** ***Martha, Vet, and Connie.***

The Boswell Sisters

The Boswell Sisters—Martha, born in 1905; Connee (originally Connie), born in 1907; and Vet (Helvetia), born in 1911—hailed from New Orleans, Louisiana, where they began playing instruments and singing before they were of school age. They had been playing clubs around the country in the twenties, before swing was the popular sound (except among a few musicians). Their first record was made in New Orleans on March 25, 1925, for Victor (before it became RCA Victor). Two of their early hits of 1930 and 1931 were "My Future Just Passed" and "When I Take My Sugar to Tea."

"The Boswell Sound," as it is still called in the music business, created a sensation. There had been sister acts before, and many since, but these three Southern girls were able to blend their voices in a way the public had never heard before—they merged harmony, rhythm, and feeling to produce a musical togetherness that has been imitated but never equaled. The records they made during the thirties for Brunswick and Okeh labels are among the most highly prized and sought after by discophiles.

In 1930 they had a popular radio program on NBC for Camel cigarettes. When, in June 1931, the girls moved over to rival CBS, it was considered a major coup for Bill Paley's network, which until that time had been unsuccessful in its competition with NBC for big-name talent. In 1932 the Boswells were heard on Chesterfield cigarettes' *Music That Satisfies* show. In 1934 they became regulars along with Bing Crosby on *The Woodbury Hour.*

Truly musicians' musicians, the group was praised by the top performers of their time—and since. No lesser names than Bing Crosby, Ella Fitzgerald, and Paul Whiteman expressed admiration for the distinct qualities of their sound. Rudy Vallee was one of the earliest Boswell enthusiasts. Not only did the girls sing great but each was also an accomplished instrumentalist. Connee, who had been confined to a wheelchair since she suffered a polio attack at the age of three, played just about every instrument but favored the saxophone. Martha was usually on piano, and Vet alternated between banjo and violin.

The girls appeared together in three pictures: *The Big Broadcast* (1932), *Moulin Rouge* (1934) with Constance Bennett, and *Transatlantic Merry-Go-Round* (1934).

When Vet and Martha decided to give up show business for marriage in 1936, the team broke up. Connee, the youngest, who had been appearing as a single as well as with her sisters since the beginning, continued alone.

During World War II, when she was entertaining troops and had to sign hundreds of autographs every day, she began spelling her name "ee" instead of the original "Connie."

Harry Leedy, Connee's husband and the man who discovered the trio and managed them and Connee, died in 1975. The same year Connee gave her last performance, at Carnegie Hall with Benny Goodman.

Harry Belafonte once called Connee Boswell "the most widely imitated singer of all time." She was also one of the most admired. Although she had to remain in a wheelchair throughout her act, her gown was draped in such a way that she appeared to be standing. Sympathy was never part of her strong appeal to an audience. She had a warmth and an energy that was contagious. When she died in 1976 the *New York Times* estimated that there had been seventy-five million Connee Boswell records sold.

Martha lived on a farm near Peekskill, New York, until her death in 1958. Vet, the second eldest of the trio, resides in Peekskill. She is a widow.

Maxine Andrews* (left) *with Vet Boswell at the opening of <u>Heebie Jeebies,</u> a musical tribute to the Boswell Sisters in 1981. The Andrews Sisters have always acknowledged the Boswell Sisters as their idols.

U.P.I.

Mary Brian was publicized and cast as the "Sweetest Girl in Pictures."

Mary Brian

The "Sweetest Girl in Pictures" was born Louise Dantzler on February 17, 1908, in Corsicana, Texas, and brought up in Dallas. Her father died when she was a month old. Her mother moved with her son and daughter to Hollywood in 1923, where Mary met one of the heads of Paramount Pictures. The studio was then looking for young, unfamiliar faces to play in its production of *Peter Pan* (1925). Her college-teacher mother was unimpressed with the profession of acting, but allowed Mary to be put under contract for seven years.

The film was a huge success and made Mary and the other two players, the late Betty Bronson and Esther Ralston, overnight stars. The children who came to see Mary on her public-appearance tours were disappointed when she couldn't fly as she did on screen.

Mary made as many as seven features a year for her studio, among them *Beau Geste* (1926), *Harold Teen* (1928), and *The Virginian* (1929). She attended school on the Paramount lot with other child actors, including Philippe de Lacy (an executive with a Los Angeles advertising agency). She thoroughly enjoyed her work and the people she met, but she never developed a driving ambition or an extravagant life-style.

The advent of sound didn't panic her and she survived easily, making quite a few talkies, among them *The Front Page* (1931) and the impressive *Royal Family of Broadway* (1930). Jimmy Cagney was her leading man in *Hard to Handle* (1933), Lanny Ross crooned to her in *College Rhythm* (1934), and W. C. Fields played her dad in *The Man on the Flying Trapeze* (1935). Nothing she did on film contradicted the "sweetest girl in pictures" image until Mary played a shrew in *The Spendthrift* (1936), with Henry Fonda. But by then her career was in such a decline that her only offers came from England, where she went for three features. It meant leaving the big love of her life, Dick Powell, with whom she was linked for about two years.

Mary returned to the United States in the late 1930s, playing presentation houses with two boys in a dancing act, and she entertained GIs in Europe and North Africa frequently during World War II. She made *No Escape* (1943) for low-budget Monogram studios and then even went one step lower for PRC in *Women at Work* (1943) before calling it quits. She came back for thirty-nine weeks in 1955, playing the mother in the *Meet Corliss Archer* TV series.

Six years after her marriage to artist Jon Whitcomb, which lasted all of three months and two days in 1941, Mary wed George Tomasini, the film editor who cut many of Alfred Hitchcock's movies, including *North by Northwest* and *Psycho.*

A widow since 1967, Mary lives in her Studio City beamed-ceiling ranch-style house surrounded by woods. Her hobby, which has proved very profitable, is painting famous people (including Conrad Hilton and Red Skelton).

She doesn't completely rule out acting again in movies. But the one real chance she had to become a star again was when she tested for the lead in *A Star Is Born* (1938). "It was almost a disappointment," says Mary now. "I say 'almost' because when I saw Janet Gaynor in the picture I realized at once that she was the one who was meant to get it. She was absolutely wonderful!"

Mary is a widow and lives in Studio City, California.

Jon Virzi

Adolph Zukor always thought of Clive Brook as the "Rock of Gibraltar."

Clive Brook

The stalwart leading man of motion pictures was born Clifford Brook in London on June 1, 1886. His mother, Charlotte Mary Brook, the opera singer, and his father wanted Clive to study law. They were able to send him to the best private schools until 1901, when they suffered financial reverses. Clive gave up plans to become a barrister when he left Dulwich College at the age of fifteen. He then studied elocution at Polytechnic, where he did so well he became a teacher. After graduation he put in a stint as the assistant secretary of the Colonial Club in London before working for a while as a newspaper reporter. He also had some success at the time writing and selling short stories before entering the British army in September, 1914, as a private. When he left the service at the end of World War I, a major, he decided to pursue the career he had really always wanted, which was nourished at fourteen years of age, when he first acted.

Brook began making silent films in England and was seen in *Debt of Honor* (1918) as well as in plays, beginning with *Just Like Judy* (1920). He married Mildred Evelyn, his costar in the play *Fair and Warmer* (1920). He made *The Royal Oak* (1923) with Betty Compson, and as soon as it was shown in Hollywood he was offered contracts with three studios. He first went with Thomas Ince and then to Warner Brothers for a short time. The period for which he is remembered best came during his eight years with Paramount, beginning in 1926. Although he complained continually that he was weary of playing only cads or terribly correct gentlemen, the studio continued to cast him in those roles. Adolph Zukor once told him that he always thought of him as the "Rock of Gibraltar." Brook always cringed whenever the title was mentioned.

Some of Clive Brook's better work was done in *Woman to Woman* (1924), *Three Faces East* (1926) with Jetta Goudal (living in Los Angeles with her husband, interior and set designer Howard Grieve,) *Underworld* (1927), *Four Feathers* (1929), *The Return of Sherlock Holmes* (1929), *Slightly Scarlet* (1930), *Shanghai Express* (1932), and *Cavalcade* (1933).

There was never any question that Clive Brook would survive the advent of sound. His precise speech made him more sought after than ever. With his old friend William Powell and the late Evelyn Brent he appeared in Paramount's first all-talkie, *Interference* (1928). When his Paramount contract expired he went to RKO, but in 1936, partly because he and his wife were beside themselves over threats to kidnap their children, they moved permanently to England. At this time the entire movie colony was alarmed as kidnapping incidents and attempts grew. For a while Brook slept with a gun under his pillow and his children, a boy and a girl, were taken to school each day by a private policeman their family shared with the late Ann Harding.

Brook had always wanted to return to the stage. In England he made more films, such as *The Ware Case* (1939) and *Convoy* (1941), but most of his efforts were in the theatre. He both acted and directed quite successfully. The movie *On Approval* (1945), which he produced, directed, and acted in with Bea Lillie (living in England), was a huge hit and was considered by Clive to be his best.

Until he died in London in 1974 Clive was lean and erect. But what fans thought of as the polish and bearing of an officer Brook dismissed as "stiff and perfectly awful." That was his assessment of how he came off in the early talkies he made opposite Ruth Chatterton and Tallulah Bankhead.

He appeared in a number of plays on BBC television and was very proud of his daughter Faith's success as an actress. His last picture was *The List of Adrian Messenger* (1963).

The last years of his life were spent in a large, luxuriously furnished flat on Eaton Square, directly across from the home of Elizabeth Bergner.

Shortly before he died he commented on Marlene Dietrich. He had known her well during his days at Paramount, when he and the late director Josef von Sternberg were close: "She was always such a beautiful, simple girl then. She used to cook delicious food and bring it to us each morning on the set. Now she's like a character from one of her films. Seems to be playing Marlene Dietrich."

Clive Brook on the terrace of his Eaton Square flat shortly before he died in 1974.

Richard Schaeffer

Rand Brooks as "Charles Hamilton," the first of "Scarlett O'Hara's" three husbands in Gone With the Wind (1939).

Rand Brooks

The featured player of the thirties and forties was born in St. Louis, Missouri, on September 21, 1918. Until he was fifteen years old Rand and his parents lived and traveled on a rather grand scale. But in 1933 his father, a wholesale jeweler, went broke and Brooks had to get a job to help support his mother and grandmother.

He worked in a stock brokerage house while attending Beverly Hills High School. After graduating he thought he might be able to make more money acting in movies. Although he did very poorly in a screen test he made for Metro-Goldwyn-Mayer, Rand was kept on at the studio and given a small part in *Love Finds Andy Hardy* (1938). Mervyn LeRoy liked him in the picture and cast him in *Dramatic School* (1938) with Luise Rainer (living in a small town in Italy), which he was directing. Then he played Miriam Hopkins's nephew in *The Old Maid* (1939).

Brooks made over one hundred films, but audiences know him today for two roles. In *Gone With the Wind* (1939) he was "Charles Hamilton," the first husband of "Scarlett O'Hara," who is killed in the Civil War. The actor Maurice Murphy was originally cast in that part, but by the time the production began he had matured too much to portray such a young man. Brooks's other famous role was "Lucky Jenkins," the young sidekick to "Hopalong Cassidy." Although he did not enjoy making the twelve features in which he appeared opposite Bill Boyd, he is well remembered as that character.

TV fans know him as "Corporal Boone," one of the principals in the *Rin-Tin-Tin* series, which starred Lee Aaker (now a carpenter in Redondo Beach, California). Rand is still a close friend of Joe Sawyer (living in Indio, California), another regular on the show.

Some of Rand Brooks's other screen credits are *Babes in Arms* (1939), *Laddie* (1940) with the late Tim Holt, *The Son of Monte Cristo* (1940) with Louis Hayward (living in Palm Springs), *Double Date* (1941) with Una Merkel, *Lady in the Dark* (1944), *Ladies of the Chorus* (1949) with Marilyn Monroe, *Riding High* (1950), and *Stagecoach to Dancers' Rock* (1962).

Rand never liked himself on the screen. Also, he grew tired of playing weaklings and bland leading men. He wanted very much to direct, and invested every cent he had to make a feature, *Bearheart,* a dog movie. Brooks directed the film, which starred Anna Lee and Fritz Feld, but it was never released. It ruined him financially, and he cut almost all ties with Hollywood after that experience.

His three children are by the daughter of the late Stan Laurel.

Brooks owns and operates the Professional Ambulance Service of Glendale, California, a prosperous business with seventy employees.

He says he would still act if someone offered him a part he felt comfortable with. "But," he adds, "I'm not going around knocking on any doors looking for movie work. I hated that part of being an actor, and thank God, I don't have to."

Rand Brooks owns an ambulance service in Glendale, California. His wife is the daughter of Stan Laurel.

John Oster

Jane Bryan in 1939, one year before she quit show business.

Jane Bryan

The almost star was born Jane O'Brian in Los Angeles on June 11, 1918. Her original goal was the stage, and she began studying with Jean Muir's Hollywood Theatre Workshop. She wasn't there long before Warner Brothers put her under contract.

From the beginning the studio had high hopes for her, and almost everything she did proved their expectations were to be fulfilled. She held her own among a cast of top pros in *The Marked Woman* (1937) and *A Slight Case of Murder* (1938). Those who felt she had been signed as a threat to Bette Davis got quite a surprise when the queen of the lot adopted her as a protégée. In fact, when Bette was once asked if she felt Jane could carry a heavy dramatic role, the star replied with a laugh, "The last time I played with her I had to hide her face in a pillow to keep her from stealing my scenes."

Many felt that while Bette Davis and the late Miriam Hopkins were pulling every trick they knew on each other while making *The Old Maid* (1939), Jane quietly walked away with the picture. Some critics said she stole *We Are Not Alone* (1939) from Paul Muni, who at that time was considered one of the country's greatest actors.

Jane was unaffected when few were and underplayed when almost no one did. Noel Coward once stopped her on the street to tell her he thought she was the best young actress in America.

Some of her pictures were *The Case of the Black Cat* (1936), *Confession* (1937) with the late Kay Francis, *The Sisters* (1938), *Brother Rat* (1938), *Each Dawn I Die* (1939), *Invisible Stripes* (1940), and *Brother Rat and a Baby* (1940).

A *Life* magazine article said she was "critical of herself and shuns publicity." Like almost everyone, it predicted major stardom. But Jane's father was a lawyer and she never pursued her career out of financial need.

When she walked away from it, as she did when she married in 1939, she proved she had no emotional need for acting. She has never returned, and she does not grant interviews.

Her life since her retirement has been as the mother of two boys and one girl and the wife of Justin Dart, the chairman of the board of Dart Industrial, a huge conglomerate that controls, among many other corporations, all the Rexall products and stores. He is also a noted philanthropist. Jane is very active in charity work and travels constantly with Dart. They are Roman Catholics.

Jane and her husband were among the first to encourage Ronald Reagan, whom she knew during her days at Warner Brothers, to run for public office. Dart marshaled huge business interests behind Reagan and has contributed generously to all of his campaigns.

A column by Hollywood reporter Hank Grant summed up filmdom's awe of Jane: "She is the only actress within my memory who gave up her successful career for marriage and motherhood and is still happily married without a single regretful look at her past."

Jane Bryan fooled all of Hollywood by having the courage when she arrived at the very brink of major stardom to say "No thank you" and mean it.

Jon Virzi

Jane Bryan recently in Hollywood.

"Buckwheat": William Thomas

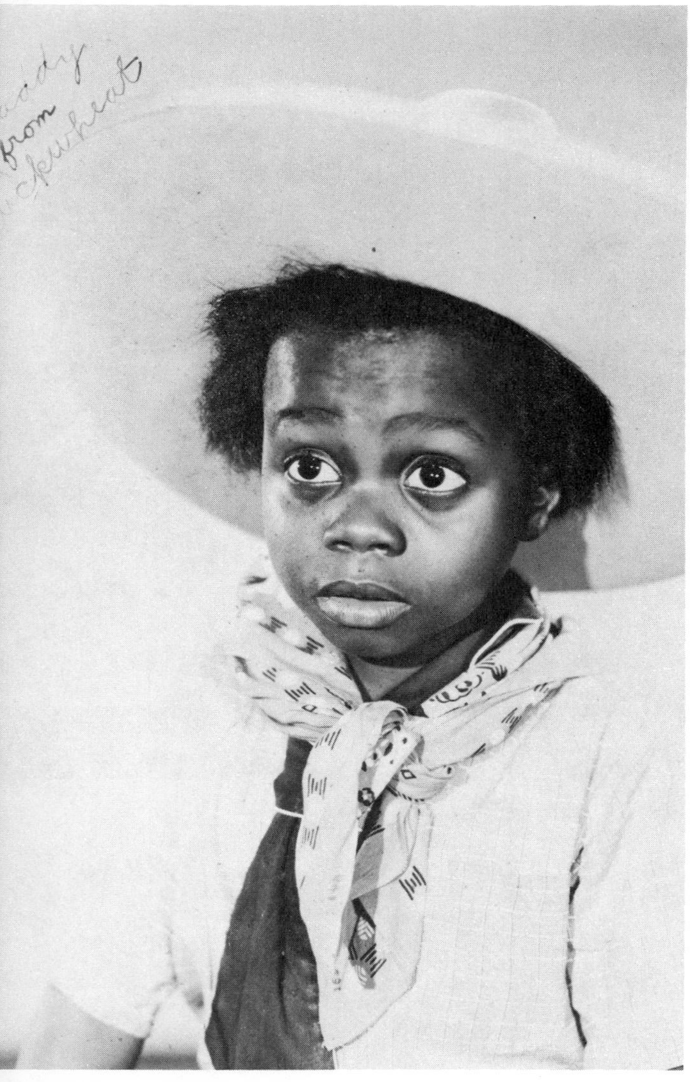

William "Buckwheat" Thomas during his <u>Our Gang</u> days.

One of *Our Gang*'s most popular members was born William Thomas in Los Angeles on March 12, 1931. He was an only child. When he was three and a half years old, his mother heard that producer Hal Roach was looking for a replacement for "Stymie," who was getting too mature to take part in the mischief-making in the famous shorts. Out of hundreds of kids, Roach picked William.

Thomas was added to the cast as "Buckwheat" in 1934. For the first few years William played the role as a little girl. His specialty of crying was particularly effective when he was in diapers or a little dress. Surrounded by some of the cutest children ever in movies, "Buckwheat" was a standout.

Most of William's earnings were put in trust for him by the court. His father was a janitor. His mother received a salary for being with him at all times on the set and when the cast toured presentation houses all over the United States. Thomas felt he was well paid for the seventy-eight comedies he appeared in.

Although he had only the happiest memories of *Our Gang,* Thomas did not keep in touch with anyone except "Stymie." They remained close friends over the years and saw each other at least once a week. The only sour note of his career came when it ended and he could no longer attend the studio school. He always cringed when he recalled how the other kids at public school teased him for the first few years he was in attendance.

When the *Our Gang* series was canceled in 1944, William's career as a film actor ended, too. After leaving the U.S. Army at the end of the Korean War, "Buckwheat" became a film lab technician. He worked at the Metro-Goldwyn-Mayer studios in Culver City, where many of the *Our Gang* shorts were filmed. Thomas once explained: "I just couldn't see going from studio to studio auditioning, and I knew even the big names had to go through that. It seemed like too much of a rat race."

"Buckwheat's" friends and co-workers didn't make a big thing about his background, and his son, who is a probation officer, got used to the fact that his dad was once famous. To the kids in his neighborhood who watched his pictures on TV under the title *The Little Rascals,* however, he was the local hero. He loved to give out autographs and pose for photos at Cub Scout meetings. At the reunion of the *Our Gang* cast held by the Sons of the Desert organization, William received a standing ovation, which moved him to tears.

Speaking of his life, he remarked in the summer of 1980: "I've got a good-looking son who's never given me one minute of trouble. I've got kids knocking on my door all the time, and I happen to love kids. I've got good friends, a nice house, and I drive a Cadillac. I think I've been a lucky person."

A divorcé, Thomas lived by himself near the University of Southern California in Los Angeles. The house was filled with his ham radio equipment and mementos of his career. Until the day he died in October 1980, he always referred to himself as "Buckwheat."

On September 27, 1980, Iris Adrian and "Buckwheat" appeared together at the Card Factory in West Hollywood, where they autographed "Hello from Hollywood" postcards carrying their pictures. In less than two weeks from that time William Thomas was dead.

Paul Adrian

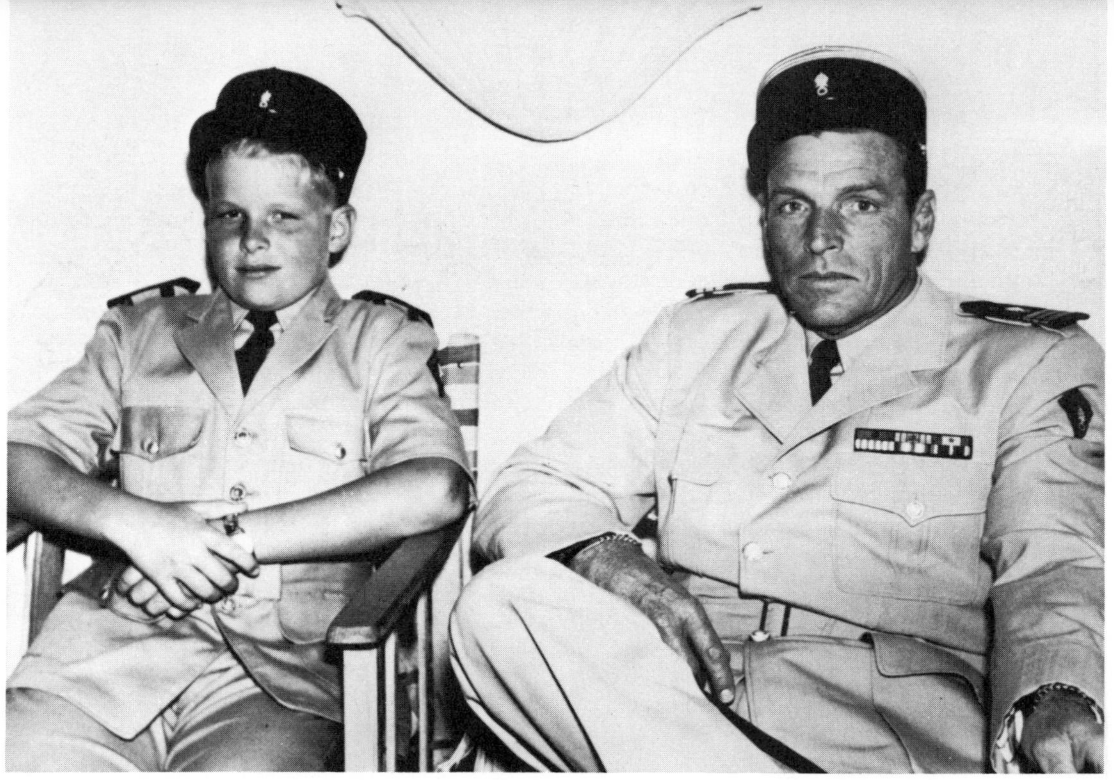

Cuffy Crabbe and his father in the mid-fifties as "Captain Gallant" and his ward "Cuffy."

"Captain Gallant of the Foreign Legion"

The adventure series was first televised over NBC from February 1955 until February 1957. The same network repeated the shows from 1960 to 1963. The half-hour programs are still being seen in some parts of the world.

Captain Gallant of the Foreign Legion was the story of "Mike Gallant" and his ward "Cuffy Sanders." The boy's father, a Foreign Legion officer, was supposed to have been killed in Indochina. Shortly afterward, when his mother lost her life in an automobile crash, "Cuffy" went to live with his father's best friend, "Captain Gallant." The title role was played by Buster Crabbe, who was born in Oakland, California, on February 7, 1908. His son Cuffy portrayed his ward.

The sixty-five shows were all filmed in black-and-white. Exteriors were shot at a French Foreign Legion outpost in Morocco. Interiors were done in Paris. Many of the two hundred Legionnaires assigned to that area were seen on the programs.

Cuffy Crabbe didn't mind acting on the shows, but he very much disliked personal appearances and being asked for his autograph. When production of the films ended, so did Cuffy's career. "My dad never encouraged me to become an actor," he said recently. "The only reason I was on the show to begin with was that the producers couldn't find the right boy to play it. At least not one whose parents would allow him to go to North Africa for all that time. The few kid actors I met I didn't get along with at all. I guess I was what you'd call a regular kid. At least that's what I wanted to be."

Speaking of his father, Cuffy has said: "We have always been real pals. Even today he's my best friend. It was great watching him on TV as 'Flash Gordon' and 'Buck Rogers' along with my friends. But lots of times he wasn't home when I was growing up because he was making a movie somewhere. That wasn't so great. I want to always be close to my family."

Cuffy was born Cullen Crabbe on September 4, 1944, in Santa Monica, California. He graduated from Arizona State University, where he took a business course and played football. Today he is in the real estate business in Arizona. His wife had never seen *Captain Gallant* when they were married.

Buster and his son are both involved with Buster Crabbe Pools, a national firm that does most of its business in the Southwest. Buster and his wife of over forty years live in Scottsdale, Arizona.

Buster Crabbe lives now in Scottsdale, Arizona.

Jon Virzi

Cuffy Crabbe today with Buster Crabbe's grandson, Cullen Crabbe, Jr.

Donna Schaeffer

Courtesy of John Tillotson Collection

Ed Prentiss posed for this Captain Midnight publicity still in 1942.

"Captain Midnight"

It may have been late afternoon by the clock on the mantel, but when boys and girls heard the sound of a plane's engine and the toll of a bell striking twelve they were transported to Midnight—the hour when radio's most famous pilot came to the rescue. The Mutual Broadcasting System presented the fictional hero Monday through Friday.

Emanating from WGN in Chicago, *Captain Midnight* was first brought to listeners in 1940, sponsored by Skelly Oil. After the first season Ovaltine dropped their sponsorship of *Little Orphan Annie* in favor of the adult, masculine character.

The Captain was as popular for his offers as for his exploits. It took the inner seal from a jar of Ovaltine to get a *Captain Midnight* "Code-O-Graph," without which a listener was unable to decipher the "secret message" he gave away at the end of each fifteen-minute episode. He also gave away an assortment of rings and winged badges (one with litmus paper that changed colors). For fifteen cents plus the Ovaltine seal one could obtain an official "Shake-up Mug."

The program was developed by Robert Burtt and Wilfred Moore, both of whom had been aviators in World War I. According to the story, Captain Midnight, whose real name was supposed to be Red Albright, had gotten his nickname from his nighttime heroism. His adversary during his lifetime on radio was the international criminal Ivan Shark, played by Boris Aplon. Then there was the equally dangerous daughter Fury Shark, who was played by both Rene Rodier and Sharon Grainger.

The title role was originated by Ed Prentiss, who left it the second season and was replaced by Bill Bouchey. The third year Prentiss was back. He stayed with the part until the end of the 1948–49 season, when he asked for a raise of $25 a week. The agency man who turned him down without consulting the sponsor was promptly fired, but by then Prentiss had gone to New York to announce for the *Dave Garroway Show*. Paul Barnes played Captain Midnight for the final season.

The hero's young friends were Chuck Ramsey, who was usually played by Jack Bibens, and Joyce Ryan, who was Mary Lou Neumayer and Angeline Orr. Their trusted but highly eccentric mechanic was Ichabod Mudd, played by Hugh Studeback. Ivan Shark had Gardo, played by Ed Hern and Earl George, to help him menace the good guys.

Kids were not the only ones to take the program seriously. In the fall of 1941 the plot concerned an unnamed foreign power that was attempting to sink a ship in order to block Pearl Harbor in preparations for an air attack. Weeks later the Japanese bombed Pearl Harbor, and the FBI visited the producers for a long and grueling interrogation about the striking coincidence.

Ed Prentiss has remained active in radio and TV, playing the part of the banker on the *Bonanza* series and parts in movies such as *The F.B.I. Story* (1959). He lives in Pacific Palisades, across the street from Walter Matthau.

In the early fifties Richard Webb played Captain Midnight on television, but the series was soon canceled. Such exciting adventures as the Captain had were not believable on TV. But for a full decade on radio the dashing hero of the skies provided the most exciting excuse a boy or girl ever had for postponing homework.

Richard Schaeffer

Ed Prentiss lives across from Walter Matthau in Pacific Palisades, California.

Sue Carol in the early thirties.

Sue Carol

The movie cutie was born Evelyn Lederer on October 30, 1907, in Chicago, Illinois. She attended Kemper Hall in Kenosha, Wisconsin, before her family moved to Los Angeles.

Director Ted Reed spotted her out of five hundred high school students on the set of *What a Life* (1926). The late Nick Stuart was then the casting director for Fox Films. He gave Sue a small part in *Slaves of Beauty* (1927). The comedian Douglas MacLean saw her in it and put her under personal contract. They made *Soft Cushions* (1927) together. The picture did nothing for its star, but it was a perfect showcase for Sue Carol.

Her career as an actress was short and profitable. None of her pictures were really important, but they all exuded the qualities Sue had in abundance—youth, energy, and sex appeal. Among them were *The Cohens and the Kellys in Paris* (1928), *Girls Gone Wild* (1929) with the late Johnny Darrow and David Rollins (single and living in Leucadia, California), *She's My Weakness* (1930), and *Secret Sinners* (1933) with the late Jack Mulhall. Shortly after making *Straightaway* (1934) she was testing for a feature at Warner's when a director told her she was "slow." She walked off the set and has never been in front of a movie camera since. "It wasn't a difficult decision," she has said. "I never enjoyed acting. But I loved movies—still do."

She became an agent and did fairly well for a while. Then she met a young actor named Alan Ladd. He had been around for a while doing bit parts when she got him a Paramount contract. Until then no one could see him as a leading man because he was exceptionally short. With one picture, *This Gun for Hire* (1942), his career took off. The same year Ladd became Sue's fourth husband. Sue had been married briefly when very young to an attorney. Her second husband was the late Nick Stuart, who costarred in many of her films. Her third husband was the actor Howard Wilson.

Some of her other "discoveries" are Julie London, whom she found running an elevator, and Rory Calhoun, who was riding a horse in Griffith Park. Peter Lawford also got his start with her help.

Sue has said that she was not nearly as influential in Ladd's career as has been reported. Maybe, but she was certainly instrumental in running up the money he made into a neat fortune. Along with her stock market manipulations, she has a keen eye for choice real estate. (Her father had been a developer.) The Alan Ladd Hardware Store in Palm Springs and the Alan Ladd Building in Beverly Hills are two of her many holdings.

Her stepson, Alan Ladd, Jr., is a motion picture executive. David Ladd, who was a child star, is now divorced from Cheryl Ladd. The Ladds' daughter, Alana, is married to Michael Jackson, who is the most popular host of talk-radio in Los Angeles. Her daughter by the late Nick Stuart is the wife of a motion picture executive. The family often congregates at Sue's Holmby Hills estate, which she and Ladd built. There are now nine Ladd grandchildren.

At the conclusion of Beverly Linet's biography of Alan Ladd, Sue Carol is quoted on her late husband:

"I'll never remarry. I'm still in love with him. . . . I'm luckier than most widows, because I still have Alan with me. I can see him in one of his pictures . . . I hear his voice, I see his face. . . ."

(Sue Carol died on February 4, 1982.)

Jon Virzi

Sue Carol-Ladd shortly before her death.

Sunset Carson in the mid-forties.

Sunset Carson

The star of B westerns was born Michael James Harrison in Plainview, Texas, on November 12, 1927.

He was eight years old when he began appearing in rodeos. By the age of twelve, Carson, who was tall for his age, had performed on horseback publicly more than forty times. In his teens he mastered bronc busting, bulldogging, calf roping, and trick riding. Tom Mix saw him at one of the events and signed the boy to travel with his circus as a trick rider. It was Mix who gave Carson the idea of becoming an actor.

He traveled throughout South America during 1941 and 1942, doing exhibition riding and shooting. His billing was as the "All-Around Champion Cowboy of South America." Returning to the United States, he took the advice of Tom Mix. He went to Hollywood and enrolled at the Pasadena Playhouse.

Producer Sol Lesser saw his picture in a newspaper article and gave him the part of "Texas" in *Stage Door Canteen* (1943) with Lon McCallister (the proprietor of the Andiron Lodge in Little River, California).

Republic Pictures was interested in him but thought he was too slender. In the meantime he entered the Armed Services. When he presented himself to the same studio after his discharge he was told he was still too light. He did a small part in *Janie* (1944) with Joyce Reynolds (widowed and living in Malibu), put on twenty pounds, and was signed to a Republic contract.

It was at Republic that he became Sunset Carson, although at first he was billed as "Sonny." Some remember him as Sunset "Kit" Carson. When his new name appeared on the screen for the first time he was billed beneath the late western comic Smiley Burnette. Very shortly thereafter he emerged a star in his own right in such B westerns as *Bordertown Trial* (1944), *Santa Fe Saddlemates* (1945) with Linda Stirling (married to screenwriter Sloan Nibley and living in North Hollywood), *Alias Billy the Kid* (1946) with Peggy Stewart (married and living in Sherman Oaks, California), and *El Paso Kid* (1946).

Don Miller summed up the appeal of Carson

in his book *Hollywood Corral:* "An honest-to-goodness cowboy. He was very young, very tall, had a baby face that the girls immediately cottoned to, and spoke slower than John Wayne, which was slow indeed, in a rather high-pitched voice."

By 1947 Sunset was among the top ten western stars in a national poll. Two years later he was among the top eight money-making western stars.

Carson made fifteen features, all horse operas, at Republic before he moved on to Astor Pictures. There he made five more, all action-packed, which was one of the features his pictures were noted for. In the early fifties Sunset starred in two short-lived TV series, *The Black Bandit* and *Ghost Rider.*

After that he became a featured attraction with the Clyde Beatty Circus. Then he toured the world with his trick riding and sharpshooting act. He has shot objects from the hands of Mme. Chiang Kai-shek and the King and Queen of Siam.

In the early seventies he turned up in Louisville, Kentucky, where he hosted western movies on station WLKY-TV.

Sunset and his wife divide their time between their Little River Ranch in Hickory, North Carolina, where he keeps his horse "Big Red," and their home in Phoenix. They often come to Hollywood in their mobile home to visit friends. Sunset is the father of a son and two daughters.

He is a big draw at western film festivals.

Producer Shelly Brodsky has the drop on Sunset Carson in this recent photograph.

Shelly Davis

Lita Grey was fifteen years old and pregnant when she became Mrs. Charlie Chaplin.

Lita Grey Chaplin

The woman who became world-famous as the teenage wife of Charlie Chaplin was born Lillita Louise McMurray on April 15, 1908, in Hollywood. Although her parents were divorced when she was eighteen months old, Lita was raised a Roman Catholic.

She first met the superstar of silent pictures in a restaurant to which her mother had taken her to celebrate her sixth birthday. She had already seen some of his two-reelers and remembers him seeming "like a god to me." Lita and her mother were bit players in Chaplin's *A Day's Pleasure* (1919), but she had no contact with him during the filming. Two years later she was playing in front of her home when his assistant director spotted her and brought Lita to Chaplin, who gave her a part in *The Kid* (1924). Thus began the relationship that resulted in their elopement to Mexico in 1924.

The comedian's new bride was fifteen years old and pregnant. In spite of her age the couple engaged in frequent bitter quarrels, in which they were joined by Lita's mother. The part Chaplin promised her in *The Gold Rush* went to Georgia Hale (living in Los Angeles) when Lita became pregnant for the second time.

They separated in 1926 and were divorced a year later. Lita was left with a sizable cash settlement and their sons, Charlie Junior and Sydney (living in Paris). During the proceedings, which were publicized around the world, Chaplin's public relations staff portrayed Lita and her mother as rather lowly born, greedy women. Mrs. Grey was related to the Lugos family, which had brought some of the first horses to the U.S. Lita's great-uncle was Henry T. Gage, a governor of California and later the U.S. Ambassador to Portugal.

After the money was spent Lita toured the country and London in a nightclub act. In 1936 she was married to a small-time vaudevillian for three months. In 1938 she remarried. When she was divorced ten years later she renounced custody of the seven-year-old boy she and her husband had adopted. In 1949 she made an unsuccessful attempt at a comeback in nightclubs, partnered with a young man who was also her lover. Today he is a successful Hollywood producer and still a close friend. In 1956 she married a man who was ten years her junior. He left her to marry another woman in 1966, although they are still friends.

In 1966 Lita published *My Life with Chaplin: An Intimate Memoir.* It had been turned down by several publishers as being too intimate. In the book and her interviews to publicize it she told stories of pettiness, greed, and sexual misconduct that many reviewers found repugnant. Chaplin was sufficiently upset to threaten litigation. Readers, however, snapped it up both in hardcover and paperback.

Lita is now working on a book of her recollections of the famous personalities she has known.

When Charlie Junior died in 1968 she filed for Social Security, claiming he had partially supported her. She and her granddaughter share in the income from the trust fund his father had set up for him over fifty years ago. In 1970, to keep occupied, Lita took the first job of her life—and loves it. She is a salesperson in the designer dresses salon of J. W. Robinson's Department Store in Beverly HIlls. She shares an apartment in West Hollywood with the man she married in 1938, a realtor.

Perhaps the most revealing glimpse into the character of Chaplin was given by Lita during an interview on radio in 1974. Commenting on the fact that both of her sons always preferred Laurel and Hardy's films to their dad's, she said, "Charlie Chaplin's genius was in comedy. He has no sense of humor, particularly about himself."

Richard Lamparski

Lita is now a salesperson in J. W. Robinson's Department Store in Beverly Hills.

Virginia Cherrill

Virginia's refined features and manner were very much in vogue in the thirties.

The actress who was once called "Hollywood's Cinderella Girl" was born on her father's farm in Carthage, Illinois, on April 12, 1908. She attended Kemper Hall, the fashionable girls' school in Kenosha, Wisconsin. She was very popular with the other students and in 1925 was chosen the queen of Chicago's Arts Ball. After finishing school she married a promising young attorney, but they were divorced after less than a year.

In 1928 Virginia came to Hollywood to visit her school chum Sue Carol. A family friend took her to the fights, where she was introduced to Charlie Chaplin. His friend, director Harry D'Arrast, had already noticed her and remarked that she had a strong potential for the screen. Chaplin signed her to play a blind flower seller in the picture he was about to make, *City Lights* (1931).

During the filming, against Chaplin's expressed orders, Virginia went to San Simeon to celebrate her birthday. When he fired her Marion Davies assured her that since scenes with Virginia in them had already been shot, Chaplin would have to rehire her. She suggested that Virginia refuse to return unless he doubled her salary. It worked out just as Ms. Davies had predicted.

Many thought that Virginia had landed the role because she was having an affair with Chaplin. "He wasn't a bit interested in me in that way," she said recently. "I was a young woman who had been married. Young girls were his thing."

She then spent a year under contract to Fox Films, followed by another year with Metro-Goldwyn-Mayer. Among her pictures were *Girls Demand Excitement* (1931) with John Wayne, *Fast Workers* (1933) with John Gilbert, and *White Heat* (1934). It was felt that her voice did not record well.

Socially, however, Virginia was a great success. When she sailed for Tahiti on Vincent Astor's yacht in 1932, it was announced that she would marry wealthy socialite William Rhinelander Stewart during the voyage. When the ship returned a few hours later, a still-single Virginia disembarked. All she would say was that the engagement had been broken by "mutual consent."

After a two-year romance with Cary Grant, they married in 1934. Many years later she told an interviewer, "Cary was really married to his career. And he was terribly jealous—even of my mother!" After a year they were divorced.

Virginia went to England, looking to revive her career in films or on stage. Instead of a contract she acquired a title. She became the Countess of Jersey. Her twenty-seven-year-old husband owned four mansions, 20,000 acres of land, and a considerable fortune. The union lasted until 1947, when they were divorced.

In 1948 she married a handsome Pole she had met at an RAF canteen during World War II. The *American Weekly* ran a piece entitled, "VIRGINIA CHERRILL'S SHIFTING LUCK: Chaplin's leading lady is still gathering four-leaf clovers, but for how long?"

Virginia is still married to the Pole, now a distinguished scientist. They live in an old, beautifully maintained house in Montecito, California. She still hears from Cary Grant, and keeps a photo of an Indian prince, another of her suitors, in her living room.

Said an old friend of hers, "Ginny has that rare quality that drew all that wealth and glamour to her, but she settled for love. In Hollywood they'd call it 'real class.' We know it as 'grace.' Hers is a true storybook life with a real happy ending."

Jon Virzi

Virginia Cherrill lives in Montecito, a part of Santa Barbara, California.

Jimmy Cagney gets in a blow for male chauvinism in this scene from Public Enemy (1931).

Mae Clarke

The promising leading lady of the thirties was born Mary Klotz in Philadelphia, Pennsylvania, on August 16, 1910. Her father was a theatre organist, well known in that area, so Mae got to see lots of free movies as a little girl. Her idol was Richard Dix.

As a child she took interpretive dancing, and at the age of thirteen began performing in nightclubs. By fourteen she was one of May Dawson's Dancing Girls. In 1924 producer Earl Lindsay saw her and put her in a show performed on the roof of the Strand Theatre in New York City. From there Mae went into small roles in such musicals as *The Noose* (1926) and *Manhattan Mary* (1927). After a vaudeville tour, Fox Films brought her and Lee Tracy to Hollywood to star in *Big Time* (1929). After that she worked with Lois Moran (widowed and living in Sedona, Arizona) in *The Dancers* (1930).

It is difficult to understand why she never became a major star after 1931, even if only for a while. In 1931 she played "Molly," the prostitute, in *The Front Page,* a smash hit of the period; had the female lead in the classic *Frankenstein;* and starred in *Waterloo Bridge* with the late Douglass Montgomery. The last production, which had Bette Davis billed seventh, is seldom seen because of the remakes. It was, however, one of the most coveted assignments in Hollywood, and her notices were excellent. That same year, she appeared in a scene that may have made her a movie immortal and/or ruined her career. The picture was *Public Enemy,* in which she had only two scenes. In one, she breakfasts with her boyfriend, Jimmy Cagney, who insults her. After the director, William Wellman, yelled, "Cut," he asked if she would do another take, "for a laugh," only this time Cagney was not going to tell her to shut up but instead would shove a grapefruit in her face. "I've always tried to be a good sport," she says. "The idea didn't appeal to me. Nobody likes having anything pushed into her face, but since it was only a gag I consented." She went home and forgot about it. When the picture was released she was astonished to find that the second version was in it. The press had a field day. Women's rights groups raised hell. It was one of the earliest and crudest examples of abuse of women on the screen and is thought by some to have triggered the fad.

Mae worked a lot after that in such movies as *Nana* (1934) with Anna Sten (living in Beverly Hills), *Hats Off* (1937) with John Payne (living in Malibu), *Women in War* (1940) with the late Wendy Barrie, *Sailors on Leave* (1941) with the late William Lundigan, *Kitty* (1945), and *Annie Get Your Gun* (1950). Because she was well liked around the studios, she has never stopped working completely, but her parts have been small and her fine work of the early years is remembered only by film buffs, who watch for her in *The Great Caruso* (1951), *Singin' in the Rain* (1952), *Voice in the Mirror* (1958), and *Thoroughly Modern Millie* (1967). When she signed for a part in *Watermelon Man* (1970), she was asked to pose in publicity stills with the late Godfrey Cambridge, threatening her with a grapefruit. "So once again I went along with the gag," she says philosophically.

Between her cameo roles, she paints and reads. Though it's been years since she last heard from her friend from her youth, Barbara Stanwyck, who started with her in chorus lines during the 1920s, she and Cagney occasionally exchange notes. One of her close friends is Robert Arthur (now an insurance broker in Los Angeles).

Mae hasn't been lucky in either money or love. "I was paid the same as the others at the time but I never really made big money," she says. "Certainly not enough to save." Her second and third marriages (to an airline pilot and an army captain) ended in divorce, as did her first, to Lew Brice, brother of Fanny Brice. "He hated being known as Mr. Mae Clarke, poor guy. But what man wouldn't?" explains Mae.

For several years Mae Clarke has lived in a bungalow on the grounds of the Motion Picture Country House. She is a convert to Roman Catholicism.

Jon Virzi

Mae Clarke lives in a cottage at the Motion Picture Country House in Woodland Hills, California.

Joyce Compton is the quintessential dumb blonde to many movie fans.

Joyce Compton

Hollywood's favorite dumb blonde was born in Lexington, Kentucky, on January 27. Her parents traveled a great deal, so Joyce was schooled in Texas, Kansas, Canada, and Oklahoma. After she won a beauty contest, the Comptons brought her to Hollywood, hoping to get her in the movies.

She was first seen in *Ankles Preferred* (1925), which was followed with *What Fools Men* (1925). Being named one of the Wampas Baby Stars in 1926 along with Joan Crawford and Janet Gaynor gave her career a boost. She was under contract at the time to First National.

In 1929 Joyce was in two Clara Bow vehicles, *Wild Party* and *Dangerous Curves.* The same year she made *Salute* with George O'Brien (living with his brother in Oklahoma) and was put under contract to Fox Films. Her next producer was Mack Sennett, who put her in a series of two-reel comedies, in which she costarred with Walter Catlett, Franklin Pangborn, and Grady Sutton (single and living in Hollywood). She found the work tiring and the atmosphere "haphazard." Although her Sennett period established her as a "name" in movie comedies, it was the men she worked with who got the laughs. The same was true in the shorts she made with Clark & McCullough and Charlie Chase. She came into her own as a comedienne when she began to freelance.

Among the over two hundred features Joyce Compton has appeared in are *Only Yesterday* (1933), *Magnificent Obsession* (1935), *The Awful Truth* (1937), *They Drive by Night* (1940), *Manpower* (1941), *Mildred Pierce* (1945), *Night and Day* (1946), *Sorry, Wrong Number* (1948), and *Mighty Joe Young* (1949). Her personal favorites include *Spring Madness* (1938), *Balalaika* (1939) with the late Ilona Massey, *Bed Time Story* (1941), and *Christmas in Connecticut* (1944).

In 1934 Joyce made *White Parade,* a story of nurses in training. She believes it was that experience that gave her the idea for a second career. "I felt it was something I could do for humanity," she said recently. "The doctors sent me out as someone 'special' to get their patients well. And the sick people flipped when they recognized me from my comedy roles." She continued to take nursing cases up until recently, long after she had left acting.

Joyce lives by herself in a large Tudor house she and her parents built in 1935. An only child, Compton was very close to her mother and father, and lived with them until they died. Her companion now is a large white cat named Taj. She takes him with her wherever she goes, the cat wearing the jeweled harness she made for him.

Joyce paints in oils and is a skilled chef, specializing in organic foods.

"I am not one to live in the past," she says. "I am an old-fashioned Christian and go the Born Again route. I like nothing better than discussing the amazing Bible prophecies that are so rapidly being fulfilled today."

Joyce Compton played waitresses, girlfriends, chorus girls, southern belles, and a drunk. In *Sky Murder* (1940) she was a detective just as smart as her costar Walter Pidgeon. Yet whenever she is recognized by fans it is always as the dumb blonde she portrayed so well and often. When film historian Leonard Maltin asked her about her image in the minds of most movie buffs, she replied: "Sometimes one has to be smart to play dumb!"

Joyce Compton recently beside a self-portrait of her during her heyday in pictures.

Bobby Downey

Marjorie Ann Mutchie's first appearance on the screen as "Cookie Bumstead" was in It's a Great Life (1943), with Penny Singleton playing "Blondie" and Arthur Lake as "Dagwood."

"Cookie Bumstead": Marjorie Ann Mutchie

The little girl who played "Cookie Bumstead" in sixteen of the *Blondie* movies was born on June 3, 1939, in Los Angeles. When she was three years old her parents enrolled her with Ethel Meglin, who trained the "Famous Meglin Kiddies," a troupe of youngsters who danced and sang in presentation houses around Los Angeles. Shirley Temple and Judy Garland were two of the child stars who blossomed under Ethel Meglin's tutelage.

The character "Cookie" first appeared in *Blondie's Blessed Event* (1942), the plot of which had "Blondie" giving birth to a baby girl. The infant "Cookie" was Norma Jean Wayne. The part of "Cookie" at age six months was taken by Majelle White in *Blondie for Victory* (1942).

Marjorie was not the first choice to play the part of "Cookie" as a little girl. The first little actress, whom she refuses to name, had a temper tantrum the first day of shooting. A talent scout from Columbia Pictures, the studio that produced all the *Blondie* films, picked Marjorie from Mrs. Meglin's school only six weeks after she joined the class.

For the next seven years she played "Cookie," baby sister of "Alexander Bumstead," who theretofore had been called "Baby Dumpling." Her starting salary in 1943 was $50 a week. Her mother, who was with her at all times on the set, was also paid.

For the first three *Blondie* pictures she made, *It's a Great Life* (1943), *Footlight Glamour* (1943), and *Leave It to Blondie* (1945), she was billed as Marjorie Ann Mutchie, her real name. Then her professional name was changed to Marjorie Kent.

Marjorie's recollections of the *Blondie* films are rather vague. She has no unpleasant memories of making the films and says everyone was nice to her. But the only other child on the set was Larry Simms, who considered himself too old to join in games with her. The only actor she remembers ever playing with her was Edward G. Robinson. After the series ended in 1950 she never saw any of the cast again, nor did she make any other movies.

During her teens Marjorie modeled for a while in a Los Angeles department store.

Asked recently if she had ever had any regrets about her career ending so early, she responded, "I never was sorry that I left show business, and there were many times I regretted that I had ever been in it."

After graduating from high school Marjorie worked in a dime store and then in a bank. Frequently people recognized her name or her face and asked, "Aren't you the girl who played 'Cookie'?" She always denied that she was. She never mentioned her film-making years to any of her friends or the boys she dated. In the only interview she has ever given she explained: "I became convinced that there were a lot of people trying to befriend me just because I was 'Cookie,' a celebrity of sorts. I deeply resented it and withdrew from everything concerned with acting as soon as I could."

Marjorie's first marriage was annulled. She and her second husband, Eugene DeLony, live with their teenage son and daughter in La Verne, California. They are Roman Catholics. There is no one in her life today who was connected with her career, and many of her friends are unaware that she was ever an actress.

The former "Cookie Bumstead" worked for a chain of stores doing floral arrangements. She reads *Blondie* every day in the newspaper and wishes the films would be shown more often on television.

Today Marjorie is Mrs. Eugene DeLony of La Verne, California.

Stanton Z. La Vey

Mark Copage costarred with Diahann Carroll on Julia from 1968 to 1971.

Mark Copage

The boy who became nationally famous as "Julia's" son was born in Los Angeles on June 21, 1962. His father was an actor before becoming a real estate broker. Mark's mother is a performer. His parents were divorced when he was three years old. His older brother is a reporter with the *New York Daily News.*

Three weeks after he was born Mark Copage made his screen debut in a brief scene in the movie *Tammy and the Doctor* (1963) with the late Stanley Clements.

His big break came when his father's agent suggested Mark to Twentieth Century–Fox, the studio that was about to produce the TV series *Julia.* He made the pilot when he was five years old and was signed to play "Corey Baker," the son of Diahann Carroll, who was cast in the title role. [*Julia* was about a beautiful widow's effort to pursue a career in nursing and raise her young son in a large city. The apartment building they lived in and the school he attended were integrated.]

Julia premiered over NBC Television on September 17, 1968, and lasted until 1971.

Mark says he enjoyed being on the show, although he admits that it somewhat distorted his concept of living during those three years. "I thought everyone got to ride in a limousine everywhere they went," he said recently. "But not being on a series had its advantages, too. I'd had a tutor until the show ended and then I went to public school. I found that a lot of girls had crushes on me from watching the show, and I had a lot more time to see my friends and family. There was never time for athletics when I was working steadily." He is a sports enthusiast.

Although he had good relations with the other members of the *Julia* cast, Mark hasn't remained close to any of them. In 1981 he hadn't seen Diahann Carroll in over two years. It was over five years since he had been in touch with Michael Link or Lloyd Nolan.

After *Julia* was canceled Mr. Copage turned down many of the offers his son received. He was determined that the boy get a really good education. The Copages moved to Beverly Hills mainly so that Mark could attend the highly accredited Beverly Hills High School. When he went to the prom in 1981 his date was Linda Morris, the sister of Gregg Morris.

Mark acts in school plays and is seen occasionally on television. He means to stay in show business, either as an actor or as a director. "It's difficult for me right now because it was easy for me earlier," he explains. "People know my name and face but I'm always thought of as 'Julia's' little boy. The trouble with that is that 'Corey' wasn't a ghetto kid. That doesn't mean I can't play a boy from the other side of the tracks. But the thinking is, 'Mark Copage—he's too apple pie for this part.'"

He does not plan to go to college, but takes lessons in singing, dancing, "just about everything that will make me a more versatile performer." Asked what his life goal is, he responded, "To be a movie star!"

Michael Knowles

Mark is a student at Beverly Hills High School.

Donald Crisp won the Academy Award as the Best Supporting Actor of 1941 for How Green Was My Valley.

Donald Crisp

The director of silent pictures and character actor was born near Abberfeldy, Scotland, on July 27.

When he was nineteen years old Donald left his father's dairy farm to become a trooper in the 10th Hussars during the Boer War. When it ended he signed up as a crew member on a ship bound for New York. While aboard, one night he sang a solo at a benefit for seamen. The head of an opera company was in the audience and liked Crisp's tenor voice. He was hired to perform in the chorus.

Once in the U.S., Donald soon moved from opera to a behind-the-scenes job with George M. Cohan. As early as 1906 Crisp was working in and around movies, as both an actor and a director of one-reelers. He was engaged by D. W. Griffith, who brought him to Hollywood, where he directed all the battle scenes of the silent classic *Birth of a Nation* (1915). He also played U. S. Grant in the picture. He said it was his sister, who was on a visit from Scotland, who suggested the title for the film to Griffith.

He gave up directing soon after sound swept the industry. The reason, he said, was that producers began insisting that relatives and friends be cast in leading roles. "Almost everything on film was making money then," he said years later. "They got the idea that anyone could be a star. I felt that was my cue to move along."

Crisp had acted in silents, but sporadically. He played parts in *The Bonnie Crier Bush* (1921) and *Don Q, Son of Zorro* (1925) with Douglas Fairbanks, Sr., two of the more than one hundred pictures he directed. He also directed the Buster Keaton film *The Navigator* (1924).

Donald Crisp is known for his acting, which he did so convincingly in dozens of talkies, including the classics: *Red Dust* (1932), *Mutiny on the Bounty* (1935), *Jezebel* (1938), *Wuthering Heights* (1939), *Lassie Come Home* (1943), and *National Velvet* (1944).

He received an Oscar for the Best Supporting Actor of 1941 playing the head of a family of miners in *How Green Was My Valley.*

Some of his other screen appearances were in *The Little Minister* (1934), *The Life of Emile Zola* (1937), *Juarez* (1939), *Dr. Jekyll and Mr.*

Hyde (1941) and *The Valley of Decision* (1945). He was in films up until the mid-sixties. One of the best of his later ones was *The Last Hurrah* (1958), in which he played a Roman Catholic cardinal.

Very few of his fans were aware of Crisp's activities away from the movie studios. During World War I he had been on the staff of General Pershing. He was a colonel in the OSS in World War II. Many major motion pictures were made because of his say-so. For twenty years he was a consultant to the Bank of America and his opinion was sought whenever the financing of a feature was being considered.

Crisp was not part of the Hollywood scene in a social sense. He built a large house in Hollywood at 1853 North Vista Street in 1924 and lived there quietly with his wife, Jane Murfin. Mrs. Crisp, who was the coauthor of the plays *Smilin' Through* and *Lilac Time,* also wrote the screenplays for *Roberta* (1935), *The Women* (1939), *Pride and Prejudice* (1940), and *Dragon Seed* (1944). Her death in 1957 left a great void in his life. They had no children.

In the early seventies Donald Crisp moved to a cottage at the Motion Picture Country House in Woodland Hills, where he died in May 1974.

In an interview he gave in 1973 he was asked the year of his birth. "I asked that myself when I was a little boy," he responded in the soft brogue so familiar to moviegoers. "They didn't remember. With ten children, I guess, it is quite difficult to keep track. But I'm either ninety-three or ninety-four. I can assure you that it doesn't matter a bit to me, and it won't to you if you live this long."

Donald Crisp in 1973, the year before his death.

Richard Lamparski

Brandon Cruz and Bill Bixby in a scene from the TV series The Courtship of Eddie's Father.

Brandon Cruz

"Eddie" of *The Courtship of Eddie's Father* fame was born on May 28, 1962, in Bakersfield, California. His parents separated and were divorced when Brandon was still very young. He is the oldest of four children.

Brandon Cruz's mother responded to an advertisement directed to parents who thought their children might have the looks and personality to act in television commercials. People had commented on how cute he was, and the financial potential was appealing. Mrs. Cruz agreed to pay to have Brandon's reactions and speech recorded on videotape. A talent agent happened to be in the studio at the time and had a brief exchange with the Cruzes. He asked to see the tape that was to be made.

Brandon was freckled, small even for his five years, and had begun to lose his baby teeth. The audtion tape made the most of all these qualities. The agent took it to the company that was about to shoot a pilot for a proposed TV series based on the feature film *The Courtship of Eddie's Father* (1962).

In the movie Glenn Ford had portrayed the widowed father and Ron Howard took the part of "Eddie Corbett." On the TV show Bill Bixby played the father to Brandon's "Eddie." The part of "Mrs. Livingston," the Corbett's housekeeper, was played by Miyoshi Umeki (now living in Japan). James Komack was Bixby's hotshot bachelor friend. Teri Garr played Bixby's secretary. The show's theme, "Best Friend," was sung by Gerry Robinson.

For some viewers the highlight of the entire series was the appearance of a very young Jody Foster, who even then exuded star quality. She played a tomboy who beat up on Eddie.

Cruz and Bixby were publicized as being

very close off camera as well. They appeared together in a special for which they went to Hungary to see the Budapest Circus. When Brandon came to visit his costar he stayed in the room kept for him in the actor's Malibu home. Bixby was then a bachelor. Brandon was a guest on *The Incredible Hulk* once with Bixby, but seldom hears from him these days.

Cruz was in the special *The Going Up of David Lev* with Melvyn Douglas and guested on such shows as *Kung Fu, Love American Style,* and *Medical Center.*

Brandon has lived with his grandparents since he was ten years old. They share a house in Camarillo, California. "He loved everything about that show," said his proud grandmother recently. Then she quickly added, "Well, I think being called 'Eddie' bothered him a lot. When fans would call him that name he'd always correct them. It was real cute."

Cruz enrolled in a course in business administration at Ventura College in the fall of 1981, but at the last minute decided instead to channel all of his energies into pursuing his acting career and working with his band. He is the lead singer in a group called "The Eddys." He describes their music as "sort of punk" or "speed rock." Most of his friends call him "Eddy." Asked if he minded, he said, "I guess not. I'm used to it now."

Brandon Cruz readily admits that he still misses being on the series and would very much like to appear in another on a regular basis. Asked what he will do if he doesn't succeed as an actor, he responded: "I've been in show business for over ten years. I know that eventually I'll do something again, maybe behind the scenes, if I don't get acting parts. But television is going to be my profession. I'm sure of that."

Brandon Cruz lives in Camarillo, California, where he is the lead singer in a rock group.

Gawain Bierne-Keyt

The daffy Cass Daley was called "radio's most popular comedienne" in 1946.

Cass Daley

The comedienne who made a career out of buckteeth and a large rear-end was born Katherine Daley on July 17, 1915, in North Philadelphia, Pennsylvania. Her father was a streetcar conductor for over forty years. In her early teens she had to drop out of school for all but one day a week so she could help her family by working in various small jobs. The most she made during this period was a $12 week.

One Saturday night in 1933, friends insisted that Cass perform during an amateur show in Gloucester City, New Jersey. She had quite a reputation for making people laugh and had once lost a job for mimicking the foreman. In her debut she sang "Please Don't Talk About Me When I'm Gone," accompanying herself on the ukulele. Until that moment she had never thought of going into show business. After that, she never thought of doing anything else.

For the next few years Cass went from nightclub hatcheck girl/singer to singer at a Walk-a-thon that was emceed by the then unknown Red Skelton. Next came the vaudeville circuits and presentation houses, where she sang briefly with Ozzie Nelson's band. She replaced Judy Canova (single and living in Hollywood) in the *Ziegfeld Follies* of 1936, and then toured the music halls of Great Britain. In 1939 she was back on Broadway with Joe Penner in *Yokel Boy*.

By this time Cass had learned to capitalize on a face and figure that would have ruined the life of another woman. In school she had been told her teeth were so big she could eat corn on the cob through a tennis racket, and so in her early act she tried to sing blues without showing her teeth. Now she featured them every time she opened her mouth, and made sure no one missed her generous backside. The audiences convulsed.

Cass signed with Paramount Pictures in 1941, just about the time she began to click on radio on such shows as *Maxwell House Coffee Time.* She pinch-hit several times for comedienne Joan Davis and even replaced radio's *Fitch Bandwagon* with her own show one summer. It was on radio that she popularized the expression "I said it and I'm glad!" She drew very well in presentation houses such as the New York Paramount Theatre. The studio, however, took 50 percent of all of her outside earnings.

Her screen debut, *The Fleet's In* (1942), was probably her best film, although her favorite was *Riding High* (1943) with Glenn Langan (living in Camarillo, California, with his wife, Adele Jergens). Among her eleven others were *Crazy House* (1943) with Martha O'Driscoll (now Mrs. Arthur Appleton of Chicago), *Variety Girl* (1947) with Olga San Juan (divorced from Edmund O'Brien and living in Los Angeles), *Here Comes the Groom* (1951), and then, after a hiatus, *The Spirit Is Willing* (1967), followed by *Norwood* (1971) with Joe Namath.

By the time her seven-year Paramount contract had expired Cass had borne a son by her husband-manager, Frank Kinsella. "We were living in Newport Beach, which is quite a drive from Hollywood," she once explained, "and you know what it's like out here—out of sight, out of mind!" She admitted, too, that she never really tried very hard to find work on TV, which would have been the perfect medium for her visual, broad comedy.

By 1970 Cass and her husband had divorced. She wanted to make a comeback, if only for the income. "Frankly, I ran out of money," she admitted in a 1972 interview. In 1971 she did *The Music Man* in St. Louis and in 1972 toured in *The Big Show of 1936* with Beatrice Kay (living in a retirement home in Hollywood). But casting directors didn't recognize her name. "And when I tell them who I am they don't seem to care," she once said.

The daffy lady, whom millions knew as a raucous, man-starved female, was by her own description "really dullsville" off the screen. She was killed in March 1975, when she fell and hit her head on the edge of a glass coffee table in her small apartment only a few blocks away from Paramount studios.

Jon Virzi

Cass Daley in 1974, the year before she was killed in a fall.

Bebe Daniels was one of the most versatile stars of the silent screen.

Bebe Daniels

The early screen star was born in Dallas, Texas, to a theatrical family. Her birth date was January 13, 1901, and her original name was Phyllis. Her parents moved to Los Angeles when Bebe (pronounced "bee-bee") was a baby, and she was educated in convent schools. She played child roles in early silent films and for several stock companies that were located in Los Angeles.

Before appearing in a feature picture as an adult, Bebe made over two hundred shorts with comedians Harold Lloyd and Snub Pollard. While she was dining one night with Lloyd, Cecil B. De Mille spotted her and offered her a part in *Male and Female* (1919). Some of her other early movies were *Everywoman* (1919), *Affairs of Anatol* (1921), *North of the Rio Grande* (1922), *Monsieur Beaucaire* (1924) with Rudolph Valentino, *Argentine Lover* (1924) with the late Ricardo Cortez, and *Lovers in Quarantine* (1925) with Alfred Lunt.

Even in the beginning, Bebe had the distinction of being liked as much by her colleagues as by her fans. She and the late Betty Compson were chosen as the two stars most popular with other stars. In 1920 movie fan magazines conducted a poll among their readers to determine the most popular film folk, and Bebe Daniels was sixth on a list headed by Mary Pickford.

In 1921 the actress was arrested for speeding and sentenced to ten days in jail. Her cell had a Persian rug on the floor, her meals were catered by a fine restaurant—and her Stutz was parked outside. Musicians serenaded her, and just about every star in Hollywood came to visit her—among the 792 who signed her guest book were Jesse Lasky, Jack Pickford, Eddie Sutherland, and Priscilla Dean (living in Leonia, New Jersey). As soon as she was released she went into a picture based on her experience, called *The Speed Girl* (1921).

Bebe Daniels was probably the most versatile star in silent films. Paramount Pictures put her in westerns, melodramas, comedies, costume epics, and flapper stories. Before the advent of sound she appeared in pictures such as *Miss Brewster's Millions* (1926), *Volcano* (1926), *A Kiss in a Taxi* (1927), *Take Me Home* (1928) with Neil Hamilton (married and living in Escondido, California), and *Feel My Pulse* (1928) with the late Richard Arlen.

When her studio refused to believe she could make a successful talkie, she bought out her contract and went to RKO, where she not only talked but sang in one of the most successful musicals in movie history, *Rio Rita* (1929). After that Bebe was a bigger star than ever, and went on to make such sound films as *Dixiana* (1930), another musical, *Reaching for the Moon* (1931) with Bing Crosby in his first important part, *The Maltese Falcon* (1931), *Silver Dollar* (1932), *42nd Street* (1933), and *Counsellor at Law* (1933) with John Barrymore.

Bebe was probably the most eligible bachelor girl in Hollywood and dated such notables as Jack Dempsey, tennis star Bill Tilden, and Rod La Rocque. The son of Wallace Reid believes that his father and Bebe were lovers early in her career. All that changed on June 14, 1930, when she married Ben Lyon with whom she made *Alias French Gertie* (1930). They toured the United States in several plays during the thirties, with time out for Bebe to do *The Song You Gave Me* (1933) in England. In 1936 the husband-wife team went to London for a three-week Palladium engagement, which was so successful they toured the British Isles with the act until 1939, when Ben became the head of the English talent office for Twentieth Century–Fox. Even after World War II broke out the Lyons stayed on in London, earning the love and respect of the English people by entertaining servicemen and civilians throughout the Blitz. In 1946 they returned to Hollywood but after a short time there decided that they had truly become Londoners, and moved back.

In England they made feature films that were never shown in the U.S.: *Life with the Lyons* (1954) and *The Lyons in Paris* (1956). Their program *Hi, Gang* ran for twelve years on radio and four years on TV.

A series of strokes, which began in 1963, made Bebe a semi-invalid during the last years of her life. Ben, who was in constant attendance, saw to it that she continued to see old friends and give interviews. Until the day she died, March 16, 1971, they were considered by those who knew them well to be a truly happily married couple. They were also one of the most admired in Great Britain.

Richard Lamparski

Ben Lyon and Bebe Daniels in their apartment in London, August 1970.

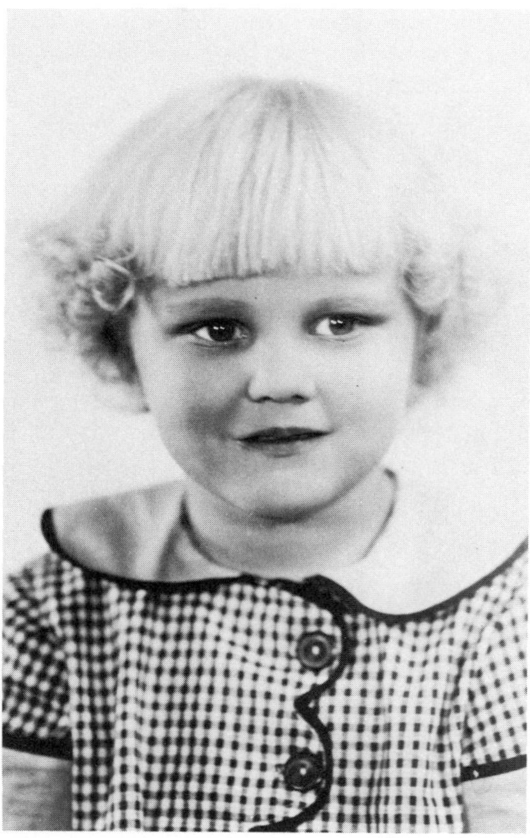

Jean Darling is remembered by her classmate, "Baby Peggy Montgomery" as "the most beautiful little girl I had ever seen."

Jean Darling

The lovely little blonde of early *Our Gang* shorts was born in Santa Monica, California, on August 23. Her parents separated when she was still a baby, and afterward, her mother changed her surname to her own middle name. At the age of six months Dorothy Jean LeVake became Jean Darling.

An executive with Hal Roach brought Jean to the attention of the producer after he saw her on the street. She was four years old when she made the first of thirty-five *Our Gang* (now known on television as *The Little Rascals)* two-reelers.

Jean was part of all of the mischief the "Gang" got into, but her screen presence was more demure than that of Darla Hood, who followed her. After appearing in *Bouncing Babies* (1929), which was her last in the series, Jean went on a public-appearance tour of the RKO-Orpheum theatres that lasted for about two years.

She returned to the Roach lot to play "Curly Locks" in *Babes in Toyland* (1934) with Laurel and Hardy. Then she portrayed Virginia Bruce as a little girl in *Jane Eyre* (1934) and a mermaid in *The Bride of Frankenstein* (1935).

At age thirteen, according to Ms. Darling, "I was sick of school and working. I went down to the Board of Education and took examinations to graduate high school, which I did with straight A's." She then moved to New York City, where she spent the next eight years studying voice, modeling, and working occasionally in vaudeville.

Lee Shubert put her under contract and presented her in *Blossom Time, The Student Prince,* and *Knickerbocker Holiday.* In 1942 she made her Broadway debut in *Count Me In.*

During World War II Jean toured Italy and North Africa for the USO. She was "Carrie" in the original Broadway production of *Carousel* (1945) for 850 consecutive performances. She was also seen in the 1949 revival of *Pal Joey.*

She worked regularly on such radio programs as *Hilltop House* and *Bobby Benson and the H-Bar-O Riders.* She had a show on TV in the early fifties, *A Date With Jean Darling,* and then hosted a women's program in Los Angeles, *The Singing Knit-Witch.*

In June 1954, Jean married "Kajar the Magician." Their son, Roy Bowen, was born in 1955. For a while she was part of her husband's act, singing and seemingly floating on air. The Bowens made a three-year tour of South Africa, South America, and Europe before settling in Ireland in 1967. They had been separated for seven years when he died in 1980.

Jean and her son, who is a numismatist and philatelist, live in Dublin. She paints African animals in watercolors. Her mystery stories have been published in Alfred Hitchcock's and Ellery Queen's magazines. Plays she has written are produced over radio in the British Isles and South Africa. She rides her motorbike from her home to the radio station, where Jean is heard as "Aunt Poppy" on *Poparama,* a kiddy show carried throughout Ireland.

Diana Serra Cary, known in silent pictures as "Baby Peggy Montgomery" and the author of *Hollywood's Children,* attended professional school in Hollywood with Jean Darling. "She was the most beautiful little girl I'd ever seen," said Ms. Cary recently. "She seemed to be everything the rest of us aspired to be. Yet I sensed no real ambition in her. Like most of us, she seemed to have a large key in her back. She'd been wound up by someone and was hitting all the marks."

Jean Darling told the author of *Our Gang:* "I got to thinking I was a little god. I lived in a world of make-believe, surrounded by people who oohed and ahed. . . . That sort of thing could have destroyed me. . . . I sometimes think the fact that I was spared was just plain magic."

Roy Bowen

Jean Darling lives in Dublin, Ireland, and works as a children's entertainer on radio. She's also the author of mystery stories.

Johnnie "Scat" Davis made Sarong Girl (1943) and Knickerbocker Holiday (1944) after leaving Warner Brothers.

Johnnie "Scat" Davis

The musician-actor was born on May 11, 1910, in Brazil, Indiana. Both his father and grandfather were concert musicians.

Davis, his brothers, and their father all played the trumpet and clarinet. Johnnie began lessons when he was three and a half years old and debuted at the age of six playing "America" with his grade school band.

After leaving high school he played with the Jimmy Joy, Smith Ballew, and Red Nicholas bands. Later he joined the Fred Waring Orchestra and came to Hollywood with that group. Records cut by those bands that are now collectors' items, such as "Waiting for the Evening Mail," "Junk Man Blues," and "Let's All Sing like the Birdies Sing," feature Davis's trumpet.

Johnnie had supporting roles in movies like *Varsity Show* (1937), *Cowboy from Brooklyn* (1938) with the late Dick Foran, and *Brother Rat* (1938). His studio, Warner Brothers, gave him one lead, the title role in *Mr. Chump* (1938) with Lola Lane.

In most of his films Davis sang and played the trumpet. His vocal is the original rendition of "Hooray for Hollywood," which he sang in *Hollywood Hotel* (1937). Even those who did not appreciate him concede that his voice and screen presence made him unlike anyone before or since. When Warner Brothers decided to cut back on its production of musicals in late 1939, Davis's option was not picked up.

The movies had made him a name and his sound was then very popular. The Johnnie "Scat" Davis band appeared at most of the country's top clubs during the forties. In 1951 Johnnie had his own TV show, which emanated from Detroit.

In the late fifties Davis settled in Arlington, Texas, with his wife and two daughters. Until 1967 he played annual dates in Las Vegas, Reno, and Lake Tahoe.

Johnnie still accepts several engagements

every year. "I'm surprised at how many gigs I'm offered," he says. "Must be from those old pictures of mine on television. But I only take a few because we don't like to be away from home for very long. Too many years on the road, I guess."

People still ask him about his middle name. "I know when they ask that they're awfully young," says Davis. "Anybody my age knows what scat is. It's a style of singing. I sing scat and play a little trumpet."

Jon Virzi

Johnnie "Scat" Davis still plays an occasional club date. He and his wife live in Arlington, Texas.

Dolores Del Rio in the late twenties.

Dolores Del Rio

The Latin beauty was born Lolita Dolores Martinez Asunsolo Lopez Negrette in Durango, Mexico, on August 3, 1905. She lived in Durango on her family's huge ranch until she was four years old, when her father, a banker, was forced to flee with his wife and daughter to Mexico City to escape the revolutionary Pancho Villa.

Dolores was educated in Mexico's capital city at the Convent of St. Joseph and, as was the custom among the class-conscious rich, was presented to the king and queen of Spain on a European trip in 1919.

Two years later Dolores married Jamie Del Rio, an attorney eighteen years her senior. Soon after, Hollywood director Edwin Carewe, while visiting Mexico, saw her dancing at a party and offered her a chance to act in his film *Joanna* (1925). It was unheard of for a young woman of her background to consider a theatrical career, but her mother and husband felt it might be fun. Only Dolores took the idea seriously. She was brokenhearted when most of her footage was edited out of her first two pictures. She was treated much better in the next two: *The Whole Town's Talking* (1926) and *Pals First* (1926). Then she won the role of Charmaine in the blockbuster *What Price Glory?* (1926). Although it was a man's picture, she did not go unnoticed. Even in an industry and city steeped in glamour and beauty, Dolores Del Rio was a standout. She appeared with the late Rod La Rocque in *Resurrection* (1927).

By the time she appeared in the title role in *Ramona* (1928) she had become an important star; meanwhile, her marriage had come apart and her director had fallen in love with her. Carewe's wife was suing him for divorce, and Hollywood expected him to marry Dolores. But before she could obtain a divorce from Del Rio, he died suddenly. Many felt Del Rio's spirit had been broken by his role as "Dolores Del Rio's husband." But it was all academic. Dolores made *Evangeline* (1929) with Carewe and then broke with him completely.

In talkies Dolores's weakness as an actress was somewhat more obvious, but she more than made up for that shortcoming with her beauty and her voice, which was also heard in song. Some of her American sound pictures were *The Bad One* (1930), *Bird of Paradise* (1932), *Flying Down to Rio* (1933), *Wonder Bar* (1934), *In Caliente* (1935) with Wini Shaw (married and living in Queens, New York), and *International Settlement* (1938) with June Lang (living in North Hollywood, California).

She was married to set designer Cedric Gibbons from 1931 to 1941. After their divorce Dolores began an affair with Orson Welles. She made *Journey into Fear* (1942) with Welles as costar and director, but their relationship ended shortly afterward when he married Rita Hayworth. In the next eighteen years Dolores made only one Hollywood picture, *The Fugitive* (1947), although she was very active in South American and Mexican cinema. In 1960 she played Elvis Presley's mother in *Flaming Star.* Since her return to Hollywood she has appeared several times on such television series as *Marcus Welby, M.D.* and in the feature films *Cheyenne Autumn* (1964), *More Than a Miracle* (1967), and *Children of Sanchez* (1978).

Dolores Del Rio travels a great deal of the time and is still considered one of Mexico's greatest stars. She has won four Arieles (Mexico's Oscar) and a Quixote (Spain's Oscar). She has appeared in stage plays in Mexico and South America.

Although her acting skills have improved considerably in the last twenty years, Dolores is best remembered by fans for her dazzling beauty, most of which she has retained to a degree that borders on the uncanny. She is undoubtedly the most beautiful of all the surviving stars of the silent era and takes great care to remain so, with strict abstinence from smoking, drinking, and overeating. Several years ago her contemporary Aileen Pringle asked her how she could look so young. Dolores answered that she was a yogi. "We think up!" she told the drinking, smoking Pringle. She reportedly sleeps as much as twelve hours a day.

Since 1959 she has been married to Lewis Riley, an American who produces in Latin-American countries. Their luxurious home is a large estate in Coyoacán, an exclusive suburb of Mexico City. It is surrounded by lush gardens and houses a large collection of pre-Columbian art.

She helped found and manages a twenty-four-hour care center in Mexico City for the children of actors and actresses.

Jon Virzi

Dolores Del Rio on a recent visit to Hollywood.

Bobby Diamond as "Joey," owner of the horse "Fury." The series is now running under the title Brave Stallion.

Bobby Diamond of "Fury"

The story of a boy and his horse premiered on NBC-TV on Saturday morning, October 15, 1955. It remained on the network for five seasons and is still in syndication under the title *Brave Stallion*. One hundred and fourteen half-hour films were made, all of them in black-and-white.

Bobby Diamond, who played the lead, "Joey," had been a professional since he could walk. His mother, who had been a vocalist with Danny Thomas, did her best to get him into movies. By the time he was two years old, he had been on the covers of *Collier's* and *Parade* magazines. She had two other children, but her efforts were concentrated on Bobby. "Probably," says Bobby, "because she got such a positive response from me. I thoroughly enjoyed everything I did in front of a camera."

Diamond was born in Los Angeles on August 23, 1943. His father was in real estate.

The opening episode of the series had "Joey" fighting in the street. Someone threw a bottle, and he was taken into custody by a policeman. "Jim Newton," who was played by Peter Graves, saw the incident and assisted in his defense in court. When the judge learned that "Joey" was an orphan, he allowed "Newton" to take him to live on his ranch, "The Broken Wheel."

"Today," says Diamond, "the kids are so hip they'd size up the situation as a gay relationship. But I was twelve years old when I signed for the series. I believed as much in those plots as our viewers did. I was so square I even ate the sponsor's product" (Post Toasties).

The other running character was the older man, "Pete," who was played by William Fawcett. He died on January 25, 1974. Bobby liked him and Peter Graves and everyone else connected with the show, including the star, the horse "Fury."

After *Fury*'s cancellation in 1960, Bobby

turned down a chance to be one of Fred MacMurray's three sons on television in favor of a role on Nanette Fabray's short-lived series. After that, he had a running part on *The Loves of Dobie Gillis.*

Since 1971, Diamond has been an attorney. His offices are in Woodland Hills and his specialties are criminal law and personal injury cases. He still acts whenever a job is offered, and in the past few years has been seen on *Banyon* and in a Johnson's Wax commercial.

Recently, he explained his change of careers: "Just when I was going into my teens, my mother died. I always felt I could do whatever a part called for, but I never had to deal with agents and casting people. She had done it for me. When *Fury* was over, I found I was really on my own. I don't miss acting like I probably would in another profession, because every time I face a jury it's like my big scene."

Diamond is also quite an accomplished gymnast. His home in Thousands Oaks, California, and his office contain equipment that he uses to work out, and their walls are covered with his oil paintings.

Bobby is still friendly with his contemporaries Paul Peterson and Tom Rettig.

Bobby Diamond has never married.

Asked if he is often recognized, he responded: "Everyone who knows me is within five years of my own age. They feel they grew up with me. Can you imagine how far ahead that puts me with chicks? It's better than residuals!"

Richard Lamparski

Bobby Diamond beside some of the oils he has painted.

Douglas Dick was on everyone's "Most Promising" list after Hal Wallis brought him to Hollywood in 1946.

Douglas Dick

The motion picture actor was born in Charles Town, West Virginia, on November 20, 1920. He was brought up in Versailles, Kentucky, and studied drama at the University of Kentucky and the University of Arizona.

After leaving the service at the end of World War II Douglas acted for a while with a group of professionals in Baltimore. A talent scout for Hal Wallis saw him in the pre-Broadway engagement of a play and brought him to the attention of the movie producer. Dick was given a contract and came to Hollywood in 1946.

Douglas got off to an impressive start in films with *The Searching Wind* (1946). In it he played the role that Montgomery Cliff had done on Broadway. In *Casbah* (1948), an unsuccessful remake of *Algiers,* he was quite effective as the sleazy informer. Then Alfred Hitchcock directed him in *Rope* (1948). The controversial *Home of the Brave* (1949) was another of his better credits. Among his other pictures were *Saigon* (1948), *The Red Badge of Courage* (1951), *The Iron Mistress* (1952), *So This Is Love* (1953), *The Gambler from Natchez* (1954) and *North to Alaska* (1960).

Professionals and fans alike were aware of Douglas Dick right from the time of his screen debut. He had the advantage of being with one of Hollywood's shrewdest and most prolific producers and was undoubtedly a gifted actor. Yet three years after *The Searching Wind* he was in a Sam Katzman cheapie, *A Yank from Indo-China,* in which he was billed under John Archer (now an executive with a Los Angeles trucking firm).

Dick received quite a bit of attention for his part in the thriller *The Accused* (1949). Playing opposite Loretta Young, he projected a sinister sensuality rarely captured on the screen in those times.

Douglas has no clear-cut explanation as to why his career faltered so early. "Perhaps I should have been more competitive for parts," he said recently, "but that's not my style. Also, I wasn't very clever socially, and that's very important in Hollywood. Hal Wallis was very good to me but he had to let me go after a couple of years because the industry was in a slump and he had no roles for me. All at once I was just another actor with some pretty good credits. To be honest, I'm very flattered that anyone noticed I was missing."

Dick acted right up until 1972, although he admits that during the last ten years he was less than dedicated to his art. "I don't regret having been an actor," he says, "and if I had to do it again to earn a living I think I could, but I'm very glad to be away from it."

Douglas married TV writer Peggy Chantler in 1963. For a while they tried to collaborate, but found it unworkable. They have several dogs but no children. The Dicks live down the street in Brentwood from Evelyn Venable (recently retired from UCLA, where she taught languages for years).

Douglas Dick spent six years in analysis before deciding to change professions. He is now a practicing psychologist.

Douglas Dick is married and practices psychology in West Los Angeles.

Zeena La Vey

The "French Bombshell" was under contract to Fox Films in the early thirties.

Fifi D'Orsay

The "French Bombshell" was born in Montreal, Canada, on April 16, 1904, with the name Yvonne Lussier. Her father, who had twelve children, worked for thirty years in the local post office. Her first job was as a typist for $6 a week. By 1924 she was making $35 a week. That was when she met a producer from New York City who told her to look him up if she ever came to Manhattan. Two family friends financed her trip, which came shortly afterward. Helen Morgan, whom Fifi had met during a personal appearance in Montreal, greeted her at the station upon her arrival in New York. She made the rounds for six months before getting a job in the chorus of the touring company of the Broadway hit *Greenwich Village Follies.* One of the show's stars, Gallagher of the team Gallagher and Shean, took an interest in her and worked Fifi into their famous act. She went over so well with audiences that they used her again in *In Dutch* (1926).

She worked steadily in vaudeville from 1926 to 1929 in an act called "Ten Dollars a Lesson." She caught the eye of Will Rogers, who asked Fox Films to test her for *They Had to See Paris* (1929). The picture and Fifi were great hits. Sound was in, and she had a cute, sexy French accent. The studio had great plans for her. She made *Hot for Paris* (1929) with Yola D'Avril (living in Port Hueneme, California), *Women Everywhere* (1930) with Clyde Cook (living in Camarillo, California), *Women of All Nations* (1931) with Greta Nissen (living in Santa Barbara, California), *The Girl from Calgary* (1932) with the late Astrid Allwyn, and *Accent on Youth* (1935). In *Going Hollywood* (1933) Bing Crosby introduced the song "Temptation" by crooning it to Fifi D'Orsay.

When she learned that her studio, which was paying her $400 a week, made huge amounts of money when she was loaned out to other studios, she was irked. Fifi left Fox, walking out on the remainder of her seven-year contract.

Fifi had played presentation houses and knew the kinds of receipts movie stars could draw in such personal appearances; in 1932 she, the late Victor McLaglin, and Edmund Lowe had headlined the bill at New York's Capitol and set records. She went out on her own, and her first booking was for $5000 a week. But what Fifi didn't seem to realize was that she was a big name because she was a movie star, and she could remain so only by continuing to make pictures. Breaking her Fox contract closed nearly every door in Hollywood to her.

By the forties, Fifi, whose trademark was

"'Ello, beeg boy!", had been working in cheap films and radio for a number of years. Her heyday was definitely over. She had no funds to fall back on; in the days when she was making $5000 a week she was spending $6000, not only supporting her family but moving about with a large entourage. "I had a very good time," she has said, "and I had a lot of people around me who were having a good time."

She attempted a comeback at the Palace Theatre in 1950. In 1952 Ralph Edwards saluted her on his *This Is Your Life* television show, which she hoped would reactivate her career, but nothing much happened. (She cashed in her gift of a round-trip plane ticket to Paris.) Fifi has done small parts in the films *What a Way to Go!* (1964) with the late Reginald Gardiner and *The Art of Love* (1965) with Miiko Taka (the proprietor of a Mexican restaurant in West Los Angeles).

She so impressed Hal Prince at an audition for *Follies* that he had a part written into the musical for her. As "Solange La Fitte" she sang "Ah, Paris!" She was with the show during its 1971–72 Broadway run and the tour that followed. Fifi still laments, however, the fact that she did not receive star billing. "When I saw zat marquee for ze first time," she said recently, "my heart, it broke."

The two husbands she divorced looked enough alike to be twins. "I like zee dark and flashing eyes," says Ms. D'Orsay. She has admitted to having been a "very, very naughty girl" in her youth, but has not had an affair with anyone since 1958. During her early days in Hollywood Fifi had a close relationship with Greta Garbo.

She lives by herself in a small apartment filled with statues and pictures of saints and portraits of herself. She is now on what she refers to as "my religious kick" and takes communion daily at a nearby Roman Catholic church in Hollywood.

The "French Bombshell" has yet to set foot outside of North America.

Richard Lamparski

Fifi lives in the same Hollywood apartment house as Betty Kean.

Ken Osmond played "Eddie Haskell."

Tony Dow played "Wally Cleaver."

Tony Dow and Ken Osmond

Although Jerry Mathers was the star of the long-running television series *Leave It to Beaver,* almost as well remembered are Tony Dow, who played Mathers's older brother, "Wally Cleaver," and Ken Osmond, who was the troublemaker, "Eddie Haskell."

Tony was born in Hollywood on April 13, 1945. His mother had been a Mack Sennett bathing beauty before working for years as the "it" girl's (Clara Bow) double. Dow's only acting experience before he got the part of "Wally" was on a television pilot that never sold. He was cast in the role when he was taken by a friend to an interview at the production offices. He canceled plans to move to Hawaii with his family when he was chosen for the series. Tony was in all of the 234 half-hour episodes. In spite of the blandness of the character he played, he developed a large and loyal following among viewers attracted to good-looking high school boys. On the shows he was a kid to his parents and an adult to his little brother.

Dow feels that he was costarred with Mathers. "The original title was *The Adventures of Wally and Beaver,*" he maintains. "They changed it because someone felt it sounded like a boy and his pet. But the stories revolved as much around me as Jerry."

The neighbor and nominal friend, "Eddie Haskell," was the program's most colorful character. While always beautifully mannered toward the elder "Cleavers," "Haskell" was usually the one responsible for getting "Beaver" or his brother or both into trouble. His name for "Beaver" was "squirt." He played a boy most people can recall from their childhoods. He was scheming and two-faced, but for the most part his guilt went undiscovered and unpunished. Osmond had the perfect expressions and attitude for the character. It was an outstanding acting job by Ken, who had been a professional since he was very young. He was born in Los Angeles on June 7, 1943.

"Beaver's" pal on the show was "Gilbert," who was played by the son of Lyle Talbot (living in North Hollywood). Steven Talbot is now a filmmaker and journalist. His TV special *Broken Arrow* won an Emmy and a Peabody Award in 1980.

Dow has a son by his first marriage, which ended in divorce. In 1980 he married a young woman whom he had met when she cast him in a McDonald's TV commercial. He and Jerry Mathers made a ten-city tour together in the play *So Long, Stanley* in 1979–80. In 1982 he appeared on a made-for-TV movie, *The Carney Case.* He lives in Venice, California.

Ken Osmond lives with his wife and two sons in the Shadow Hills area of the San Fernando Valley. He has repeatedly denied the persistent rumor that he works in porno movies under the name John Holmes or Johnny Wadd. Ken is a traffic enforcement officer for the Los Angeles Police Department.

Police officer Ken Osmond with his youngest son, Christian.

Richard Lamparski

Lauren and Tony Dow in their Venice, California, apartment.

Mathew Tombers

Dixie Dunbar is best known for her appearances in Pigskin Parade (1936), Sing, Baby, Sing (1936), and Alexander's Ragtime Band (1938).

Dixie Dunbar

The dancing doll of Hollywood and Broadway musicals of the thirties was born Christine Elizabeth Dunbar in Montgomery, Alabama, on January 18, 1918. She took dancing lessons from a very early age in Atlanta, where she was brought up. In those days she was called "Tootsie."

In 1932 Mrs. Dunbar took her daughter to New York City. Her southern drawl was so heavy that minutes after she met Harry Richman he had dubbed her "Dixie." Lying about her age, she got a job dancing at Nils T. Granlund's Paradise Restaurant.

She made her screen debut in *George White's Scandals* (1934) and then bowed on Broadway dancing with Ray Bolger in *Life Begins at 8:30* (1934). She was signed to a Twentieth Century–Fox contract from that show and brought to Hollywood, where she made *Professional Soldier* (1936) with Freddie Bartholomew (living in Leonia, New Jersey; he is a vice-president with a large New York advertising agency), *Girls' Dormitory* (1936) with Simone Simon (single and living in Paris), *Life Begins in College* (1937) with Gloria Stuart (widowed and living in West Los Angeles), and the Shirley Temple classic *Rebecca of Sunnybook Farm* (1938).

Dixie's personal favorites among her pictures are *King of Burlesque* (1936), in which she had a flashy dance number, the Sonja Henie movie *One in a Million* (1937), and *Walking Down Broadway* (1938) with the late Michael Whalen and Claire Trevor (widowed and living in Manhattan). She was also in several of the *Jones Family* series.

"I did whatever I was told to do," Dixie recalls, "but I never really enjoyed making movies like I did being in a show."

During her Hollywood years she dated Tyrone Power, Wayne Morris, Johnny Downs, and mogul Carl Laemmle, Jr.

Ms. Dunbar left Hollywood for good when she returned to Broadway in *Yokel Boy* (1939) with Buddy Ebsen and Judy Canova.

In 1940 she married the codirector of the Rockettes of Radio City Music Hall fame. Dixie had a nightclub act for a while and made appearances in presentation houses, but her husband discouraged her from working.

The last the public saw of Dixie Dunbar was her legs. From 1949 to 1951 she danced in television commercials wearing a huge Old Gold cigarette box as her costume.

After her 1952 divorce she owned and operated a steak house in Florida. For over twenty years Dixie has been the wife of the wealthy Jack L. King. "Jack just goes right up the wall if he hears anyone refer to me as 'Dixie,'" she said recently in a pronounced drawl. To her friends these days she is "Christine," although her husband calls her "Mama."

Asked if she missed the limelight, Ms. Dunbar replied: "Not a bit. I enjoyed my career but it was my mother who had all the ambition. I find the work I do today for our hospital and church very fulfilling. And I discovered that I have a green thumb." Dixie teaches Sunday school at the Congregational church in Miami Beach and belongs to the same garden club as Toby Wing.

Dixie Dunbar in Miami Beach, Florida, where she lives with her husband.

Don Koll

The amiable Irish face of James Dunn in the mid-thirties.

James Dunn

The actor who came back from professional oblivion to win an Oscar was born on November 5, 1905, in New York City. He was raised mostly in New Rochelle and for a while worked there selling lunch wagons.

In 1927 Dunn began hanging around the Paramount Pictures studios in Astoria, Long Island, hoping to get work as an extra. By 1929 he was doing bit parts. Then he got a role in the Helen Morgan show *Sweet Adeline* (1929). Fox Films, like all the other studios at the time, was signing up young stage actors for talking pictures. James was put under contract and brought to Hollywood.

James Dunn became a star in the first part he was given. *Bad Girl* (1931) was based on a best-selling book of the period. The picture was a box-office smash and was nominated for an Academy Award as the Best Picture of the year. Its director, Frank Borzage, and its scenarist, Edwin Burke, both won Oscars. The title role was played by Sally Eilers.

In hopes of capitalizing on the popularity of the Eilers-Dunn combination, Fox cast them in several more movies, such as *Sailor's Luck* (1933) and *Hold Me Tight* (1933).

Dunn was used frequently during the four years he spent under contract to Fox. Some of his pictures during that time were *The Girl in 419* (1933) with Gloria Stuart (now a sculptor living in Beverly Hills), *Have a Heart* (1934) with Jean Parker (single and living in Glendale, California), and *The Daring Young Man* (1935) with Mae Clarke (living at the Motion Picture Country House in Woodland Hills, California). His most important screen appearances then were with the studio's biggest star, Shirley Temple. He supported her in *Stand Up and Cheer* (1934), *Baby, Take a Bow* (1934), and *Bright Eyes* (1934).

In 1933 James was very much the man about town. He and the late Lona Andre, the winner of Paramount's "Panther Woman" contest, announced their engagement, but when the day of the wedding arrived the prospective bride changed her mind on the way to the courthouse. On New Year's Day 1938, he married Frances Gifford. The marriage ended in divorce.

Shortly after Darryl F. Zanuck merged his company with Fox Films to create Twentieth Century–Fox, Dunn was called into producer Sol Wurtzel's office and told that his option would not be renewed. Years later James told an interviewer that it was at that point that he ruined his career by "looking at my fee in the contracts rather than my parts in the scripts." His other mistake was heavy drinking.

Dunn made pictures after leaving Fox, but none with any distinction. In 1940 he was back on Broadway in *Panama Hattie* with Ethel Merman.

In 1931 Dunn was making a personal-appearance tour when he met Gloria Grafton. She was a singer and they were on the same bill at a Pittsburgh presentation house that had Dick Powell as its emcee. James and Gloria never got to know each other very well, but he made an impression on her. Over a decade later she overheard two executives at Twentieth Century–Fox talking about the difficulties they were having in casting a role of the father in the upcoming screen version of the best-seller *A Tree Grows in Brooklyn.* Ms. Grafton interrupted them to suggest Dunn. "He's unreliable," said one. "And a drunk," the other added. Gloria persisted, telling them that the person they had described was the character they were looking for: weak, charming, and slightly inebriated.

The idea was taken to Zanuck. The studio head, against strong advice to the contrary, cast James as "Jimmy Nolan," the Irish waiter. "They needed a bum, so they hired me," a jubilant Dunn announced to the press.

Dunn was perfect as the father who couldn't properly support his family or stay sober. His scenes with Peggy Ann Garner are especially touching. Not only did he receive the Oscar as the Best Supporting Actor of 1945 but he had the satisfaction of playing the part while wearing a discarded tuxedo he'd found in the studio wardrobe department. Inside the coat was the name of its former owner, Sol W. Wurtzel.

But the success did not really revive his career. By 1951 he was forced to declare bankruptcy. The following year his breezy style helped make *It's a Great Life* a hit of the television season.

After winning the award his pictures were *Killer McCoy* (1948), *The Bramble Bush* (1960), and *Hemingway's Adventures of a Young Man* (1962).

In 1966 his last film, *The Oscar,* was released. The next year, on September 3, James Dunn died after abdominal surgery. His friends Robert Young and Jackie Coogan were among the mourners at his funeral.

Jon Virzi

James Dunn shortly before he died in 1967.

The late John Cromwell, who directed Irene Dunne in five films, said she always had the look of a cat who had swallowed the canary.

Irene Dunne

The motion picture star was born in Louisville, Kentucky, on December 20 (some sources give the year as 1901, others as 1904). Her mother, who was an accomplished pianist, saw to it that Irene received expert vocal coaching. After years of study in Indianapolis, Irene was auditioned by the Metropolitan Opera but was turned down.

Her stage career began in the touring company of *Irene* in 1920. Ms. Dunne had supporting parts in Broadway productions of *The Clinging Vine* (1922), *The City Chap* (1925), and *Sweetheart Time* (1926) before getting the title role in *Luckee Girl* (1928).

The first of the forty-two feature films Irene made was *Leathernecking* (1930). Then Richard Dix, who had been impressed by her stage work, requested her for his leading lady in the epic *Cimarron* (1931). The picture was a huge hit, and she received an Oscar nomination. Although she never won an Academy Award, Irene Dunne was nominated four other times for the Best Actress award: *Theodora Goes Wild* (1936), *The Awful Truth* (1937), *Love Affair* (1939), and *I Remember Mama* (1948).

The career of the versatile actress seems almost ideal. Ms. Dunne's voice proved as lovely in film musicals, such as *Roberta* (1935), as it had been on the stage. She was very effective in women's pictures, and her light touch at comedy holds up extremely well when viewed today.

Her screen image—that of the discreet, cultivated, and well-groomed woman—is not the sort idolized by movie cultists. She never played the common or neurotic characters with whom so many fans of today seem to identify.

Some of her best pictures, such as *Back Street* (1932), *Magnificent Obsession* (1935), *Show Boat* (1936), *My Favorite Wife* (1940), and *Anna and the King of Siam* (1946), are seldom seen because they have been remade and the originals were withdrawn from distribution.

Among her other films are *Symphony of Six Million* (1932) with the late Ricardo Cortez,

The Age of Innocence (1934), *Sweet Adeline* (1935), *High, Wide and Handsome* (1937), *Penny Serenade* (1941), *Unfinished Business* (1941), *The White Cliffs of Dover* (1944), and *Life with Father* (1947). Her last, *It Grows on Trees* (1952) with Joan Evans (the proprietor of a private school in the San Fernando Valley), disappointed everyone concerned.

The off-screen Irene Dunne is very much the same person her admirers enjoyed in motion pictures. When her husband, a dentist, died in 1965, they had been married for thirty-seven years. She is a grandmother by her one child, a daughter. Her religion, Roman Catholicism, which was often mentioned in her publicity, is very much a part of her life today. The altar of St. Teresa in the Church of the Blessed Sacrament in Hollywood was a gift from Irene. She has been very effective in raising funds for charities, especially St. John's Hospital in Santa Monica.

Not everyone enjoyed her in movies. Film critic James Agee wrote, "I am not among those who take to Irene Dunne—as a rule she makes my skin crawl." In another context he said, "She would probably keep her tongue in her cheek uttering the Seven Last Words."

President Eisenhower appointed Dunne U.S. Delegate to the 12th General Assembly of the United Nations in 1957. Although in recent years she has become less active in politics, she was a staunch supporter of her old friend Ronald Reagan's bid for the presidency.

Irene Dunne lives in a large home in the exclusive area of Los Angeles that is known as Holmby Hills.

Jon Virzi

Irene Dunne is very active in Los Angeles socially and in charitable fund raising.

Sally Eilers in the early thirties.

Sally Eilers

The star of early talkies was born Dorothea Sallye Eilers to an Irish father and a Jewish mother in New York City on December 11, 1908. She was in her early teens when, for the sake of her brother's health, her family moved to Los Angeles.

While attending Fairfax High School, Sally became a close friend of a classmate named Jane Peters, who would later become famous as Carole Lombard. Both haunted the studios to get work as extras and bit players. Then Carole introduced her to Mack Sennett. The producer tested Sally and signed her for the ingenue in his feature *The Goodbye Kiss* (1928). The same year Hollywood publicists chose her as one of the Wampus Baby Stars.

In 1929 she was seen in the prestigious *Show of Shows* and married the popular star Hoot Gibson. She acted opposite her husband in several of his westerns. She was with Buster Keaton in *Dough Boys* (1930) and played opposite Spencer Tracy in his second picture, *Quick Millions* (1931).

Sally's big year was 1931, when her movie *Bad Girl* was released. Not only was it a hit at the box office, but its director and writer both received Academy Awards for their efforts. But while it put her on top professionally for a while, it also forged an image of Sally as a girl from the wrong side of the tracks, an image she never escaped. The chemistry between her and leading man James Dunn seemed so strong that they were for a few years one of the screen's most popular couples. Their films together include *Dance Team* (1932), *Hold Me Tight* (1933), and *Don't Get Personal* (1936).

Even after she turned in an excellent performance in *State Fair* (1933) as a respectable young woman, her studio continued to feel Sally was best when she was bad.

The titles of her pictures are indicative of not only their plots but of Sally's parts: *She Couldn't Say No* (1930) with the late Winnie

Lightner, *Hat Check Girl* (1932) with the late Ben Lyon, *Sailor's Luck* (1933), *Second Hand Wife* (1933), and *She Made Her Bed* (1934).

Shortly after her 1932 divorce from Gibson, Sally married the producer Harry Joe Brown. She was definitely part of the Hollywood "in" crowd. She was a frequent visitor at the William Randolph Hearst ranch, San Simeon, and a favorite of Marion Davies, who relied on her for the latest gossip and off-color stories. Not everyone, however, appreciated Sally's humor. Someone once said to Louis B. Mayer that Carole Lombard had the filthiest mouth in all of Hollywood. Mayer asked the man if he'd ever met Miss Eilers.

She worked often through the thirties and forties but in unimportant films, such as *Pursuit* (1935) with the late Chester Morris, *Condemned Women* (1938), *I Was a Prisoner on Devil's Island* (1941), *Strange Illusion* (1945), and *Coroner Creek* (1948). Her last film was *Stage to Tucson* (1950).

Sally has a son by Brown, from whom she received a large financial settlement when they divorced. Her third husband was a handsome naval officer. Marriage number four was to movie director John Hollingsworth Morse. They were divorced in 1958.

Even after Sally's career faded, she was a familiar face among Hollywood's social set. She had money, dressed well, and had a reputation for a quick, if outrageous, wit. She had long ceased to be a big name, but she would still pop up in Louella Parsons' column now and then. Sally may have been the "bad girl" to her fans, but among film folk she was known as a good sport.

Jon Virzi

Sally Eilers photographed with one of her Yorkies in her Beverly Hills home shortly before her death in 1978.

During the last years of her life serious illness and heavy drinking curtailed her socializing, yet her behavior remained outlandish and her language seemed to worsen.

She lived with her two Yorkies in a house in Beverly Hills until her death on January 5, 1978.

James Ellison in the late thirties.

James Ellison

The handsome leading man and western star was born James Ellison Smith on May 4, 1910, in Guthrie Center, Iowa. He moved to Los Angeles with his widowed mother when he was eight years old.

Ellison won a scholarship to Loyola University, but before he could enroll, his mother suffered a stroke. Jim went to work in the film vaults of a studio and in the evenings he attended classes in dramatics held at Hollywood High School. "Not," he says, "that I had any interest in acting, but because I'd heard a lot of cute girls went there." He found, however, that he enjoyed performing, and soon joined the Pasadena Playhouse. From the Playhouse he won parts with Laura Hope Crews and Billie Burke. He toured with the latter in a play for nine months.

James Ellison first appeared on the screen in *Play Girl* (1932) with Loretta Young and the late Norman Foster. Then he did a play with Pauline Frederick. Jim was tested by M-G-M and appeared briefly in a few of M-G-M's films before his option was dropped.

He sailed for Hawaii, planning to remain there with his brother, but when no jobs were available he came back to Hollywood, with only two dollars to his name. His agent at this point was Jerry Mayer, the brother of Louis B. Mayer. The first day back Mayer took him to meet "Pop" Sherman, who was looking for a young sidekick in a series of westerns he was about to produce starring Bill Boyd. Jim was signed for the role of "Johnny Nelson" in the "Hopalong Cassidy" pictures and played the part until Cecil B. De Mille picked him for a role in *The Plainsman* (1937). His friend and roommate during this period was the late Russell Hayden, who eventually played "Lucky" in most of the "Hoppy" westerns.

Jim feels he was miscast as "Buffalo Bill" in *The Plainsman,* a picture that starred Gary Cooper and Jean Arthur. Neither he nor De Mille was happy with his performance.

After two more "Hoppy" films Sherman sold his contract to RKO, where he made *Vivacious Lady* (1938) with Ginger Rogers. Jim's flair for light comedy surprised everyone, including himself. The studio didn't pick up his option, but before he left the lot he made *Next*

Time I Marry (1938) with Lucille Ball and the late Lee Bowman. It did so well he was resigned.

After RKO Ellison went to Twentieth Century–Fox for two years but was in mostly B's. The most notable pictures he made there were *Hotel for Women* (1939), in which he gave Linda Darnell her first screen kiss, and *The Gang's All Here* (1943).

James Ellison made over eighty feature films. Among them were *The Winning Ticket* (1935), *Mother Carey's Chickens* (1938) with Anne Shirley (widowed and living in Los Angeles), *Fifth Avenue Girl* (1939) with Veree Teasdale (the widow of Adolph Menjou lives in Beverly Hills), *Zenobia* (1939) with Oliver Hardy, *Charley's Aunt* (1941) with Jack Benny, *I Walked with a Zombie* (1943), and *Johnny Doesn't Live Here Anymore* (1944) with Simone Simon (single and living in Paris) and Chick Chandler (living in Laguna, California).

It was in the late forties that Jim became involved with real estate. It proved lucrative right from the start and quickly replaced what little interest he had in acting. He continued to make movies and even co-produced some low-budget westerns with Russ Hayden. "I found myself thinking about the construction business even when I was supposed to be acting," he admitted recently. "I had no illusions about my abilities on the screen. The best review I ever got was when a woman came over to me in a bank and asked if I was James Ellison. I thought she was a fan. It turned out she just wanted to tell me how much she and her family were enjoying the home I'd built a number of years before. I was delighted. I think I'll be remembered more for Ellison Drive, which I developed in Beverly Hills, than for any of my pictures."

Ellison's first wife, the sister of child star Junior Durkin, died in 1970. Their daughter, who acted for a while, is also deceased. His son, an engineer, lives in Finland.

Jim is now married to the former ballerina Shelly Keats. They live in a home they purchased from Jennifer Holt, the daughter of Jack Holt and sister of the late Tim Holt, in Montecito, California. Jane Russell was married in the small chapel on their property.

He seldom hears from anyone he worked with in pictures but is very flattered to get letters from fans.

Richard Lamparski

James Ellison is a retired contractor living in Montecito, California.

John Ericson in the early fifties.

John Ericson

The heartthrob of the fifties was born in Dusseldorf, Germany, on September 25. His original name was Joachim Meibes. His parents, increasingly aware of the political turmoil in Germany, took him to Belgium when he was one year old. In 1935 they migrated to the United States.

His mother, who was Swedish, had abandoned her career in light opera when she married. His father was a chemist and strongly encouraged his son to follow in his footsteps, but John was more interested in art.

Ericson enrolled in the dental school at Hofstra University, more to please his father than to satisfy his own inclinations. He wasn't there long before another student told him he had decided to be an actor. "I was really surprised," says John. "I'd lived in Detroit and Chicago before going to college. The kids I grew up with thought acting was for sissies. Then this really tough guy announced that he wanted to spend his life in the theatre." Shortly afterward John Ericson enrolled at the American Academy of Dramatic Arts. While studying there he spent his summers acting with the Gateway Stock Company in Tennessee.

After graduating from the Academy he gave himself three years in which to establish himself as an actor. It wasn't long before he got a walk-on in *Studio One,* the weekly TV drama. He was at a rehearsal when he got a call to attend an open audition for a screen role. John taxied to the audition on his lunch hour and did a brief reading. The next day he was called back. Four days later he was given a screen test. Forty-eight hours after that Ericson was on his way to Italy to play opposite Pier Angeli in *Teresa* (1951).

The film was a success and he photographed beautifully, but when M-G-M offered him a contract John sensed that they saw him only as a neurotic young man, the part he had played in *Teresa.* Instead he accepted a meaty role in *Stalag 17* (1951) on Broadway. He created the part that brought William Holden an Oscar in the movie version. Ericson played it 688 times altogether in New York and on the road tour.

After appearing opposite Elizabeth Taylor in *Rhapsody* (1954) Ericson was put under contract to Metro-Goldwyn-Mayer. He was less than happy with most of his assignments there but is grateful that he had the chance to work with Spencer Tracy in *Bad Day at Black Rock* (1955). After turning down three scripts in a row, he was suspended.

Some of his other screen roles were in *The Student Prince* (1954) with Edmund Purdom (living in Rome), *Green Fire* (1954) with Grace Kelly, *The Return of Jack Slade* (1955), *Day of the Badman* (1958), *Under Two Flags* (1960), and *Seven Faces of Dr. Lao* (1964). The part he very much wanted to do was that of Charles Lindbergh in *The Spirit of St. Louis.*

John free-lanced in features and on television after leaving M-G-M. The only thing of any note he did, however, was the title role in *Pretty Boy Floyd* (1960). The picture wasn't well made but he was convincing in it. He made six "spaghetti westerns" in Europe and in 1967 made a tour of dinner theatres with Kathryn Grayson in *Camelot.* He was a regular on *Honey West,* the TV series that starred Anne Francis in 1966.

John has two children by his first marriage. His son is a musician and his daughter appears on TV commercials. He was in the process of getting a divorce when he met his present wife, the actress formerly known as Karen Huston. She now uses his surname. They were married in 1975 and spent their honeymoon making a Spanish-language film in the Philippines.

Ericson has had a one-man show of his paintings. His landscapes in oil are hung throughout his duplex apartment in Sherman Oaks.

Speaking of his career recently he said: "I insisted on playing different parts—a sensitive sadist, an artist, a criminal, etc.—but that has left me without a screen image. As an actor that's much better than being typecast, but I would like to work much more than I do. I'd also like very much to direct."

The January 1974 issue of *Playgirl* magazine carried several pages in color of John Ericson cavorting about in the nude with a lion cub. He agreed to the piece thinking it would reactivate his career. "All that happened," he admits, smiling, "is quite a few friends called me. Some said very complimentary things. Others said very amusing things. Professionally it didn't mean a thing."

Richard Lamparski

John Ericson and his wife live in Sherman Oaks, California.

In 1946 Frank Faylen was under contract to Paramount Pictures.

Frank Faylen

The character actor of movies and television was born Frank Cusik on December 8, 1909, in St. Louis, Missouri. Much of his childhood was spent touring with his parents, a vaudeville team known as "Ruf & Cusik." For several years he attended St. Joseph Preparatory School in Kirkwood, Missouri.

Frank worked for a while in his parents' act. After the death of his father he formed a team of his own, a comedy duo billed as "Cusik and Hughes." The other half, Carol Hughes, he married in 1928.

By the early thirties Frank realized that he would have to change his surname. Many old-timers in the profession had told him that theatre owners still bristled when they heard his father's name. The senior Cusik had been one of the most effective organizers of the White Rats, the original actors' union.

The talkies had slowed vaudeville considerably and Frank and his wife were having a hard time getting bookings even with his new name. Then they were offered a tour of Australia and New Zealand; at the same time, a talent scout suggested them to Warner Brothers. Before they were screen-tested by the studio their agent warned them to pretend they were both single. Publicity in those days for young players almost invariably came from having them date stars from the same lot. They both received contracts, and it was over a year before the word reached Jack Warner that Frank and Carol were married. The next time their options came up for renewal they were dropped. In the meantime he had made appearances in twenty-six movies. In nineteen of them he was in a uniform of one kind or another. All of them were character roles.

Frank free-lanced until he was signed by Paramount in 1943. There he did some of his best work, including the part of the sadistic nurse in *The Lost Weekend* (1945). Both Lee Tracy and Jack Oakie were tested for the role, but Faylen got it in spite of Billy Wilder's lack of enthusiasm for his abilities. In the release print Frank is on the screen for only a few minutes, but it is an appearance that filmologist Don Miller rates as "the single best performance I've seen in *any* movie." To the dismay of many, he wasn't even nominated for an Academy Award.

Frank Faylen was an excellent actor and an extremely versatile one. He played detectives, reporters, drunks, an old saloonkeeper, and a Russian pianist. In *Bring On the Girls* (1945) he was a youthful sailor. In *Two Years Before the Mast* (1946) he was a Swedish farmer turned seaman. He played a crooked Indian agent in *Blood on the Moon* (1948) and an albino in *Whispering Smith* (1949).

But for all of his range as an actor, Frank is

probably best known for playing the father of Dwayne Hickman on the television series *The Loves of Dobie Gillis,* which ran on CBS-TV from 1959 to 1963. Carol Hughes, his wife, is usually thought of by movie fans as "Dale Arden" in *Flash Gordon Conquers the Universe* (1940).

Some of his other credits are *Bullets or Ballots* (1936), *Headin' East* (1938), *The Grapes of Wrath* (1940), *The Canterville Ghost* (1944), *To Each His Own* (1946), *California* (1947), *Road to Reno* (1948), *Detective Story* (1951), *Gunfight at the O.K. Corral* (1957), and *Funny Girl* (1968).

The picture he enjoyed the most, because of Frank Capra's sensitive direction, was *It's a Wonderful Life* (1946).

Frank and Carol live in a large house in the Las Feliz district of Los Angeles. Their oldest daughter, Kay, was for a while an impressionist in nightclubs. Their other girl, Carol Faylen, played Bing Crosby's daughter on his television series. Frank spends much of his time at his club, the Masquers, a building in Hollywood that was once the home of silent star Antonio Moreno. Frank was for some years the club's president. The Faylens are Roman Catholics.

Frank Faylen recently, beside a picture of his wife, Carol Hughes.

Richard Lamparski

Author Charles Higham called Edith Fellows "Totally believable. She was a real kid."

Edith Fellows

The movie moppet was born in Boston on May 20, 1923. Her mother disappeared when Edith was two years old, and her grandmother took her to North Carolina. She was so pigeon-toed that an osteopath suggested she be given dancing lessons. By 1926 she had developed into a local name entertainer in school plays. An agent saw her and suggested she be brought to Hollywood, where he felt he could get her into pictures. When Grandmother Fellows and Edith arrived they found the agent's address to be a vacant lot. Her grandmother did housework to support them, taking Edith along. When one matron objected, she left the girl with a neighbor. The neighbor's boy, who was an actor, got a call from the casting director of Hal Roach Studios. His mother had to take Edith along on the interview. The boy got the part in *Movie Night* (1929), but then came down with chicken pox. Edith filled in, making her debut in the Charlie Chase two-reeler. After that she began working regularly as an extra and bit player.

She was in *Cimarron* (1931) and *Daddy Long Legs* (1931), but briefly. She still has fond memories of Richard Dix's kindness during her first real part, in his picture *His Greatest Gamble* (1934). She was a standout in *She Married Her Boss* (1935) and was signed to a contract by Columbia Pictures.

The guiding force behind Edith's career and personal life was her grandmother, a fiercely ambitious woman who insisted on perfection from Edith in everything she did. When in 1936 her mother reappeared and demanded her daughter's return, the grandmother fought her successfully in a messy and, for Edith, painful court fight. One thing Grandmother Fellows could not be accused of was spoiling her granddaughter. Harry Cohn, the studio head, called her to his office once and strongly suggested she get Edith some decent clothes.

Edith specialized in brat and wallflower roles. She developed quite a following from her appearances in *Mrs. Wiggs of the Cabbage Patch* (1934), *Pennies from Heaven* (1936), and a series that began with *Five Little Peppers and How They Grew* (1939). Filmologist Don Miller has written of her: "Of all the precocious tots at the time she was the least affected and certainly the best actress." She also had a very pleasant singing voice.

Her teenage pictures were *Her First Romance* (1940) with Julie Bishop (married to a Beverly Hills physician) and Alice White (single and living in Hollywood), *Her First Beau* (1941), and *Girl's Town* (1942). Then she replaced Joan Roberts (living in Rockville Centre, New York) in *Marinka* (Broadway wags dubbed the musical "Marinka the stinker") in 1945. Her greatest professional disappointment was when she lost the lead in the road tour of *Peter Pan* in 1950 because of her height—4 feet 10½ inches. Her last Broadway play was *Uncle Willie* (1956).

Edith has one child, Kathy Fields, an actress, who is married to David Lander, "Squiggy" of the *Laverne and Shirley* cast. Kathy's father is Freddie Fields, the movie producer.

Edith divorced for the second time in 1970.

Edith Fellows is again living in Hollywood and is a founding member of "The Survivors," a club of former child stars. In 1981 she was seen in *Brothers*, a made-for-TV movie, and *The Brady Brides*, a TV special.

Edith lives by herself in an apartment in Hollywood.

Richard Schaeffer

Stepin Fetchit was once billed as "The Laziest Man in the World."

Stepin Fetchit

The first black actor to receive featured billing on the screen was born Lincoln Theodore Perry on May 30, 1902, in Key West, Florida.

Little is known about Fetchit's early years. He was adopted when he was eleven years old and taken to live in Montgomery, Alabama. The next year he ran away and joined a carnival. For a few years he earned his living as a singer and tap dancer in small traveling shows.

He has always claimed that the name Stepin Fetchit came from a racehorse on which he won $30. Early in his career, however, he was part of a pair who were billed as Step & Fetchit, "Two Dancing Fools from Dixie."

Although blacks had appeared in pictures before his arrival, Stepin Fetchit was the first to strongly register in films as a personality. He has been called the "first black movie star." As soon as he began making a big salary Fetchit set about to live like a movie star—or at least as he thought a movie star should live. By his own count he owned sixteen different automobiles during the thirties. One, he claims, was the first pink car ever seen in Hollywood. Another was a limousine driven by a white chauffeur. His favorite had his name in neon across the back. Then there was his wardrobe, which included fifty shirts and two dozen custom-made suits.

Fetchit vehemently denies that he epitomized on the screen the slow-witted, shuffling, head-scratching black. He has claimed that "an international conspiracy of atheists, who oppose my strong belief in God, ruined my career." Yet in spooky pictures his eyes would begin to roll and his knees would begin to shake at the slightest creak of a floorboard. Stepin walked, talked, and thought seemingly in slow motion.

The features he made with his friend Will Rogers, such as *David Harum* (1934), *Judge Priest* (1934), and *The Country Chairman* (1935), are studies in race relations of the period. It was considered acceptable for the greatly loved comedian to talk to Fetchit in much the same manner as one would address a not-too-bright house pet. Threats of a kick in the pants to get Stepin moving sent audiences into hysterics. With eyes always half closed and his slue-foot gait, he played to a fare-thee-well the stereotype of the southern field hand.

The popular *Amos 'n' Andy* character "Lightnin'" was based on Stepin Fetchit.

After his screen debut in *In Old Kentucky* (1927) he made *Hearts in Dixie* (1929), a musical with an all-black cast headed by the late Clarence Muse. Both pictures were made by the William Fox studios, where he was under contract. At one point his option was not picked up because, stated a studio spokesman, "Fame and prosperity proved too much for him."

Some of his other credits are *Swing High* (1930), *The World Moves On* (1934), with Madeleine Carroll (single and living in Paris), *Showboat* (1936), *His Exciting Night* (1938), *Miracle in Harlem* (1949), *Bend of the River* (1952), and *Sudden Fear* (1954) with Joan Crawford. His last were *Amazing Grace* (1974) and *Won Ton Ton, the Dog Who Saved Hollywood* (1976).

During the forties he worked in small clubs and carnivals and appeared in a review, *Flamingo Follies*. It was rumored then that he could not find screen work because civil rights groups objected to his portrayal of blacks.

In 1943 he was sentenced to thirty days in jail for impairing the morals of a minor.

He has stated that he made over $2 million, and while it is doubtful that his contract and free-lancing could have brought that much, he worked a great deal and certainly should have done very well. Yet in 1947 Stepin declared bankruptcy, with assets of $146.

Little was heard of Fetchit until Heavyweight Champion of the World, Muhammad Ali, after knocking out Sonny Liston in 1965, announced he did it with a punch taught him by his good friend Stepin Fetchit. Fetchit was on hand to explain that he had learned the "secret punch" from another black champion, Jack Johnson. Muhammad Ali, perhaps the world's most famous and proud black, had in his entourage for a while the actor who probably has done more than any black man today to label his race all the things that Ali is not.

Since suffering a stroke in 1976 Fetchit has lived most of the time at the Motion Picture Country House in Woodland Hills, California. His manner is totally at odds with his public image. Although his speech is somewhat impaired now, he talks nonstop and moves about constantly. During his time with Ali it was rumored that he had converted to Islam, but today he claims to be a devout Roman Catholic.

Stepin Fetchit in his room at the Motion Picture Country House.

Michael Knowles

Susanna Foster in 1944.

Susanna Foster

Suzanne DeLee Flanders Larson was the original name of the movie songstress. She was born in Chicago, Illinois, on December 6, 1924, and reared in Minneapolis, Minnesota. When she was eleven years old, Carl Johnson, a violinist, and Merle Potter, a reporter, recorded her voice and sent the record to Metro-Goldwyn-Mayer. The studio had only recently let Deanna Durbin out of her contract, whereupon she had gone straight to Universal and rescued that studio from bankruptcy with her immediate popularity. M-G-M was therefore quite receptive to having under contract a pretty little girl so young and talented. She wasn't as cute as Judy Garland or as pretty as Deanna Durbin, but her voice was phenomenal, and it was the era of child stars. Susanna was promptly given a vocal coach, who—according to Susanna, who had never taken lessons—nearly ruined her voice. After a year she was called into the office of Nicholas Nafack and told that she was not a singer, but might have some acting ability. Nafack was the nephew of Eddie Mannix, one of the studio heads, and married to a girl who considered herself to be a singer. Susanna's option was dropped.

Paramount auditioned her for a walk-on in *The Great Victor Herbert* (1939), and she so impressed the director, Le Roy Prinz, that he got her a big part in the movie. She was put under contract and did three more pictures: *Glamour Boy* (1941) with Jackie Cooper, *The Hard-Boiled Canary* (1941), and a bit in *Star Spangled Rhythm* (1942). When her option was up for renewal they offered to continue her contract without her entitled raise. Susanna, who was her own manager, turned them down flat and, with no other offers or prospects, left the lot.

Forty days later she signed with Universal for her best part: she played opposite Nelson Eddy and Claude Rains in *The Phantom of the Opera* (1943). Actually, Susanna was brought to the Valley lot to act as a threat to Deanna Durbin, and it was to Durbin that all the plum parts went. Susanna was unaware of the situation. In fact, she was and is an avid Durbin fan. Other films followed: a bit part in *Follow the Boys* (1944), *This Is the Life* (1944), *Bowery to Broadway* (1944), *Top Man* (1943) with Donald O'Connor, and *That Night with You* (1945) with Franchot Tone. She made two films with Turhan Bey, her boyfriend at the time: *The Climax* (1944) and *Frisco Sal* (1945).

When option time came around she informed the front office that she was retiring. Susanna knew that they simply could not give her the vehicles suited to her talents and that she would continue in one mediocre film after another. The best they could offer was the lead in *The Countess of Monte Cristo,* which was made by Sonja Henie in 1948.

She says of rumors that she wanted to go into opera: "I knew enough about opera to know that the politics were even worse than in the studio. I was never really ambitious. At least not in the cut-throat way that's required to succeed. The truth is that I hated a career and everything that went with it." Word did reach her that the Metropolitan Opera was interested in her for *Der Rosenkavalier,* but she never followed it up.

In 1948 Susanna married Wilbur Evans, a well-known singer of light opera who was over twenty years her senior. The marriage lasted eight years and produced two sons, Michael and Philip. The divorce was quite bitter and was followed by litigation over custody of the children.

For years Ms. Foster lived in Manhattan, supporting her boys by working as long as sixteen hours a day, sometimes seven days a week. She received almost no financial help from her ex-husband. What little he did contribute was by order of the court.

After a gap of many years she is now back in touch with Turhan Bey, whom she referred to recently as "the one real love of my life." They correspond and speak on the telephone frequently. He lives in Vienna with his mother and works as a commercial photographer.

Although she made no phonograph records, Universal has recently released an album of the sound track of *Phantom of the Opera.* She is pleased by how well it is selling but does not receive a cent from its sales.

Since 1974 Susanna Foster has lived in Los Angeles. She presently shares an apartment with her son, Michael, and his little boy, Eric. Her younger son lives in Manhattan. Both sons are musicians.

Susanna has very mixed feelings about resuming her career. She still sings very well, but does not want to concertize or appear in a film unless she has complete control over her material.

Her autograph is still one of the most sought-after among collectors, and her fans all over the world outnumber those of many former major stars.

Richard Lamparski

Susanna Foster with her son Michael and grandson Eric Evans.

Mona Freeman was named a "Star of Tomorrow" by the Motion Picture Herald in 1948.

Mona Freeman

The blonde almost-star was born Monica Elizabeth Freeman on June 9, 1926, in Baltimore, Maryland. She was raised in Pelham, New York, by parents who had been hit hard by the Depression.

When Mona was fourteen years old she was taken by a friend of her uncle's to meet John Robert Powers. Although the Freemans couldn't afford the $300 tuition for the Powers modeling course, she somehow managed to get the necessary training. Immediately she became a very popular "Junior Miss" model. In 1941 she became the first "Miss Subways." She had never been in a subway. The same uncle had another friend who worked for Howard Hughes. When he brought her photos to the attention of the billionaire she was put under personal contract to him.

Mona was sent to Hollywood, where for the first two months she sat around a hotel room awaiting a call from Hughes's office. Then she was turned over to various coaches and "experts." Before Hughes could find a role for her Paramount asked for Mona to play a small part in *Double Indemnity,* but after viewing the rushes Paramount decided that she looked too young. The studio was, however, impressed with how well she photographed, and bought her contract from Hughes. The first and only time Mona ever saw Howard Hughes was on the day the sale of her contract was completed.

Loaned to M-G-M for *National Velvet,* she was replaced after one day. Mona looked too mature to play Elizabeth Taylor's sister. She usually was cast as either a brat or a sweet young girl. She never objected to any of the parts she was assigned to and had difficulty only once. She found working with director Charles Vidor in *Together Again* (1944) a disagreeable experience.

Some of her other credits are *Junior Miss* (1945), *Black Beauty* (1946), *Dear Ruth* (1947), *Mother Wore Tights* (1947), *The Heiress* (1949), *Copper Canyon* (1950), *Dear Wife* (1950), *Dear Brat* (1951), *Jumping Jacks* (1952), *Battle Cry* (1955), *Dragon Wells Massacre* (1957), and *The World Was His Jury* (1958).

Mona had just turned twenty when she married a wealthy young auto dealer. After their divorce in 1953 he married Jane Powell.

She says she never had real ambition. "I did it for the money," she said recently. "I didn't dislike acting, but when I no longer needed the income I lost all interest. Not only don't I watch my pictures on TV, I haven't ever seen some of them." She last acted on a *Mission Impossible* segment.

Mona dated Bing Crosby for three years. They never married, says Ms. Freeman, "because I had been married in the Catholic Church. For Bing that was insurmountable."

In 1961 Mona married a businessman. "I'm a fallen-away Catholic and he's what he calls 'a bad Jew.' Our friends pray for us like mad."

Mona's daughter, who is by her first husband, married the son of her present husband. They are now divorced, but they all get together often since their daughter is the only grandchild of Mona and her husband. "Thank God," says grandmother Mona, "that we all have very, very good manners."

Mona had painted since childhood but took it up seriously after she retired from the screen. She has had several one-woman shows of her specialty, oil portraits of children.

Mona and her husband travel a great deal. Their Beverly Hills home was once the residence of Dick Powell and June Allyson.

Her best friend is her contemporary Phyllis Thaxter (married and living in Portland, Maine).

Asked if she would accept a really exceptional role, she replied: "I would spend a full week throwing up. Then I might—mind you, only might—say yes."

Frank Christi

Mona Freeman in her Beverly Hills home with her Maltese, "Lily."

The Gogi Grant of the mid-fifties.

Gogi Grant

The recording star of the fifties was born Myrtle Audrey Arinsberg on September 30 in Philadelphia, Pennsylvania. She was the oldest of six children in a family that she describes as being of "less than moderate means." The Arinsbergs moved to Los Angeles when Gogi was twelve years old. No one in her family was connected with show business, nor was music an important part of her home life. But Gogi listened faithfully to *Your Hit Parade* on the radio and never missed a movie musical.

After graduating from Venice High School she entered into a marriage that produced a daughter but ended soon afterward in divorce.

Friends who had heard her sing encouraged Gogi to try her luck at the monthly amateur night held at the Mocombo on Sunset Strip. Eddie Oliver, whose group was the house band there, told her he thought she had great potential and sent her to his sister, who was a vocal coach. When she cut her first demo record the owner of the recording studio, Stan Ross, liked her voice so much he recommended her to the huge talent agency MCA.

At first she sang under the name Audrey Brown at the Hotel Coronado and small clubs. Then she became Audrey Grant. When she signed her contract with RCA Victor its president, Dave Kapp, gave her the name Gogi.

By the autumn of 1955 her first hit, "Suddenly There's a Valley," had broken onto the charts, where it remained for eleven weeks. Selling over 700,000 copies, the song made the number three position on *Variety's* "Top 40" list. *Billboard*'s "Hot 100 Chart" listed "Who Are We?" for seven weeks, and "You're in Love" for another seven weeks in 1956.

Gogi's smash hit, one of the most popular records of the decade, was "The Wayward Wind." Recorded during the last fifteen minutes of a long session, it was, according to Gogi, "a throwaway." But Howard Miller, the Chicago disk jockey, broke the cut, which went to the top of every hit list everywhere, knocking even Elvis Presley out of the number one position. It remained on *Billboard*'s chart for twenty-eight straight weeks in 1956. When it was revived five years later it appeared again on the chart for nine weeks. Gogi's gold record of "The Wayward Wind" is displayed on the wall of her mansion.

Warner Brothers was about to star Ann Blyth in *The Helen Morgan Story* (1957) when their musical director, Ray Heinsdorf, decided that Ms. Blyth's light operatic voice was unsuitable for such torch songs as "Why Was I Born" and "Mean to Me." The studio had tested just about every name female vocalist in the business, but none had the quality that they were seeking. Then, driving home one evening, Heinsdorf heard Gogi on the radio singing "The One I Love." She was signed to dub all of the Helen Morgan songs for the film. Gogi never sounded better, and many felt her singing was the best thing about the picture. Although out of print, the album is a much sought-after collector's item. It remained on *Variety*'s list of the nation's best-selling albums for two years.

Gogi Grant was a songwriter's dream, combining the warmth of a pop singer with the vocal discipline of a semiclassical artist. Her interpretations brought out the best in a song, underlining the meaning and emotion of the lyrics.

By the late sixties Gogi had married a very successful attorney. Their son was about the age her daughter had been when Gogi's career began to take off. "I remembered how my girl had been without me when I was on tour," said Ms. Grant. "It created a gulf between us that took years to bridge. I wanted to be a full-time mother to Josh. So I quit."

Gogi and her second husband have been separated for several years. She and her son, who is an honor student in high school and an aspiring actor, live in Beverly Hills. Their next-door neighbor is Loretta Young. Ms. Grant plays tennis and is a gourmet cook. She is very involved in charity work and is often asked to sing at benefits for a child-care center.

"I'm very glad I retired when I did," she said during a recent interview. "My son and I are very close."

Asked about the possibility of a comeback, she replied, "I know this business very well. No one comes looking for you, and I don't see myself going knocking on doors. I'm thrilled that fans remember me, but I don't honestly feel any void."

Howard W. Hays

Gogi Grant and her son live next door to Loretta Young in Beverly Hills.

The cast of Father Knows Best in 1960: Jane Wyatt, Robert Young, Billy Gray, Lauren Chapin, and Elinor Donahue.

Billy Gray

William Thomas Gray, who portrayed what many considered to be the typical teenage boy of the fifties, was born on January 13, 1938, in Los Angeles. Just before his birth his mother, Beatrice, who had appeared in westerns with Bob Steele and Johnny Mack Brown, was dropped by her studio, RKO, because she was pregnant and couldn't make a publicity tour for *New Faces of 1938,* her last movie.

Billy was a precocious boy and began doing bit parts when he was only six years old. His first real role came in the 1946 M-G-M short *Our Old Car,* one of the John Nesbitt *Passing Parade* series. Billy had a Warner Brothers contract and then moved over to Twentieth Century–Fox. He was seen in such features as *The Guy Who Came Back* (1951) and *By the Light of the Silvery Moon* (1953).

Gray's real fame came when he played "Bud Anderson," son of Robert Young in the highly successful television series *Father Knows Best.* He calls it "an embarrassment right from the beginning." Even a thirteen-year-old boy knew something was wrong when instead of the weekly $500 he had been getting in movies he made $250. And his objections to a "Gosh" or "Golly" in almost every line of "Bud's" were dismissed without discussion. He settled down to what he felt was a real acting chore.

Father Knows Best premiered on CBS on October 3, 1954. It epitomized "togetherness," an expression coined by *McCall's* magazine, which was supposed to be the desired state of the American family. The fictional insurance salesman, his wife, and their three children from the small town of Springfield might have seemed close-knit on the screen, but to Billy the show's set had an atmosphere of "strictly business mixed with a lot of pretense."

On March 25, 1962, about a year after production had ceased on the series, Billy was stopped by police on suspicion of drunk driving. Gray admits that he has smoked marijuana at times but on that night, he insists, he had used neither drugs nor alcohol. The officers found a small amount of marijuana seeds and stems under the front seat of his car, and the story hit every newspaper in the country. The actor drew a three-month jail term and was on probation for three years afterward. He found that upon his release he was persona non grata around the studios. Even his agent told him that he would no longer be able to represent him. The only person from *Father Knows Best* days to contact him was a propman.

Gray traveled for a while, bought some income property in the Topanga Canyon section of Los Angeles, and settled down with a woman for eight years. They were married for the last two years but have since been divorced. In 1981 he married the actress Donna Wilkes.

Billy has no regrets about being a child actor except for the studio schools. They were so lax, he claims, that he is still learning to read and write properly. He recalls with real pain that if the producers of his TV series had agreed to shoot around him for two weeks he would have been in the James Dean movie *Rebel Without a Cause* (1955).

Billy Gray was one of the top motorcycle racers on the West Coast until he gave it up a few years ago. He still considers himself an actor, although the only things of note he has done in the last decade are *Dusty and Sweets McGee* (1971) and the *Father Knows Best* reunion special in 1979.

Any mention of the series that made him famous still makes him wince. "So many guys tell me they tried to be like 'Bud Anderson' because that was who their parents really wanted for a son. I tell them that there never was such a person. That character, like those shows, was idealized. It was very unfair to hold up a plastic character to boys as an example of how to behave. I'm sorry about the harm it did."

Dick Lynch

Billy Gray lives in the Topanga Canyon area of Los Angeles.

In 1939 Anne Gwynne was signed to a contract with Universal Pictures that began at $75 a week.

Anne Gwynne

The movie actress and popular pinup girl of World War II was born Marguerite Gwynne Trice in Waco, Texas, on December 10, 1918.

The summer before she was to enter her sophomore year at Stephens College, Anne accompanied her father to a convention in Los Angeles. He was with Catalina Swimwear, and she got a job modeling bathing suits. This led to a part in a little-theatre production. Soon she was making the rounds of studios and agents' offices.

One day she had appointments at Universal in the morning and at Warner Brothers after lunch. Anne never made it to her second date. After a thirty-minute interview, she was signed to a contract that began at $75 a week in June 1939.

Even though she didn't have a single line in a short she made with Edgar Bergen and Charlie McCarthy, fans noticed her and wrote in asking who she was. Anne's appeal was very visual.

Her relatively low salary, combined with her willingness to pose for endless hours of cheesecake photography, made her a favorite in the front office. Her reward, however, was to be overworked in one B picture after another: *Unexpected Father* (1939) with Baby Sandy, *Mob Town* (1941) with the late Dick Foran, *The Glass Alibi* (1942), *Frontier Badmen* (1943), *Murder in the Blue Room* (1944), and *Dick Tracy Meets Gruesome* (1947). In 1941, just one year alone, she had the lead in thirteen feature films.

Anne was also in two Deanna Durbin movies, *Spring Parade* (1940) and *Nice Girl* (1941), and was a bridesmaid at the star's wedding.

It was Anne Gwynne's ability to emit blood-curdling screams that has kept her face familiar to movie fans over the years. She was seen and heard shrieking her lungs out in horror pictures that are still popular: *Black Friday* (1940), *The Black Cat* (1941) with the late Claire Dodd, *The Strange Case of Doctor Rx* (1942), *The House of Frankenstein* (1944), *Weird Woman* (1944), and *The Ghost Goes*

Wild (1947). Two of her other films that remain favorites on TV are *Flash Gordon Conquers the Universe* (1940) and *Ride 'Em Cowboy* (1942) with Abbott and Costello.

When Anne married a theatrical lawyer-producer in 1945, Evelyn Ankers was her maid of honor. The two still correspond. (Evelyn Ankers and her husband, Richard Denning, live on Maui in Hawaii.) Another close friend from the old days, whom she still sees, is Lois Collier (married to a Beverly Hills attorney). Her daughter, Gwynne Gilford, and Gwynne's husband, Robert Pine, both act on TV. Anne is a grandmother by her daughter. Anne's son, a musician, is single.

Widowed since 1965, Anne lives by herself in the San Fernando Valley. To keep herself occupied she works as a receptionist in a department store beauty salon.

She would very much like to act again, but a bit part in *Adam at 6 A.M.* (1970) has been her only role in a long time. She speaks wistfully of her career: "I wish I had been more insistent on better pictures. Maria Montez complained about absolutely everything and told me not to be so cooperative. They made her a star, and I'm sure her demands had a lot to do with it. It was a busy, happy time in my life, and I have no regrets, but I must admit that every now and then I wonder what might have happened if I'd kept that appointment at Warner's."

J. Nicolesco-Dorobantzou

Anne Gwynne in her apartment in Studio City, California, holding the cover of Look magazine with her photo. The date was January 1940.

Jack Haley was under contract to Twentieth Century–Fox in 1938.

Jack Haley

The light comedian of stage and films was born on August 10, 1902, in Boston, Massachusetts. He came from a poor Irish-Catholic family. After Jack saw a comic in a Christmas benefit for underprivileged children, he decided to be a famous funnyman, and rich. Within forty years he was both.

Haley made his debut at the age of six, singing a song called "Leapfrog Jump" in a Catholic church play. After graduating from Dwight Grammar School, he bummed around at a number of odd jobs. First he worked in a New York law firm for $3.50 a week. Then he went to Philadelphia, where he made as much as $60 weekly as a song plugger in vaudeville houses. He used a pointer and encouraged audiences to sing along with him. His first act was with six girls. Within six months he was booked into the Palace Theatre in New York City, minus the girls. His partner was Charlie Crofts and their act was called Crofts and Haley. Jack described it as "the Martin and Lewis of our day." He also worked with Benny Rubin, who for years was his closest friend. Jack's most successful liaison, professionally and privately, was with a girl named Florence McFadden in an act not unlike "Burns and Allen." They were husband and wife for over fifty years.

Jack had his first big break in 1929, when he introduced the song "Button Up Your Overcoat" in the hit musical *Follow Through.* In 1930 he did the screen version with Zelma O'Neal, both in secondary leads, and Buddy Rogers and the late Nancy Carroll, the stars. The film set the pattern for most of Jack's movie work: he never got the girl unless she was a Patsy Kelly or a Joan Davis. In 1932 he was back on Broadway in *Take a Chance* with Ethel Merman and the late Olsen and Johnson.

Among his fifty or so films were *Sitting Pretty* (1933) with the late Jack Oakie, *Coronado* (1935) with Johnny Downs, *Wake*

Up and Live (1937) with Alice Faye, *Alexander's Ragtime Band* (1938), *Rebecca of Sunnybrook Farm* (1938) with Shirley Temple, *The Wizard of Oz* (1939), and *George White's Scandals* (1945).

Undoubtedly, Jack remains best remembered for *The Wizard of Oz,* the motion picture classic that "at the time seemed like just another movie," according to Haley. In it he played "Hickory" and the "Tin Man."

He was in the stage version of the musical *Higher and Higher* (1940), repeated his role for the movie in 1943, starred on Broadway in *Show Time* (1942) with the late Ella Logan, and followed that with *Inside U.S.A.* (1948) with Bea Lillie, which they also took on the road.

Jack had little interest in performing during his last years. As a favor to his old friend Jackie Gleason he did a 1969 guest shot on Gleason's TV show. Jack and Jackie were partners in several highly successful business ventures. In 1969 he was directed by Jack Junior in *Norwood,* playing Joe Namath's father. Jack was reluctant to do it but it was his son's first picture and Jack junior wanted his father in it for good luck. Jack also had a daughter, Gloria, who twice made him a grandfather.

Haley had extensive holdings in real estate, oil, and cattle. Although he never became a major star, he was much richer than many superstars.

Until his death in June 1979 Jack and his wife hosted parties at their ultramodern home just behind the Beverly Hills Hotel. Their guests were an unusual mixture as Hollywood parties go. Millionaires mingled with former stars of movies and vaudeville who now lived on small pensions. "We invite rich people and people who are not doing so well these days," he once said. "They're all welcome because they're all our friends."

Jon Virzi

Jack Haley shortly before his death in 1979.

Jon Hall in the late thirties.

Jon Hall

Mrs. Locher's train was stopped in Fresno, California, on February 26, 1913; Charles Hall Locher was born moments later. His father was a Swiss figure-skating champion in 1910 and 1911. His mother was Tahitian. Their son studied engineering, languages, and science in England and Switzerland.

He said he had no interest in acting until Samuel Goldwyn noticed him sitting in his outer office. Hall was waiting for his uncle, writer Norman Hall, coauthor with Charles Nordhoff of *Mutiny on the Bounty* and *Hurricane.* Goldwyn offered him a contract for $500 a week and cast him in *Hurricane* (1937) opposite Dorothy Lamour. At least, that was the story Jon Hall liked to tell interviewers. The truth was that he made at least five pictures in 1935 and 1936 under the name Charles Locher; he even had a contract with Twentieth Century–Fox under that name. One of those films was *Charlie Chan in Shanghai* (1935). Under another name, Lloyd Crane, he made *Mind Your Own Business* (1936) and *The Girl from Scotland Yard* (1937) with Karen Morley.

After *Hurricane* he was a hot property and billed as "Goldwyn's Gift to Women." Because he had swum well since his fifth birthday, he was able to do his own water stunts, including a 131-foot dive. His young-man-in-the-loincloth image held on, despite quite a few westerns to his credit. Some of those South Seas films are *Aloma of the South Seas* (1941), *On the Isle of Samoa* (1950), and *Forbidden Island* (1959). His other specialty was exotic locales: *Arabian Nights* (1942), *Ali Baba and the Forty Thieves* (1944), *Lady in the Dark* (1944), *Cobra Woman* (1944) with Maria Montez and Sabu, *Sudan* (1945), and *Zamba* (1949). Aside from *Hurricane, Lady in the Dark* is his only picture taken seriously today. The rest were matinee fare, particularly *When the Redskins Rode* (1951), *Brave Warrior* (1952), and *Beach Girls and the Monster* (1965).

Hall made a great deal of money on his *Ramar of the Jungle* television series, syndicated nationally in the fifties. He received a share of its profits. In 1955 Jon and Frances Langford, his wife of seventeen years, were divorced. He then married Racquel Torres. After they divorced he married a psychiatrist. After his third divorce Jon and Racquel lived together again for a while.

By the mid-sixties Jon had lost what little interest he had in acting. He told an interviewer: "I never liked acting. I don't like to be told what to do and what to say and how to say it. I'm grateful to it, as it provided me with the money to do other things such as I'm in now, but as a profession it's a bore."

By then Hall had immersed himself in the business side of movies. Even before he retired from acting, Hall owned and managed companies that built boats and underwater camera housings for the navy. He also operated a fleet of airplanes and a flying school. He developed and patented Fantascope, a lens that can be adapted to any camera to provide a wider view of the subject, similar to the wide-screen process in motion pictures. His firm rented camera equipment to independent producers. The Oscar for Cinematography in 1966 (for *Who's Afraid of Virginia Woolf?)* was won with his cameras. Jon produced a low-budget motorcycle picture, *The Side-Hackers* (1969).

The last time the public saw Jon Hall was in April 1979 at the premiere of the remake of *Hurricane.* Although it was not generally known, he had been undergoing chemotherapy treatments in hope of arresting his cancer. Early in the morning of December 13, 1980, his sister found the sixty-six-year-old actor dead. He had shot himself in the head. He left no note.

Jon Virzi

Jon Hall in 1979, at his last public appearance, the premiere of the remake of Hurricane.

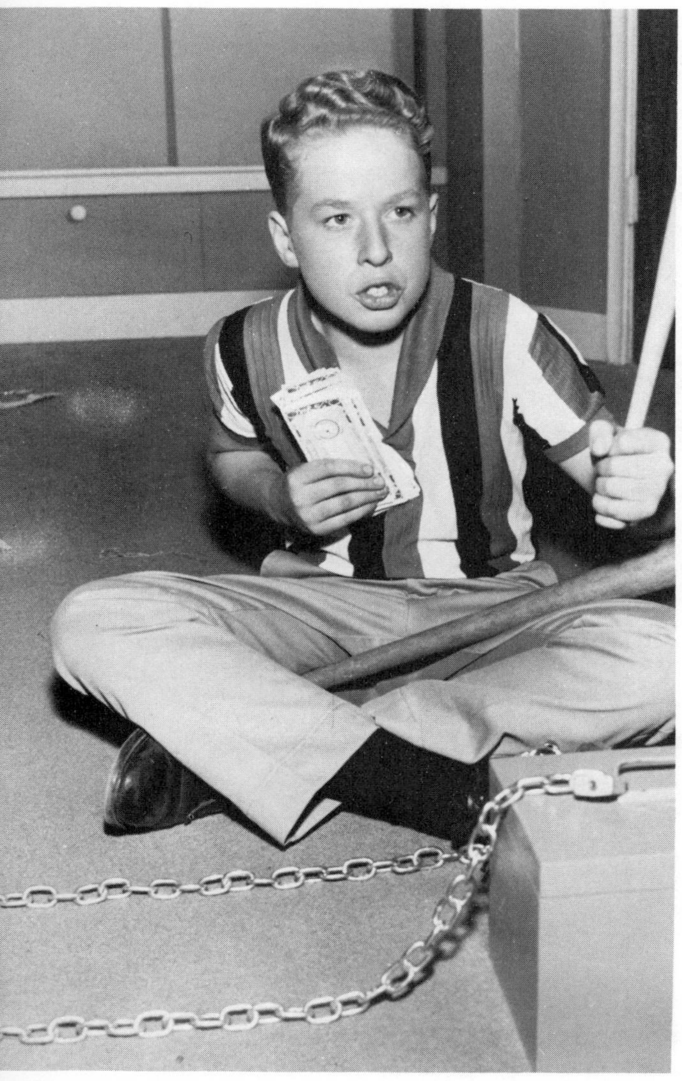

Rusty Hamer played the son of Danny Thomas on Make Room for Daddy.

Rusty Hamer

The boy who became nationally famous playing Danny Thomas's son on television was born Russell Craig Hamer in Tenafly, New Jersey, on February 15, 1947. He was the youngest of three boys, whose parents were very active in local little theatre. Russell was only four years old when he debuted in one of their productions.

The Manhattan Shirt Company, which employed his father, moved the Hamers to Los Angeles in 1951. Shortly after they settled there Rusty began rehearsing for the lead in the play *On Borrowed Time.* At the same time his parents learned that Danny Thomas was holding an open call for a boy to play his son in a new TV series. The five-year-old Rusty was among the several hundred kids who came to the auditions. Thomas chose Rusty and signed him to a contract before seeing the boy in the play. After the final curtain he came backstage and said, "I picked you because you were so cute, and now I find out you're a great little actor, too."

The first of over 200 half-hour episodes of *Make Room for Daddy* premiered over CBS in September 1953. That first series of 195 films were all in black-and-white. They are still popular in syndication around the world.

He played "Rusty Williams," the son of a Lebanese nightclub performer and the brother of Angela Cartwright (the proprietor of Rubber Boots, a gift shop in Toluca Lake, California). The plots had him in trouble often enough for his frequent smart-aleck remarks. Thomas was usually the butt of his humor. Actually, Rusty says he likes and admires his former boss. He has similar feelings for Angela Cartwright, but he had not seen or heard from either in years until they were reunited in 1981 for the *Whatever Became Of . . .?* TV special.

In 1970, the sitcom was revived for twenty-four more shows, this time in color, called *Make Room for Granddaddy.* Rusty was on some of them as a serviceman with a wife and children.

When the shows ended, Rusty says, he felt the need to be free. There were no offers of employment as an actor, nor did he seek them.

Because he went back and forth between private tutors and a Roman Catholic school, Rusty feels he did not receive an adequate education. At the time he felt cheated, if only by the fact that he was never able to be part of a sports team. His gym teacher in high school was Bob Denver. He says he was "hated" by many of the other students and "tormented a lot." The top of his new convertible was slashed and its body scratched. Once another boy spat on him. In school and since, he has found it difficult to fight excessive weight gain.

Financially Rusty didn't fare as well as might be expected. Part of his earnings went into a trust fund. A goodly portion, however, helped support the Hamer household. Mr. Hamer had died when Rusty was six years old. Mrs. Hamer was paid by the show for coaching Rusty and any other children who appeared on the show. When he turned twenty-one he cashed in his trust, but by then a mutual fund in which much of his salary had been invested had gone bust. Since then his average yearly income, including residuals, has been less than $10,000. He no longer receives residuals. Rusty has worked as a house painter and messenger in the last few years.

Hamer was married to an actress for about a year in the late sixties. They are divorced.

He does not regret being on the Thomas series but feels he was seen as one character for too many years and was harmed professionally. He believes he has suffered personally, too: "A show like ours was a very nurturing experience. We had a happy, close cast and crew. I've found the real world a very hard place."

Rusty Hamer now lives with his mother and brother in De Ridder, Louisiana. He never mentions his background to people and is seldom recognized. He wants to settle down in that area and find a good job.

Peter Schaeffer

Rusty Hamer lives now in De Ritter, Louisiana.

June Haver was publicized as "Hollywood's Sweetest Star."

June Haver

The girl who was publicized as "Hollywood's Sweetest Star" was born June Stovenour on June 10, 1926, in Rock Island, Illinois. When she was six years old June made her debut at the Cincinnati Suburban Theatre in *Midnight in a Toyshop.* The following year she won first prize in the Cincinnati Conservatory of Music's Poet-Music contest: a solo piano appearance with the Cincinnati Concert Orchestra conducted by Eugene Goossens. At eight, she was offered a screen test, which her mother declined, explaining that she wanted her daughter to have a normal childhood. June studied drama at the Little Theatre at Mariemont and the Schuster-Martin School, and at nine won the annual oratory contest at Hamilton Carnegie Public School. The next year her family moved back to Rock Island, where June sang at a school opening and won a spot on a local radio program. By eleven, she had her own radio show, sponsored by an ice cream company, in which she sang, emceed, and played piano for $2 a week.

At thirteen, June was soloist with Dick Jurgens's orchestra and then went with the Freddie Martin aggregation. By the time she was fifteen, she and her mother were touring with Ted Fio Rito and his band, which took them to Hollywood. While there, she made two shorts for Universal, one with Rito, the other with Tommy Dorsey. The rest of the Havers came out to join them, and June enrolled at Beverly Hills High School, where she was voted the most talented student and won first prize in an interscholastic debate. She played the lead in the high school production of *Ever Since Eve.* A talent scout from Twentieth Century–Fox spotted her and signed her to a contract, but it stipulated that she be allowed to finish the school term. Later, her option was not picked up because it was thought she looked too young. But in 1943, less than a year later, she was signed again by Fox.

Her image was of a sweet young thing, and her pictures were perfect examples of the period's slick, glossy musicals. June was groomed to succeed Fox's Betty Grable, who had replaced Alice Faye at that studio. But though June was prettier than Betty Grable and considerably softer, she lacked a strong screen personality. Some of her pictures were *Home in Indiana* (1944) with Lon McAllister,

Irish Eyes Are Smiling (1944) with the late Dick Haymes, *Where Do We Go from Here* (1945), *The Dolly Sisters* (1945), *Three Little Girls in Blue* (1946), *I Wonder Who's Kissing Her Now* (1947), *Scudda Hoo! Scudda Hay!* (1948), *The Daughter of Rosie O'Grady* (1950), and *Love Nest* (1951).

In 1953, while making $3500 a week, she announced she would not renew her Fox contract but would become a nun. When she entered the novitiate of the Sisters of Charity at Xavier, Kansas, she was warned that she might be doing so to run away from life: a romance with composer David Rose in 1946 had come to nothing; she had been married to musician Jimmy Zito in 1947 and been divorced the following year; and in 1953 her fiancé, Dr. John Durzik, a dentist, had died of hemophilia. She left the convent after seven months.

In 1955 June married Fred MacMurray, who is seventeen years her senior. Her last time before a camera was when she guested on the *Lucille Ball–Desi Arnaz Show* in 1958. June has turned down many offers since, including a part on her husband's TV show and the role of Danny Thomas's wife in his series.

The lady who personified the title of her movie *The Girl Next Door* (1953) says she does not miss her profession. "With Fred so active I still feel a part of the business," she told one interviewer. She does regret the trend toward violence and obscenity in films and feels the stars of today would have a wider appeal if they kept their freer life-styles to themselves. "I realize there was a lot of hypocrisy in my time," she admitted recently, "but I prefer discretion. There's a lot to be said for ladylike behavior."

June always planned to retire early, "while I was still *under* rather than over the hill." But now that her adoptive twin daughters are out of college she admits that a really good part might tempt her. In the meantime she keeps busy following Fred around the golf links.

When the MacMurrays are not traveling (they made seven trips to Europe in one year) they live in a Williamsburg Colonial mansion that was built by Nelson Eddy.

How does the former star feel about her life now? "When I look at what's happening in the world these days I can only feel that I have been very blessed."

Sarah Richardson

June Haver and her husband, Fred MacMurray, live in Brentwood in a mansion built by Nelson Eddy.

Horace Heidt became so popular on radio that during the late thirties he was heard on both the Red and the Blue networks of NBC.

Horace Heidt

The popular bandleader of the thirties and forties was born in Alameda, California, on May 21, 1901. For the first thirty years of his life nearly everything went wrong. His mother bought him a piano, but he hated to practice. While a student at the Culver Military Academy, he finally became interested in a musical career. He attempted to join the Culver Jazz Band but was rejected. (The late "Red" Nichols also auditioned, and made it..)

While at the University of California, he fractured his back during a football game and was told he could never again play that sport. While recuperating, Horace heard Guy Lombardo on the radio and decided to form a group of his own.

Horace Heidt and his Musical Knights played one-night stands at theatres and hotels up and down the West Coast. Between engagements Heidt worked in a real estate office and as a service station attendant. There were many "Knights" during those years, since the orchestra had to be disbanded over and over due to a lack of bookings. Finally, they got a national tour for the Fanchon Marco circuit of theatres.

By 1930 Heidt and his men had arrived at the legendary Palace Theatre in Manhattan. The emcee was Ken Murray, and although they were second to last on the bill, just playing the Palace was a big boost to Heidt's career. Next they went to Paris and the Riviera and rested on past laurels. When they returned the following year they had rehearsed so little that their second Palace engagement was a complete flop.

But Heidt hit his stride in radio. His first success in the medium came in 1932 with *Answers by the Dancers,* a show of dance music mixed with informal interviews from the Drake Hotel in Chicago. Two years later he came up with *Treasure Chest,* one of the first giveaway programs, in which couples from the audience who were celebrating their wedding anniversary competed for prizes. In 1935 he changed the format to include couples who were about to be married and brides and grooms fresh from the altar. The title was changed to *Anniversary Night with Horace Heidt,* and the show was so popular that the

National Broadcasting Company carried it on both Red and Blue Networks on Saturday nights. His *Pot o' Gold* show, which began in 1938, was the first to give away large amounts of money and was an overnight sensation. The Musical Knights supplied the music and there were big-name guests, but the real appeal was the long-distance call to someone somewhere in the United States who just might win the *pot o' gold.* The gimmick worked so well that movie theatre attendance dropped sharply and many theatre owners were forced to offer $1000 to anyone whose home was called while he was at the movies. United Artists bought the title and made a feature with it in 1941, starring Paulette Goddard (widowed and living in Manhattan) and James Stewart. Everyone thought it would go on forever, but the Federal Communications Commission declared it to be in violation of its rules and eventually forced it off the air.

Heidt started many successful careers. A few who admit their association with Heidt boosted them professionally are Art Carney; Dick Contino (living in Las Vegas and married to Leigh Snowden); the King Sisters; Al Hirt; Frankie Carle; and Fred Lowery (the blind whistler) who is living in Johnsonville, Texas.

Heidt utilized his knack for discovery of talent on radio, television, and on the road in his *Youth Opportunity Program.* Boys and girls with no experience whatever were given a chance not only to perform before an audience, but to act as stage manager, publicist, or advance person. Many of the top people in the entertainment industry today acknowledge the training they got as part of the company that toured the nation from 1948 to 1953.

In 1953 Horace decided to devote all of his time to the real estate holdings he had been acquiring in Southern California during his lucrative years in show business. He is the resident landlord of a 170-unit apartment complex in Van Nuys. (Roberta Sherwood is one of his tenants.) Adjacent to it is the former home of Oliver Hardy, which Heidt also owns. Horace Heidt Manor features several waterfalls, a large collection of exotic birds, and a recreation hall that houses memorabilia of his career. Some of the items on display are the original wheel that was spun every week on the *Pot o' Gold* program, a huge hand-carved ivory eagle, and the personal golf clubs of Hermann Goering.

Heidt is a widower. One of his sons is the president of the United Bank of California. Another is in the construction business. The youngest is studying law. His daughter owns and operates a gold mine.

John Oster

At age eighty-one Horace Heidt says, "I never felt better in my life."

In 1947 Wanda Hendrix was named "Bright New Star" in a poll of foreign press correspondents in Hollywood.

Wanda Hendrix

The pretty movie actress was born Dixie Wanda Hendrix near Jacksonville, Florida, on November 3, 1928.

She once said that her earliest recollections were of movies and screen personalities and that by the age of four she had set her mind on becoming a movie star. "By the time I was six everyone in the neighborhood knew about my ambition," said Wanda. "My dad was in the insurance business. Both he and my mother thought it was a childish fantasy at first. But they continued taking me to a lot of pictures, and I never stopped talking about the star I was going to become." After a local drama teacher told Mrs. Hendrix that her daughter had talent, her ambition was taken seriously.

Wanda was fourteen years old when a little theatre in Jacksonville presented her in the lead role of *Snow White and the Seven Dwarfs.* A talent scout from Warner Brothers saw her and recommended that the studio sign her. She and her mother, who by then was convinced of her cherubic daughter's destiny, moved to Hollywood. The teenager was groomed and schooled on the Warners lot.

Wanda took to acting in films immediately. She loved the clothes, makeup, and constant attention. About the other side of being a young girl under contract she once said, "On one hand I was treated like a child. On the other I had greater responsibilities than most adults."

She debuted with the late Charles Boyer in *Confidential Agent* (1945). The late Robert Montgomery saw it and borrowed her to play the Indian girl in *Ride the Pink Horse* (1947), which gave her career a big boost. She returned to her home lot for *Nora Prentiss* (1947) and then was put under contract by Paramount Pictures, where she made *Variety Girl* (1947), *Miss Tatlock's Millions* (1948), *Song of Surrender* (1949), and *Captain Carey, U.S.A.* (1950).

When the late Audie Murphy left the U.S.

Army as the most decorated GI of World War II, Jimmy Cagney signed him to a personal contract. At their first meeting the young veteran showed Cagney the Valentine Day's issue of *Coronet* magazine, which had a photo of Wanda on the cover. "That's the girl I want to meet," said Murphy. "I'm going to marry her." A highly publicized whirlwind courtship was climaxed by their marriage in January 1949.

The newlyweds were costarred in *Sierra* (1950). At the insistence of his young wife, Audie Murphy received top billing. But he was a deeply disturbed young man. "He despised his father," Wanda confided years later. "He told me that every time he shot one of the enemy during the war he pretended he was killing his dad. Audie had the most terrible nightmares. He had guns all over our home. He even slept with a loaded gun under his pillow."

A year after they became America's favorite young couple they were divorced. His obsessive gambling had used up all of her savings.

Four years later Wanda became the wife of Jim Stack, wealthy brother of Robert Stack, in a wedding that was the social event of the season. At his request, Wanda abandoned her career. The union was a stormy one and ended amid harsh accusations from both sides.

"I'd love to work again," she disclosed in a 1971 interview. "But young people are now in casting and they don't know my name or my work. The industry has changed so very much."

Among her films were *Prince of Foxes* (1949) with Tyrone Power, *My Outlaw Brother* (1952), *Sea of Lost Ships* (1953), *The Black Dakotas* (1954), *The Boy Who Caught a Crook* (1961), *Johnny Cool* (1963), and *Stage to Thunder Rock* (1964).

Wanda had some cosmetic surgery done and was working toward a comeback when she was taken seriously ill in 1979. For over a year she lingered in a semiconscious state. Her mother sat with her in the hospital all day, every day. Friends Terry Moore and Connie Haines visited her frequently. During this period the somewhat younger man she had married in 1969 divorced her.

Wanda Hendrix died in February 1981.

Once, when told about a fan of her age who had long identified with her, Wanda remarked, "I just hope she has found more happiness in life than I have."

courtesy of Mrs. Mary Hendrix

Wanda Hendrix shortly before she became seriously ill.

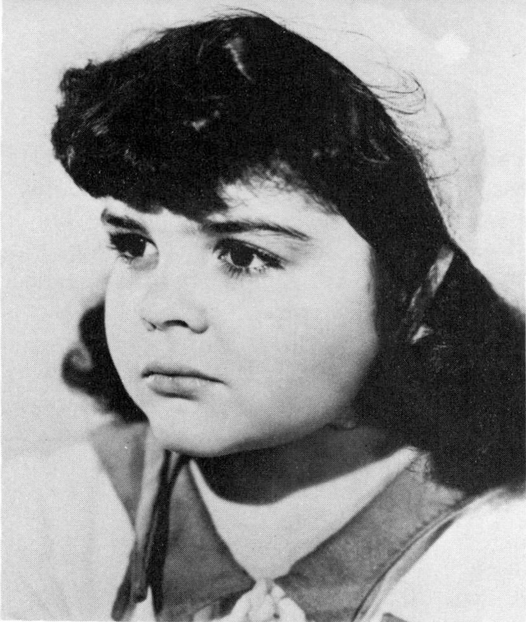

Darla Hood, the "sweetheart" of Our Gang.

Darla Hood

The distaff member of the screen's best-remembered series of comedy shorts, *Our Gang* (now known on television as *The Little Rascals),* was born on November 4, 1931, in Leedy, Oklahoma. Her father was the banker in their town of five hundred. Darla was an only child, whose mother was determined that her daughter was going to be a success in show business. When Darla was only three, Mrs. Hood enrolled her for dancing and singing lessons in Oklahoma City, necessitating a 150-mile round trip once a week. As Diana Serra Cary, author of *Hollywood's Children,* put it, "Darla was her mother's ticket out of that small town."

In 1935, Kathryn Duffy, Darla's coach, took her to New York City on a trip. One night they were dining at their hotel, the Edison, in Times Square, when the orchestra leader asked Darla if she would like to lead the band. The tot guided the group through a number, to the delight of the audience. Afterward Ms. Duffy and Darla were joined by Joe Rivkin, a talent scout for Hal Roach Studios. They were looking for a "little sweetheart" for the mischievous boys in the *Our Gang* series. Darla was tested in New York, signed to a nine-year contract, and sent to Hollywood, where she was joined by her mother. Mr. Hood commuted as much as possible from Leedy. From 1936 until 1945 Darla appeared in over 150 of the famous shorts.

The "Gang" was tutored on the Roach lot by Mrs. Alma Rubens. When the series was sold to Metro-Goldwyn-Mayer they attended the famous "little red schoolhouse" on the M-G-M lot.

Darla said that being the only girl among a group of preadolescent boys was often quite lonely. While the boys were always nice to her, most of the games they played excluded girls, and more often than not she was left alone with her dolls.

Few *Our Gang* pictures were made during World War II because of the shortage of film, which was reserved for feature pictures. By the time they were ready to revive the series, Darla was too mature for the role. In 1945 she left the group and enrolled at Fairfax High School in Hollywood, from which she was graduated as an honor student. She planned to continue her studies at the University of Southern California, but Ken Murray offered her vocal group, "The Enchanters," a good spot in his famous *Blackouts of 1949,* which had a long run in Hollywood before it went to Broadway. In 1950 she started the first of four seasons as Murray's leading lady in his TV series. After that Darla made numerous appearances in nightclubs in Las Vegas, San Francisco, and New York.

Darla was first married when she was seventeen years old. It lasted eight years. Darla had two children, Brett and Darla Jo, from her first marriage. In 1957 she became the wife of a music publisher.

Darla received a great many fan letters from children about as old as she was when she played in *Our Gang.* They watched *The Little Rascals* on TV and usually wanted an autographed photograph. She sent out stills from the thirties because she found that kids were disappointed when they discovered she was a grown woman. This was often true when she was introduced to adults who had known her from their childhood on the screen. "I often felt that I had let them down by not remaining a child," Darla once said. "They'd be dying to meet me and yet I could see their faces fall when I walked into the room. What do you say to someone whose fantasy has just been disturbed?"

Until the last day of her life, June 13, 1979, Darla Hood worked at working in show business. Her glossy photos and résumés were in her handbag when she died of heart failure. She was often discouraged as she made the rounds of casting offices. "People just want to talk with me out of curiosity when I go for a job," she told interviewer Bob Garner in 1977. "They're interested in learning all about my life, but end up not hiring me. . . . I'm still hoping something fantastic will happen in show business for me again."

When Darla did work, it was doing voice-overs for cartoons and commercials. The most money she ever made in her entire career came from the Chicken-of-the-Sea jingle. Her parents never gave her a penny of the salary she earned from *Our Gang.*

When her widowed mother looked at Darla in her casket, she sobbed, "Oh, Darla honey, you were such a *good* girl, and you had such a *hard* life!"

The sweetheart of *Our Gang* is entombed in crypt number G-4 in the Abbey of the Psalms in the Hollywood Memorial Park Cemetery.

Richard Stanley

Author Richard Lamparski and Darla at a book-autographing party in Los Angeles in 1978.

Miriam Hopkins's biographer, George Ellis, described her in Ginger, Loretta and Irene Who? as a combination of "thistledown and steel wool." Author David Shipman has written of her "hostessy graciousness and cracked-ice delivery."

Miriam Hopkins

The mercurial and controversial star of stage and screen was born on October 18, 1902, in Bainbridge, Georgia. While not wealthy, she came from a family that could trace its roots back to the American Revolution.

From her earliest days in the theatre, dancing in the chorus of *Music Box Revue* (1921), Miriam was noticed. To some she was a brilliant actress of great range and a genuine intellectual. Others thought her a frightful ham and a hysterical neurotic.

About the only consistencies in her life seem to be her firm belief in astrology and numerology and her frequent screaming tantrums.

Her choice of roles and her performances in them were as unpredictable as her behavior. Yet when she arrived in Hollywood in 1930 she was already considered a star. On Broadway she had had great success in *An American Tragedy* (1926), *Excess Baggage* (1927), and *Lysistrata* (1930).

She was married to and divorced from a young actor, an older writer, director Anatole Litvak, and a *New York Times* man. In between husbands she startled even close friends when she adopted a baby boy. When he wasn't in military school, where he spent most of his early years, Miriam saw to it that he had piano lessons from Jose Iturbi and tennis instructions from Big Bill Tilden. When he expressed an interest in flying she brought him to Igor Sikorsky. But the only guidance she ever offered was when she warned him never to be "boring in bed."

She had a well-publicized and long-running feud with Bette Davis, with whom she appeared in *The Old Maid* (1939) and *Old Acquaintance* (1943).

Her other screen roles were in *Dr. Jekyll and Mr. Hyde* (1932), *The Story of Temple Drake* (1933), *Design for Living* (1933), *Barbary Coast* (1935), *These Three* (1936), *The Heiress* (1949), *The Children's Hour* (1962), and *The Chase* (1966). She was seriously considered for the part of "Scarlett O'Hara," but will probably be remembered best for starring in *Becky Sharp* (1935), the first all-Technicolor feature, and the delicious Lubitsch comedy *Trouble in Paradise* (1932).

On stage she took over the lead from Tallulah Bankhead in *Jezebel* (1933) and *The Skin of Our Teeth* (1944) without suffering by comparison. Some of her other Broadway appearances were in Tennessee Williams's *Battle of Angels* (1940), *The Perfect Marriage* (1944), and *Look Homeward, Angel* (1958).

Although Miriam Hopkins was a classic case of egocentricity, the subject of her own career bored her. She much preferred telling stories about her many lovers. Among them were Bennett Cerf, Leland Hayward, Maurice Chevalier, John Gilbert, and John Gunther. She had a staccato speech pattern, softened by traces of a southern drawl.

Ms. Hopkins died in October 1972. Confounding her friends and fans to the very end, she wrote her own epitaph: "If I had it to do over again, I'd do everything different."

Jon Virzi

Miriam Hopkins shortly before her death in 1972.

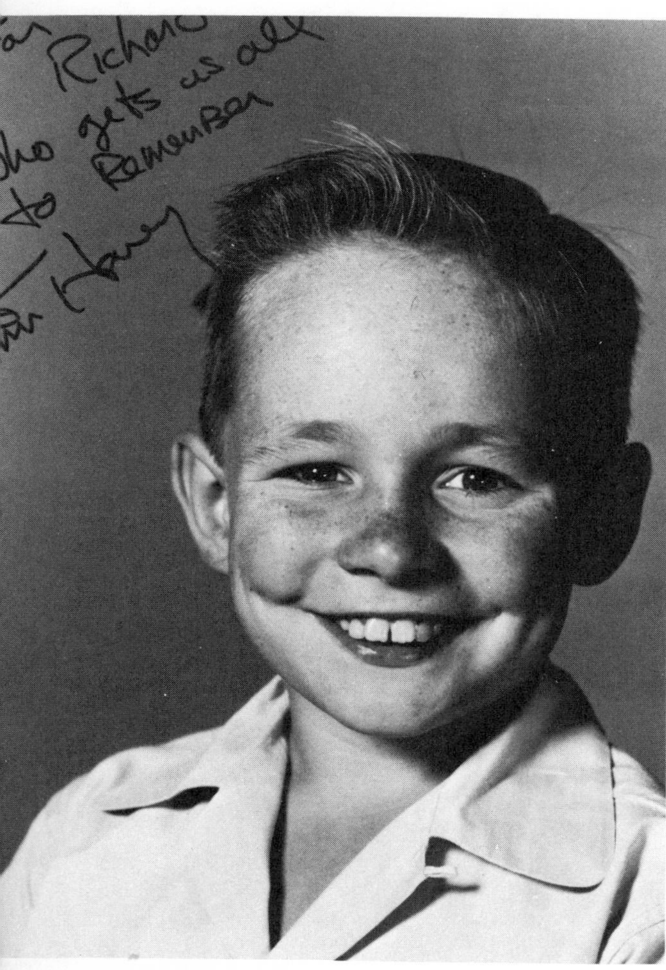

Tim Hovey in 1956.

Tim Hovey

The child star of the fifties was born in Los Angeles in June. His father owned a large sporting goods store in the San Fernando Valley. Tim began talking when he was only ten months old. He taught himself to read before he started grade school.

Tim was "discovered" for the first time when he was six months old. The secretary to his pediatrician suggested him for a part in a movie, but his prosperous parents never bothered to follow up on the opportunity. The second time, his picture in a photographer's shop window caught the eye of an agent who called the Hoveys, but they didn't take him seriously. Then his mother became acquainted with a woman who represented child actors. She sent him on a call for boys to work on Milton Berle's television show. After that he did a part on *Lassie*.

Mrs. Hovey took Tim to an open call for the part of a very small, very young cadet at a military academy. Out of the hundreds of children who auditioned, Tim and David Ladd were among the handful of finalists. Tim Hovey was chosen to play opposite Charlton Heston in *The Private War of Major Benson* (1955). Tim was small even for his six years, and his squeaky voice and almost homely features stole the picture.

Signed to a seven-year contract with Universal, he was cast in *Queen Bee* (1955) with Joan Crawford, *Toy Tiger* (1956) with Laraine Day (married and living in Beverly Hills), *Everything but the Truth* (1956), *Man Afraid* (1957) with George Nader (single and living in Los Angeles), *Slim Carter* (1957) with Jock Mahoney (living in Del Mar, California, and married to the mother of Sally Fields), and *Money, Women and Guns* (1958).

In a recent and very rare interview Hovey spoke of his life during that time: "I think my experience as a child star is unique. I never had to struggle to further my career. My parents didn't need the money I made and never pushed me in any direction. I never did a role in which I was uncomfortable. I rode in parades and on a fire truck. I was given keys to cities. I not only met J. Edgar Hoover, he let me fire a real tommy gun. If I missed out on anything, I'm not aware of it."

He found some of the stars he worked with

"pretentious and silly," but refuses to name them. He likes Charlton Heston and says that Tommy Rettig was the nicest of all of his contemporaries. Tim was so impressed with Ronald Reagan when they worked together on a *General Electric Theatre,* one of Hovey's last roles, that he voted for him in 1980 even though he is a Libertarian.

As Tim began to mature he became increasingly aware of his fame, which he always refers to as "notoriety." "Why anyone wants to be famous is beyond me," he says. "But then I suppose you have to actually be famous to realize what limitations it places on your life."

When Hovey was fifteen years old Otto Preminger offered him a role in *Critics Choice* on Broadway. To the astonishment of his studios, friends, and family, he not only refused to consider it but announced that he would no longer be available for any parts.

Hovey was educated by Jesuit priests in high school and then studied with Arnold Toynbee at the University of Colorado.

He tried to join the air force as a helicopter pilot but was too short (5 feet 5½ inches) to be accepted. He toured Europe for several years and then went to Asia, where he worked for a while as a photojournalist and then for the CIA, dropping propaganda from helicopters. From Vietnam he went to Africa, where he spent two years. At one point he was detained and beaten up by members of the Ugandan army. He has been in seventy-seven countries.

Upon his return to the U.S. Tim was arrested for draft dodging, but the charges were immediately dropped when the judge learned that on the day Hovey was to report for induction he was in Saigon.

From 1971 to 1977 Tim Hovey was the chief sound engineer for the Grateful Dead and Kingfish. "Fame as a movie star doesn't even compare to being on the road with a rock group," he says. "Just the fact that I knew Bob Weir had girls climbing through my hotel room windows."

Tim and his wife, Helen, share their apartment in Beverly Hills with their English bulldog, named "J. Edgar Hovey." He has an income from investments made for him years ago and does, according to Tim, "as little as possible." He is still recognized but says that he now finds it rather enjoyable.

About his career Hovey says: "I'm very grateful to have done what I did in movies, even though I think that was the most sterile period in Hollywood history. I'm equally thankful that I got out when I did."

Donna Schaeffer

Tim Hovey and his wife live in Beverly Hills.

In September 1934 John Howard signed a seven-year contract with Paramount Pictures.

John Howard

The actor who was publicized as "the American Ronald Colman" was born Jack Cox on April 14, 1913, in Cleveland, Ohio. He was an honor student and won scholarships in high school and college.

When his family was hard hit by the Depression, John began earning extra money by playing piano over local radio station WHK. He was studying at Western Reserve University when he joined other students in a dramatic reading of *John Brown's Body.* A studio talent scout approached him about a screen test, but Howard thought it was a joke and brushed him off. Then he got a call from Paramount Pictures with an offer of a contract beginning at $75 a week.

Howard began a seven-year association with Paramount in September of 1934. He debuted in *Car 99* (1935), supporting Fred MacMurray and the late Ann Sheridan. The following year he was in one of the great tearjerkers of all time, *Valiant Is the Word for Carrie,* which starred Gladys George and featured Jackie Moran (living in Leucadia, California).

Ronald Colman's portrayal of "Bulldog Drummond" had made the character a popular one with movie audiences. Paramount had John grow a mustache and starred him in a number of features playing the famous sleuth. Howard was able to project the intelligence necessary for the role, but audiences still thought of Colman as the authentic "Drummond."

Most of his many films were programmers: *Prison Farm* (1938) with the late Shirley Ross, *The Mad Doctor* (1941), *The Isle of Missing Men* (1942), and *I, Jane Doe* (1948) with Vera Hruba Ralston (married and living on the Hope Ranch in Santa Barbara, California).

John summed up his career in a recent interview: "If it hadn't been for Frank Capra and George Cukor, I would be remembered only as the man who made love to *The*

Invisible Woman." He was referring to the feature he made in 1941 with the late Virginia Bruce. John was loaned out for Capra's *Lost Horizon* (1937) and for Cukor's *The Philadelphia Story* (1940) only because those two directors asked for him. At the time, Howard strongly objected to his parts in both pictures. Although he is glad he played in them, he feels both roles were weak, foolish men. The only role he ever really wanted was in *Gone With the Wind.* Like dozens of other young leading men, he tested for the role of Ashley Wilkes, which was played by Leslie Howard. He thinks his best work was in *Dr. Hudson's Secret Journal,* an exceptionally well-written TV series that ran from 1955 to 1957.

For his service during World War II Howard was awarded the Navy Cross. After his discharge he went under contract to Twentieth Century–Fox. He secured his release from that studio to star in Broadway in the musical *Hazel Flagg* (1953). He has done little since in Hollywood except *The High and Mighty* (1954) and a few television commercials.

Howard lives with his wife and two children in West Hollywood. When he was hired away from his studies he promised himself that someday he would complete his education. Thirty years later he did just that. He now teaches English and drama at a private high school in the San Fernando Valley.

Bobby Downey

John Howard teaches English and drama at a private high school in the San Fernando Valley.

Will Hutchins as "Sugarfoot" in the late fifties.

Will Hutchins

The star of TV's *Sugarfoot* was born Marshall Lowell Hutchason in Atwater, California, on May 5, 1932. He is an only child of parents who divorced when Will was quite young.

In school he was considered the class clown, and his first ambition was to become a burlesque comic. He studied drama at Pomona College until he went into the army in 1952.

The first time Will Hutchins auditioned for a part he was hired—the lead on the live, daytime drama *Matinee Theatre.* Warner Brothers was preparing the *No Time for Sergeants* television series and signed him to a contract. It was originally intended that Will would play the role that eventually went to Sammy Jackson (a disk jockey in Southern California). Instead he was cast in small roles in some of Warner's features and used frequently in the *Conflict* series.

Sugarfoot was inspired by the 1951 Randolph Scott movie of the same name. In it Will played "Tom Brewster," a young man so green about the ways of the West he was called a "sugarfoot," which in the jargon of cowboys is one step below even a tenderfoot. He was friendly, trusting, thoroughly honest, and a bit bashful—a character not unlike Hutchins. Whenever the trouble in the plots subsided, "Sugarfoot" would study law, which he was being taught by mail.

The hour-long series premiered on ABC-TV in September 1957 and ran for four seasons. All of the shows were in black-and-white. Because Hutchins was under contract, he never received any residuals from any of the sixty-nine *Sugarfoot* episodes after they went into syndication. By the time the series was canceled in 1961 the writing had deteriorated to the point where he no longer enjoyed acting in it. He left Warner's shortly thereafter.

In 1964 Will replaced Orson Bean in the play *Never Too Late,* which he did on Broadway and on the road for two years.

Will was starred in two other TV programs, *Hey, Landlord!,* which lasted on the network from the fall of 1966 until the spring of 1967, and *Blondie,* which began in September 1968 and was canceled after thirteen weeks. Sandy Baron, who played Will's roommate on the *Hey, Landlord!* shows, recalls how generous he was to him and other cast members. "He was a big name, a star, and I was nobody," said Baron recently, "but there was never the crap coming down on his set that you get from most stars. I never worked with anyone I enjoyed and respected more."

Some of Will Hutchins's movie credits are *No Time for Sergeants* (1957), *The Shooting* (1965), *Spinout* (1966), *Clambake* (1967), *Shanghai Patrol* (1970), and *The Happy Hooker Goes to Washington* (1976).

Will Hutchins's home is in the Hollywood Hills, just across the street from the house where Lenny Bruce died. He has lived by himself since his divorce several years ago. He has a daughter by that marriage. Will is a graduate of *est*, studies Zen Buddhism, and practices yoga. He is a familiar face at screenings of classic films in Hollywood.

After a trip around the world Will joined a small circus as its ringmaster. In 1975 he became one of a troupe of performers who entertain at senior citizen homes and playgrounds. It was during that period that he developed his clown character "Patches." He spent 1980 and 1981 touring Australia and New Zealand with a circus, as the chief clown.

When he isn't made up as "Patches" Will is recognized constantly and approached by fans as "Sugarfoot." He has turned down lucrative offers for dinner theatre tours and TV parts because "the money might seduce me and I'd get back into the rut I hated. I'm now an actor who works all the time and I love it. I hope I can be 'Patches' forever."

Will Hutchins lives in the Hollywood Hills. He performs these days as "Patches," a clown.

Richard Lamparski

Marion Hutton was paid a flat fee of $50 for her recording of "Don't Sit Under the Apple Tree," a big hit of the war years. She introduced another hit of the period, "My Dreams Are Getting Better All the Time."

Marion Hutton

The songstress of the big band era was born on March 10, 1919, in Fort Smith, Arkansas. When she was three years old her father deserted the family. Marion and her sister, Betty Hutton, who is nineteen months younger, spent several years in foster homes before their mother brought them to Detroit in the early thirties.

Mrs. Hutton used to take her girls to the bars near the factory where she worked. There they would sing and dance, earning nickels and dimes from the customers. Later the bar owners paid them a few dollars to perform. Marion began working as a single. While Betty was singing at a hotel in Atlanta she was hired as the vocalist for the Vincent Lopez Orchestra. When Marion's engagement ended she joined Lopez, although the sisters did not sing together. The only time after leaving Detroit that the Huttons ever performed together was once on Betty's TV show.

In September 1938, Marion went with the newly formed Glenn Miller orchestra as the vocalist. Since she was underage and her mother was always with Betty, Miller became her legal guardian. When Twentieth Century–Fox offered a contract, Miller refused to release her.

Marion Hutton is often dismissed as "Betty Hutton's sister," but Don Miller has written of her: "She has never been given enough credit for her part in the Miller orchestra's huge success. She was instrumental in putting across a certain style. Marion looked good on the bandstand and had a solid personality—not nearly so flamboyant as her sister, but perky and vivacious in true forties tradition."

In 1944, when Glenn Miller went into the army, Marion struck out on her own. By then she had married a song plugger who was a close friend of Miller. For a while she sang on radio with Perry Como. Her screen debut had been in *Orchestra Wives* (1942). Then she made *In Society* (1944) with Abbott and Costello and *Love Happy* (1950) with the Marx Brothers.

In 1949 she divorced her first husband and married writer Jack Douglas. Five years later they, too, were divorced. The oldest of her three sons is an agent. She has not heard from him in over ten years. Her second son sings with a group. "I don't know how they ended up in show business," says Marion, "because I did everything I could to keep them away from it."

In 1954 Marion married Victor Schoen, who had been married previously to Kay Starr and was for many years the musical director for the Andrews Sisters. She decided then to retire. She hasn't sung a note in over twenty years.

Eventually Marion admitted to herself that she had a serious drinking problem. "Once I got the booze out of my system," she says, "I went to work on my mind. I'd been using amphetamines for years and so I had to stop that, too. I began to see how terribly guilty I'd been about traveling constantly when I should have been looking after my kids."

In 1972 she resumed the education she had abandoned when she was fifteen years old. Marion has a Master's degree in family counseling. In 1981 she and her husband moved to Seattle, where she is the program director of a rehabilitation center for women. She also works with alcoholics at a local clinic.

Recently Ms. Hutton spoke of her famous sister: "I love Betty because she's my sister, but I seldom hear from her and when I do there's not much to be said. I'd like to be her friend someday, but until she realizes what I came to know—that we and no one else make our lives what they are—communication is impossible. Betty's always blaming an ex-husband or a false friend or the state of show business. The problem is and always was Betty herself."

Marion Hutton, who now lives in Seattle, with composer-lyricist Howard W. Hays.

Don Koll

Claude Jarman, Jr., received a miniature Oscar as the outstanding child actor of the year, 1946, for The Yearling.

Claude Jarman, Jr.

The boy who won an Oscar for his first movie role was born on September 14, 1934, in Nashville, Tennessee.

When Claude was ten years old a man who was supposed to be a building inspector spent a few minutes observing his class one day. After school Claude was called to the principal's office, where the man told him that he would drop by his house that evening to speak with his parents. When the man arrived he found that the boy was out at a Cub Scout meeting and had neglected to mention the incident to his mother and father. The man introduced himself to the Jarmans as Clarence Brown, the director of such movies as *Anna Christie* and *The Human Comedy.* He had picked Claude, who was much in need of a haircut at the time, as a candidate to star in the screen adaptation of the Marjorie Kinnan Rawlings best-seller *The Yearling.* Disappointed at not being able to interview the boy further and photograph him, Brown left. Mr. Jarman, a railroad employee, and his wife were also disappointed, as the director told them that he had to leave that night and it was unlikely that he would be able to see Claude again.

That evening a snowstorm, rare in Nashville,

grounded all planes. Brown returned, talked with Claude, took a photo of him, and promised the Jarmans they would hear from him, one way or the other, within a month.

Three weeks later, Claude, who had acted in a few school plays but had no theatrical ambitions and had never heard of *The Yearling,* was on his way to M-G-M, where he remained under contract for five years.

Brown, who earlier had brought Butch Jenkins and Liz Taylor to prominence, coaxed a smooth, natural performance out of Claude. It brought the boy a special, miniature Academy Award for his portrayal of the boy who loved a baby deer in the 1946 film.

Claude's second film was *High Barbaree* (1947), and then came *Intruder in the Dust* (1949), a Faulkner story, which was a critical success but too far ahead of its time to win much favor with the public.

Claude never enjoyed making pictures—at least not the acting end of it. "I didn't hate it," he says now, "but neither did I find it at all fulfilling." Before his last, *The Great Locomotive Chase* (1956), he appeared in *The Sun Comes Up* (1949), *Hangman's Knot* (1952), and *Fair Wind to Java* (1953) with Vera Hruba Ralston.

During his layoff periods at the studio he would return to Tennessee, where he worked in an ice cream factory. After M-G-M he went home again to attend Vanderbilt University, thereafter joining the navy. In 1959 he got a discharge, got married, and appeared on a segment of TV's *Wagon Train.* He was divorced in 1967.

From 1960 to 1968 he was the West Coast public relations director for John Hancock Insurance. His firm Medion Productions produced the rock documentary *Fillmore* (1972). Claude was the director of the San Francisco Film Festival for twelve years. He resigned after the Festival of 1979. The same year he joined the Shaklee Corporation as vice-president in charge of corporate communications and government relations.

Claude has two sons and a daughter by his first marriage. He and his second wife, Mary Ann, have two girls in grammar school. Jarman and his family live in San Francisco. He would not permit any of his children to perform until they were out of school and capable of making a career decision for themselves.

He is still in touch with Clarence Brown, who lives in Palm Springs.

In 1978 Jarman acted for the first time in many years when he guested on the TV show *Centennial.* "I really enjoyed it, much to my surprise," says Claude, who did the part as a favor to an old friend. "I began wondering why I ever left a profession that was so much fun. Then as the production drew to a close everyone but me was on the phone to his agent trying to find another job. I'd forgotten the insecurity that reigns in that business. So I walked away from *Centennial* feeling very glad to be where and who I am."

Claude is now a vice-president of Shaklee Corporation and lives in San Francisco.

Wayne Parks

In the late thirties Sybil Jason went under contract to Twentieth Century–Fox.

Sybil Jason

The child star of the thirties was born on November 23, 1929, in Capetown, South Africa. She was on the stage for the first time when she was carried on during an opera at the age of three months. She began taking dancing lessons when she was eighteen months old. After appearing at a few benefits along with a group of children, she began going on alone to do her impressions of Jimmy Durante, Mae West, and Maurice Chevalier.

When she was four years old Sybil was taken to visit her uncle in London. He was the accompanist to Gracie Fields and Frances Day. Both took an immediate liking to her. The former got Sybil on the bill at the Palladium. The latter did a recording with her. Archie Pitt, who was married to Gracie Fields, then arranged for her to do a walk-on in a film he was making. What was originally supposed to be a one-day job for her in that picture, *Barnacle Bill* (1934), evolved into a showy part. Buddy Rogers was in London then making *Dance Band* (1935), and Sybil was signed for that, too. Irving Asher, who headed the Warner Brothers operation in the British Isles, made a test of her and sent it to Hollywood. A wire came back: SIGN HER. JACK WARNER.

Sybil's first feature in Hollywood was *Little Big Shot* (1935), which was followed by *I Found Stella Parrish* (1935) with Kay Francis. Then she made *The Captain's Kid* (1936) with Guy Kibbee, *The Great O'Malley* (1936), *The Singing Kid* (1936) with Al Jolson and Beverly Roberts (sharing a house in Laguna Niguel, California, with Wynne Gibson), and *Comet Over Broadway* (1938).

Sybil also made some shorts at Warner Brothers, including *A Day at Santa Anita* (1937), in which she rode the famed "Seabiscuit." Al Jolson, Ruby Keeler, and Bette Davis were in it also. Another was *The Little Pioneer* (1937). Ronald Reagan was ordered away from the location on that one when the director felt that his presence was distracting to Jane Wyman, who was Sybil's costar.

When Sybil Jason made a record album for Decca on which she was backed by Victor Young and his orchestra, she received a request for a copy from Princess Elizabeth.

Before moving from Warner's to Twentieth Century–Fox she free-lanced in *Woman Doctor* (1939) at Republic with the late Frieda Inescourt.

At Fox Sybil supported Shirley Temple in *The Little Princess* (1939) with Richard Greene (living in London) and *The Bluebird* (1940) with Gale Sondergaard (living in Los Angeles). Sybil and Shirley were supposed to do *Topsy and Eva* for Samuel Goldwyn on loan-out, but the picture was never made.

Twentieth Century–Fox sent the moppet on a worldwide public-appearance tour. During the second week of her trip the U.S. entered World War II and Sybil was stranded in her native country. Unable to travel, she was featured on her own radio program and entertained the troops.

At the end of the war she returned to Hollywood and went into a theatrical production of *The Wizard of Oz.* It was during the run of that play that she met her husband, writer Tony Drake. He had just been discharged from the navy and it was his first day in Hollywood. They married on New Year's Eve 1947.

Although she considers herself retired, Sybil lectures from time to time on her career, which she thoroughly enjoyed. "No child, no matter how rich, had a studio back lot to play on," says the former star. "All of the stars I worked with were nice to me and I made a lot of good friends among my contemporaries."

The Drakes live in Studio City and often host get-togethers with other child stars, such as Dickie Moore, Gloria Jean, Peggy Montgomery, and Edith Fellows. They call themselves "The Survivors" and hold their meetings in the little theatre behind the Drake home, where they screen the movies they made years ago.

Sybil's only child, Toni, is married to the producer of *The Price Is Right.*

Sybil today alongside the Shirley Temple doll in the den of her San Fernando Valley home.

Howard W. Hays

The singing star of the forties.

Gloria Jean

The girl who was to replace Deanna Durbin—and didn't—was born Gloria Jean Schoonover on April 14, 1926, in Buffalo, New York. By the age of three she was making occasional singing appearances in vaudeville and on radio in Scranton, Pennsylvania, where the family had settled. Her billing was as "Baby Schoonover."

A string of bad breaks that plagued her continually throughout her career began with an illness when she was six years old, making it impossible for her to accept an offer to tour with Paul Whiteman. Nevertheless, she became so popular locally that at Scranton's Capitol Theatre she packed the house.

When she was thirteen, her teacher took her to New York to pursue an operatic career. But Joe Pasternak, Deanna Durbin's producer, heard her sing, and she was signed to a contract by Universal Pictures. The thinking on the lot was that since their biggest star, Deanna Durbin, was now ready for ingenue roles, Gloria could take over in the preteen parts.

Her debut film, *The Under-Pup* (1939), although inexpensively made, was a perfect showcase for her and was quite successful. Universal was convinced she had great potential. Her second, *If I Had My Way* (1940) with Bing Crosby, was disappointing as a film but proved again that Gloria had a certain personal appeal and a lovely soprano voice. She made *Never Give a Sucker an Even Break* (1941) with W. C. Fields, who she remembers was very considerate of her, although she was disturbed by his nose: it reminded her of a melting popsicle.

It is remarkable that Gloria Jean ranks so high in popularity among old-movie buffs and still collectors, since she never was a major star. Her films were at best mediocre. Some of them are *What's Cooking?* (1942) with the Andrews Sisters, *When Johnny Comes Marching Home* (1942) with Jane Frazee (now a real estate agent in Newport Beach, California), *River Gang* (1945), *Copacabana* (1947), and *There's a Girl in My Heart* (1949) with Elyse Knox (married to sportscaster Tom Harmon and the mother of TV star Mark Harmon).

What didn't happen in Gloria Jean's career is much more interesting. She turned in a memorable performance as the blind girl with the late Alan Curtis in *Destiny* (1944), but the picture, originally supposed to be the opening episode of *Flesh and Fantasy,* was instead released on its own, with footage added—

hastily and cheaply shot. The following year her appearance at London's Casino was a critical disaster. Gloria, who had never experienced bad notices or an unappreciative audience, broke down on stage. A vaudeville tour scheduled to follow was canceled and she returned to Hollywood, very shaken and somewhat embittered. Gloria was seen a few times on television in the early fifties, and by 1954 was reduced to starring in a poverty-row programmer entitled *Air Strike.* The real heartbreak came when Jerry Lewis announced that she would make her comeback in his film *The Ladies' Man* (1961). She left her job as hostess at a restaurant across from Republic Studios and was promised a big part and songs. In the print that was released she didn't have a single line. It would have been her first color movie.

Gloria Jean shares a small house in Canoga Park, California, with her mother and sister and her son from an unsuccessful marriage. She works as a receptionist at Redkin Cosmetics.

Gloria feels that those she helped in Hollywood when she was on top turned away from her when she needed them. "Bing Crosby once told me to stay close to my family," she said. "It's a good thing I did, because they're all I have now." All the money she had saved during her peak years went for back taxes. About her future she commented: "I thought that making movies was going to be my life. I loved it so much and I'd just give anything to be able to work again, even in small parts, but I know that I'm too heavy and my age is against me."

A few years ago Sammy Davis, Jr., in a chance encounter with Gloria Jean and her son, Angelo Cellini, told her that the boy should model or act in pictures. Davis had no idea who the boy's mother was. "I just couldn't bring myself to tell him," Gloria said. "I've changed so much I was afraid of how he'd react."

John Oster

Gloria Jean and her son, Angelo, who is a natural science major at Pierce College.

By the late thirties the face of Allyn Joslyn was familiar to moviegoers throughout the world.

Allyn Joslyn

The character actor-comedian was born on July 21, 1901, in Milford, Pennsylvania, and brought up in New York City. His father was a mining engineer who lived in Dutch Guiana much of the time. Allyn's mother, who was a nurse, took him to all the Broadway plays and encouraged his interest in acting. He left prep school at sixteen and took a job as an office boy, but after six months of boredom he left to go on the stage.

Margaret Mayo, author of *Twin Beds,* gave him letters of introduction to twenty-three Broadway producers. The last on the list gave him a small part in *Toot Toot* (1918). Allyn worked a great deal through the twenties but somehow never hit it big until *Boy Meets Girl* (1936) put his name in lights. It was his thirty-sixth play. Before that he had carried a spear in John Barrymore's *Richard III* (1920), appeared in *The Firebrand* (1924), and had the lead in George M. Cohan's flop *Vermont* (1929). He supported himself during the lean Depression years by working as an assistant stage manager and radio actor. In one play he had only one line, consisting of two words. In one period of eighteen months he was in six flops in a row.

Director Mervyn Le Roy saw him in *Boy Meets Girl* and signed him to a two-picture contract. His debut was also Lana Turner's first, *They Won't Forget* (1937). His others included *Sweethearts* (1938), *Only Angels Have Wings* (1939), *No Time for Comedy* (1940), *The Immortal Sergeant* (1943), and *Junior Miss* (1945).

Joslyn returned to Broadway several times, most notably for the smash hit *Arsenic and Old Lace* (1941). Although he wasn't cast in the movie version of it or *Boy Meets Girl,* he was not greatly disappointed. He took his acting seriously, and Hollywood was always something of a joke to him.

He was not temperamental, or overly impressed by money and power. He turned down a $40,000 offer from Ernest Lubitsch because he didn't like the role, and risked suspension at Twentieth Century–Fox when he refused a part in which he was to rape Peggy Ann Garner. Two of his favorite pictures are *Café Society* (1939), in which he played a homosexual, and *Titanic* (1953), in which he played a coward who got into drag to save his skin.

Allyn worked less and less over the last twenty years. He appeared now and then on the television series *The Addams Family* in the sixties, but his appearances were usually as a favor to someone. He didn't miss acting and wasn't a bit tempted by the scripts that were sent to him.

In 1936 Allyn married the stage actress Dorothy Yockel. Their only child, Linda May, is a psychologist. Mrs. Joslyn died in 1978.

Allyn Joslyn spent the last five years of his life as an invalid. Something went amiss during what was supposed to have been a minor operation and he was never able to walk again. Always a voracious reader, he spent the rest of his time chatting and playing cards with his contemporaries at the Motion Picture Country House, where he died in January 1981.

Shortly before his passing he told a visitor, "I don't want anyone feeling sorry for me. I'm not in pain and there's not a day goes by that I don't have a few good laughs. I've had a wonderful career and now I'm being well looked after."

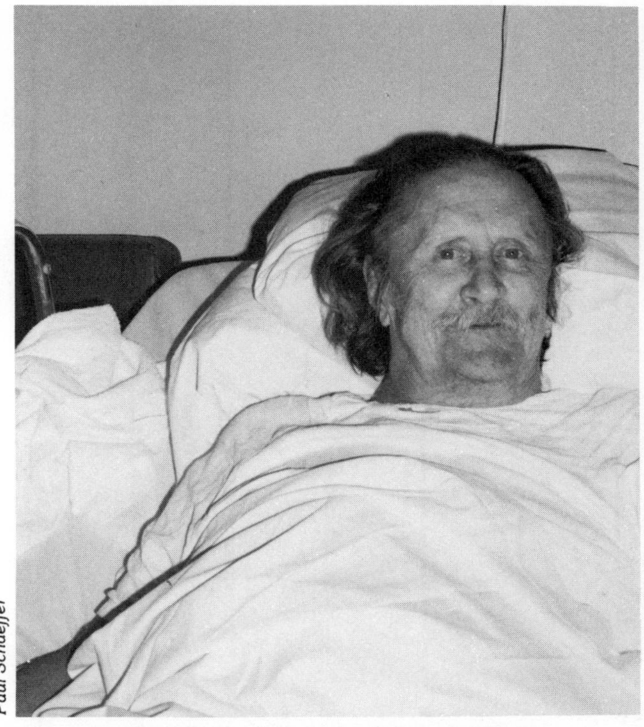

Paul Schaeffer

Allyn Joslyn shortly before his death in January 1981 at the Motion Picture Country House.

To the end Joslyn delighted in telling stories about the pomposity of some of those he had worked with in movies. His favorite targets were the producers.

Much of the popularity of bobbed hair during the twenties was due to her mannish coiffures.

Leatrice Joy

The star of silent pictures was born Leatrice Zeidler on November 7, 1896, in New Orleans. Her mother gave her the name Leatrice to tease her father; it had been the name of his former girlfriend. She took her mother's maiden name when she decided to become an actress.

Leatrice was a young girl when she first appeared in movies made in New Orleans by the Nola Film Co. She then spent almost a year working for the Diamond Film Co. in Wilkes Barre, Pennsylvania. In 1913 she was signed to a contract in New York City that began at $150 a week and was sent to Hollywood to play opposite Billy West, the imitator of Charlie Chaplin. She was also an extra in the Mary Pickford vehicle *The Pride of the Clan* (1917) and the love interest in several slapstick comedies with Oliver Hardy.

When Gloria Swanson went on to work with other directors, Cecil B. De Mille chose Leatrice Joy to replace her. Under De Mille's direction in such pictures as *Manslaughter* (1922) and *Ten Commandments* (1923) she became a major star. They worked so well together De Mille took her with him when he left Paramount to become an independent producer. She headed an all-star cast in *Java Head* (1923) and in 1924 costarred with Rod La Rocque in *Triumph*. Her other credits include *The Dressmaker from Paris* (1925), *Vanity* (1927), *Man Made Women* (1928), and *The Bellamy Trial* (1929).

Leatrice was neither a vamp nor a sweet young thing. In many of her films she played a severely tailored career woman. Much of the popularity of bobbed hair during that period was due to her mannish coiffures.

It is doubtful that anyone ever enjoyed being a star more than Leatrice Joy did. Her life-style seemed extravagant even to her contemporaries. When she bought herself a Rolls-Royce in 1926 her friend Conrad Nagel told her he thought it was extravagant. "What, darling, does 'extravagant' mean when you are making thousands of dollars a week?" she asked. She has described those years this way: "I was young, beautiful, rich, and famous. It was the most lavish and romantic time in history and I was right in the middle of it. There wasn't a moment I didn't savor."

On Christmas morning 1921 John Gilbert, who was one of the most handsome men in the world, gave her a twelve-piece vanity set of fourteen-karat gold. A short time later they eloped to Mexico, where a mariachi band played "Alexander's Ragtime Band" as their wedding march. She is still addressed as "Mrs. Gilbert," although she and the matinee idol were divorced long before he died in 1936. "What John and I had happens only once in a lifetime and only then if you are very lucky," she has said. "It was mutual, instantaneous, and very intense. I've been married twice since but it was never the same."

Joy went into semiretirement in the thirties, living in Beverly Hills. She appeared occasionally in featured parts in talkies such as *First Love* (1939) and *Red Stallion in the Rockies* (1949). At that time she fostered the career of one of the most popular black character actresses, Louise Beavers, who was for twelve years Joy's personal maid before peeling grapes for Mae West.

In 1951 Leatrice had a supporting role in a picture called *Love Nest.* Also in the cast was a comedian who had not been very successful. His name was Jack Paar. The ingenue was played by a blonde whom Ms. Joy noticed at once in spite of her small part. "She had the bearing of a real star and was gifted with that wonderfully innocent sex appeal that is so rare," recalls Leatrice. Her name was Marilyn Monroe.

Leatrice Joy lives by herself in a charming house right on the water in Riverside, Connecticut. It is called "The Magic Cottage." Her daughter, Leatrice Fountain, who is writing a biography of her father, lives close by. Now a great-grandmother, Leatrice Joy lectures, gardens, and visits her contemporaries in Hollywood.

There is more than a trace of a southern drawl in her speech. The farther back into the past she goes the heavier it gets: "I'm never lonely on cold, snowy nights. I have the delightful memories of a wonderful, happy childhood and a terribly romantic youth."

Leatrice Joy is a Christian Scientist.

Sandy Brown Wyeth

Leatrice Joy with her longtime friend, author Richard Lamparski.

In the early thirties Ruby Keeler was the star of Warner Brothers musicals and the wife of Al Jolson.

Ruby Keeler

The musical star was born on August 25, 1909, in Halifax, Nova Scotia. When she was three years old her family moved to New York City. During the Roaring Twenties Ruby became a dancer in speakeasies because it was the only job in which a teenage girl could work nights. The money she made came in very handy at home, where her mother had a houseful of children to care for.

Ruby was in the chorus at Texas Guinan's El Fey Club when she caught the eye of a man who was at that time the biggest name on Broadway, Al Jolson. She became his wife in 1928. Jolson was instrumental in getting Ruby featured in Ziegfeld's *Show Girl* (1929). Every night she would do a tap dance on stage while Jolson strolled down the aisle of the theatre to a front-row seat singing the song "Liza." Jolson received no billing and no money. It was the one and only time he ever worked for Flo Ziegfeld.

Jolson and Ruby were married in New York and came to Hollywood in the early thirties, when nearly all of the films being made were taking advantage of the new sound systems by adding songs to pictures.

Ruby was unknown to movie audiences when Warner Brothers took a chance on her by giving her the lead in *42nd Street* (1933). It was one of the most successful pictures that the studio ever made and today is considered the classic musical of the early 1930s. Her costar was a young man not much better known than Ruby, Dick Powell. Ruby and Dick costarred in a series of singing and dancing films, such as *Dames* (1934) and *Shipmates Forever* (1935). Also in 1935, she and Al Jolson appeared together in a picture about backstage life called *Go Into Your Dance.*

Altogether Ruby Keeler made nine films, her last, *Sweetheart of the Campus* (1941), before she retired in 1941. She and Jolson had been divorced a year before she gave up movies. Ruby was awarded custody of their adopted son, Al junior.

When Columbia Pictures decided to make *The Jolson Story* (1947) they offered her a goodly sum of money for the use of her name. She refused to grant permission, and when the picture was made Mrs. Jolson, played by Evelyn Keyes, was given a fictitious name.

In 1966, when tributes to Busby Berkeley,

her former director, were held in nine cities throughout South and North America and Europe, Ruby toured and appeared with her old friend. As her films were screened she stood in the back of one of the theatres and shook her head. "It's really amazing. I couldn't act. I had that terrible singing voice, and now I can see I wasn't the greatest tap dancer in the world, either."

All of what Ms. Keeler said may be true, but she had a quality during those bleak Depression years that people could identify with. Her roles, those of a kid trying to get a break on Broadway, were so close to her own story that it didn't matter how she read the lines, because she felt them, and audiences were rooting for her to make good.

Ruby Keeler made one of the most successful comebacks in recent show business history when she starred on Broadway in *No, No Nanette* in 1971. She and the musical revival were huge hits.

For the past few years Ruby, who was widowed by her second husband, has lived quietly in her home at the Thunderbird Golf Club in Palm Desert, California. She also maintains an apartment at the Balboa Bay Club in Balboa, California.

She has recuperated nicely from a bout of serious illness but no longer plays golf, a game that brought her several championship trophies.

Ruby Keeler is a grandmother and a Roman Catholic.

Jon Virzi

Ruby Keeler divides her time these days between Palm Desert and Balboa, California.

Patsy Kelly in the late thirties.

Patsy Kelly

The natural comedienne of stage and screen was born on January 12, 1910, in the Williamsburg section of Brooklyn. She was baptized in the Roman Catholic Church as Bridget Veronica Kelly. Raised in Manhattan, Patsy spent much of her childhood hanging around a fire station. Concerned about her daughter's ambition to be a fire fighter, Mrs. Kelly sent her to dancing school. It was there that she met Ruby Keeler, who became a close friend.

Patsy developed into an exceptional tap dancer, but when her brother brought her to the Palace Theatre to audition for Frank Fay, the star was taken instead by her funny attitude and quick wit. Fay, one of vaudeville's biggest stars, was known for his timing and sarcastic remarks. He hired Patsy as a stooge in his act. For the rest of her life Patsy credited Fay not only for discovering her but for what she learned from him about comedic delivery.

Patsy Kelly did *Harry Delmar's Revels* (1927) on Broadway before impresario Charles Dillingham put her in *Three Cheers* (1929) with Will Rogers. She went from that show into Earl Carroll's *Sketch Book* in 1929 and his *Vanities* the following year. After appearing in *Wonder Bar* (1931) with Al Jolson, she was brought to Hollywood by Hal Roach.

Patsy made 21 two-reeler comedies with Thelma Todd for Roach. When her costar was killed in 1935 Patsy made one short with Pert Kelton and then two with Lyda Roberti.

Her debut in features was in *Going Hollywood* (1933) with Bing Crosby and Marion Davies. Among the more than three dozen pictures she made were *The Girl from Missouri* (1934), *Page Miss Glory* (1935), *Pigskin Parade* (1936), *The Cowboy and the Lady* (1938), and *Topper Returns* (1941). By World War II she was free-lancing in low-budget fare such as *Danger! Women at Work* (1943).

There were many who considered Patsy Kelly bad luck. A remarkable number of stars she knew well or had worked with had died: Jean Harlow (suddenly), nightclub headliner Jean Malin (by drowning in a freak occurrence that almost killed Patsy, too), Thelma Todd (mysteriously), Carole Landis (by suicide), and Lyda Roberti (from a heart attack when she bent over to tie a shoelace). Others whispered that she couldn't work because of her drinking. Tallulah Bankhead, whom Patsy supported in a cross-country tour of *Dear Charles* in 1955, responded to both accusations in a 1969 interview: "Patsy never missed a cue in her life, much less a performance. She is a thorough professional. She brings nothing but good luck with her. I consider myself lucky just to know her."

When asked why there were lapses of so many years when the public didn't see her on screen or stage, Kelly replied: "I don't honestly know, but I believe in cycles. There are just times when it seems you can't do anything wrong. Then there are other times when whatever you do is wrong." Then she added, "I think I could have had more drive. I was never very ambitious."

Although she is thought of strictly as a comedienne, there was a tragic role that she seriously considered playing at one time. The late William Inge and Patsy had long talks about the possibility of her doing the lead in his drama *Come Back, Little Sheba.*

In 1960 Patsy made her first film in many years, *Please Don't Eat the Daisies,* and began to appear on TV. But her only screen role of note since then was in *Rosemary's Baby* (1968).

Then in 1971 she was back on Broadway in one of the decade's biggest hits, *No, No Nanette,* and working for the first time in her career with her old friend Ruby Keeler. She also made a lengthy tour in the musical.

Patsy Kelly had far more fans than many major stars. Often when her movies are shown on TV newspapers will highlight them with such comments as "worth watching for the Patsy Kelly scenes."

Patsy Kelly and the author in her Hollywood apartment.

The *New York Times* called her "the pert, rumpled farceur of knockabout movie comedies" when she died on September 24, 1981, at the Motion Picture Country Hospital.

Victor Kilian was under contract to Columbia Pictures for three years in the mid-thirties.

Victor Kilian

The character actor who was blacklisted during the McCarthy era was born in Jersey City, New Jersey, on March 6, 1891. The youngest of eight children, he began working when he was twelve years old. Before he acted, he labored as a longshoreman, ditchdigger, and brickmaker.

The first time Victor was on a stage was in Exeter, New Hampshire, in 1909. The play was a pirated version of a Broadway hit. Afterward, he toured the country in road shows and stock companies. For a while he played in a vaudeville act called "Say It with Flowers." One of the other actors in the sketch was Jimmy Cagney, who got fired.

The original production of Eugene O'Neill's play *Desire Under the Elms* (1925) was in its ninth week when Kilian replaced one of the actors. It was his first time on Broadway.

Victor, the late Brian Donlevy, and Kay Francis made their movie debuts together in *Gentlemen of the Press* (1929), which starred his close friend Walter Huston.

After doing *Valley Forge* (1934) on Broadway, he was signed up by Columbia Pictures. It was his only contract, and it lasted for three years.

Among his many films were *The Road to Glory* (1936) with June Lang (sharing a house in North Hollywood with her daughter), *Tovarich* (1937), *The Adventures of Tom Sawyer* (1938), *Huckleberry Finn* (1939), *Young Edison* (1940), *Western Union* (1941), *This Gun for Hire* (1942), *The Ox-Bow Incident* (1943), *Spellbound* (1945), *Gentleman's Agreement* (1947), and *The Flame and the Arrow* (1950).

Kilian always preferred the stage to pictures, but he remained in Hollywood and made about six features a year until he found himself unemployable. Although he never testified before the House Un-American Activities Committee, his name came up during the hearings. Victor was unacceptable to any major studio after 1951. It was six and a half years before he got another job. When he finally was cast in a movie, the late Ward Bond made a great effort to get him fired. Kilian always denied any bitterness about the blacklist.

In 1958 Victor returned to the stage, replacing Hugh Griffith in *Look Homeward, Angel.* Two years later he was again on Broadway, in

All the Way Home. His last play was *Gideon* (1961).

During a fight scene with John Wayne in *Reap the Wild Wind* (1942) Kilian lost an eye. Asked about the incident in 1976, he said: "It was not his fault, but I don't like him. Not for what he did but for the person he is." He called the late George Sanders "the biggest snob I have ever known."

When asked whether he sees any of the stars he worked with, he replied: "Stars and character actors do not mix socially in Hollywood. In New York I had close friendships with many stars, but in all the years I've lived here the only star who ever invited me to his home was Fredric March."

Victor's portrayal of "Grandpa Larkin" on TV's *Mary Hartman, Mary Hartman* won him a whole new set of fans. Kilian played the "Fernwood Flasher," a senior citizen who loved to eat peanut butter and expose himself to women.

Victor Kilian, a widower, lived by himself for many years in an apartment in the heart of Hollywood. One evening in 1979 he was having a late snack while watching TV when an intruder broke in and beat him to death. The murder has never been solved.

Victor Kilian in 1976, three years before he was murdered.

Donna Schaeffer

In <u>Broadway Limited</u> (1941) Leonid Kinskey played a tempermental Russian movie director.

Leonid Kinskey

The Russian character actor was born in St. Petersburg on April 18, 1903. He performed as a mime with all three of the imperial theatres before leaving his homeland in 1921.

Kinskey came to the United States via South America as a principal in the highly acclaimed Firebird Theatre. The company's failure at the box office on Broadway left him stranded in New York City without money or a knowledge of English. Then Leonid managed to get a part in the silent film *The Great Deception* (1926), starring Aileen Pringle and the late Ben Lyon. When he learned that his scenes had been almost completely lost in the editing, he accepted a position in Chicago, running a theatre-restaurant with a Russian theme. It was quite a success until the stock market crash of 1929.

Al Jolson hired him for the road tour of *Wonder Bar,* which brought Kinskey to Hollywood. Ernst Lubitsch caught him in the show and signed him for *Trouble in Paradise* (1932). The film is considered a classic comedy of the period.

Although he was never under contract to any studio, his Pinocchio nose and half-moon grin became famous in the hundreds of appearances they made in such pictures as *Duck Soup* (1933), *Les Misérables* (1935), *The Road to Glory* (1936) with June Lang (sharing a house with her daughter in the San Fernando Valley), *The Great Waltz* (1938) with the late Miliza Korjus, *I Married an Angel* (1942), *Monsieur Beaucaire* (1946), and *The Man with the Golden Arm* (1955).

Although he is usually remembered as "that crazy Russian," Kinskey's film credits show he had much more range as an actor than the image he left in the minds of most moviegoers. In *We Live Again* (1934) with Anna Sten (living in Beverly Hills), he was a murder victim. In *Algiers* (1938) he played an oily informer. *So Ends Our Night* (1941) presented him as a sniveling coward. He gave a delightful performance in *On Your Toes* (1939) as an eccentric and excitable composer. His most incongruous scene came in *Rhythm on the Range* (1936). Leonid harmonized with Bing Crosby, Martha Raye, and Bob Burns in introducing the song "I'm an Old Cowhand." It is his personal favorite. He is usually recognized as "Sascha," the bartender in *Casablanca* (1942).

In his early, lean years, he supplemented his income by writing articles and short stories for

Russian-language publications. During World War II he began working with the Soviets in choosing Hollywood movies for showing in the USSR. He is still consulted. His countrymen and -women, however, think he is an American acting the part of a Russian. Explains Leonid, "When I play Russians in movies they made me so exaggerated, no real Russian believed me." Kinskey is a U.S. citizen.

His claim, that *The Spot Lite Club,* a program he did over KTLA in Los Angeles in 1948, was the first situation comedy ever on TV, has never been disputed. He was a regular on Jackie Cooper's TV series of the fifties, *The People's Choice.*

Kinskey has been widowed by both of his wives. He has no children. He lives by himself in North Hollywood. During the past twenty years he has written and directed quite a few large industrial shows. He makes rare appearances on television but adamantly refuses to do commercials. He admitted not long ago that his interest in acting is all but dead. He did the pilot for the series *Hogan's Heroes* but then decided against signing for the show. Said Kinskey in his still heavy Russian accent, "The premise was, to me, both false and offensive. Nazis were seldom dumb and never funny."

Richard Lamparski

Leonid Kinskey frequently lunches at Sorrentino's, a restaurant near his home in the San Fernando Valley.

Martin Kosleck portrayed Nazi propaganda minister Joseph Goebbels on the screen four times.

Martin Kosleck

The character actor was born in Pomerania, Germany, on March 24, 1909. His mother was German. Martin's father was Russian with a family tree that could be traced back to the thirteenth century.

Kosleck was brought up on a small family estate in Germany. When he left at age ten to visit his grandmother in Italy, it was the first time he had ever seen a town or city.

Martin was a student of Max Reinhardt, who directed him in a small part in the Berlin stage production of *Saint Joan,* which starred Elisabeth Bergner (widowed and living in London). He made two German films, but Hollywood was his goal. "I was completely movie-struck," he said recently. "Marlene Dietrich, whom I had known well in Berlin, took me to dinner the very first night I arrived in Hollywood in 1932. Afterward we sat in a projection room at Paramount watching the picture she had just finished, *Shanghai Express.* It was all so exciting and glamorous. I don't think I ever got over it, because here I am, still."

While he perfected his English and settled himself in Hollywood, Kosleck supported himself with his painting. He has done several portraits in oil of Marlene Dietrich and two of Bette Davis, who is his favorite actress. In 1938 he was given a one-man show in New York City. While there, he appeared in a production of *The Merchant of Venice* in Brooklyn. The late Anatole Litvak saw him in it and cast him in the film he was making, *Confessions of a Nazi Spy* (1939).

Martin Kosleck is probably best remembered for his portrayals of Dr. Joseph Goebbels, a role he played four times in movies, the first being in *Confessions of a Nazi Spy.* Although he did not closely resemble the Nazi propaganda chief, he was convincing in the part because he was small in stature, like the Nazi, and was able to project the brooding menace that Goebbels always conveyed.

He worked frequently during the 1940s in the pictures Hollywood made to boost morale during World War II, playing spies, double agents, resistance fighters, and Gestapo officers. A few of these features were *Underground* (1941), *All Through the Night* (1942), *Chetniks* (1943) with Anna Sten (living in Los Angeles), and *The North Star* (1943) with the late Ann Harding.

He was also seen frequently in pictures with European casts and settings. Hitchcock used him in *Foreign Correspondent* (1940). He was with the late Ilona Massey in *International Lady* (1941). The other genre for which he is well known is the horror film. He appeared in such chillers as *The Mad Doctor* (1941), in which he played the jealous companion of the late Basil Rathbone, *The Spider* (1945), *She Wolf of London* (1946), and *The Frozen Ghost* (1946) with the late Douglas Dumbrille. Among his last films were *Something Wild* (1961) and *Agent for H.A.R.M.* (1966). He was cast against type as the hero in *The Wife of Monte Cristo* (1946), in which the heavy was played by John Loder (living in London).

Martin did *The Madwoman of Chaillot* (1948), starring the late Martita Hunt, both on Broadway and on the road. Also in it was Kosleck's late wife, the wealthy and titled Eleonora von Mendelssohn.

During a recent interview Martin Kosleck spoke of his performances as Goebbels: "I never met him or saw him. In fact, I've never spoken with a Nazi in my life. The fools were all over the streets of Berlin when I left in 1931. No one I knew took them seriously. I never regretted playing Goebbels so many times, although I realize that I became too closely identified with him. Twice when I have been in New York City within recent years, men have shouted at me from car windows, 'Heil Hitler!' I understand how my German accent has limited me as an actor. This is very ironic, because I have never felt the slightest patriotism toward Germany. I've been a U.S. citizen for many years, and I'm delighted to be here."

Kosleck shares a house in West Hollywood with a friend. It is filled with his antiques collection and the oils he has painted. His close friends are Peter Lorre's widow and Angela Lansbury, whom he has known since she was a teenage salesclerk at Bullocks Wilshire.

Martin says the happiest moments of his life were spent in front of a camera or on stage. But since suffering a heart attack while on location in the Sierras a number of years ago, he has been in semiretirement. One offer that would bring him back to work would be to play with Carol Burnett. He considers himself her greatest fan.

Richard Lamparski

Martin Kosleck lives today amid his antiques and oil paintings in a house in West Hollywood.

By 1945 Kurt Kreuger was a familiar face to American moviegoers.

Kurt Kreuger

The handsome blond movie actor was born on July 23, 1916. Contrary to studio publicity during World War II, which for a while had him a Swiss ski instructor and another time a Dutch student, he was born in Michenberg, Germany, and brought up in St. Moritz, Switzerland. Kurt's father disapproved of his son's wanderlust and interest in acting. For a while Kreuger attended the University of London's School of Economics and then transferred to Columbia University in New York City. When he dropped his studies his allowance was cut off, and in 1939 he took a job as a travel agent and enrolled with the Provincetown Players on Cape Cod. By 1941 he had landed a small part in *Candle in the Wind* on Broadway with Helen Hayes and understudied one of the leads.

Kreuger made his movie debut in a small part in *Edge of Darkness* (1943) and did bits in *Action in the North Atlantic* (1943) and *Unconquered* (1947). During his six years under contract to Twentieth Century–Fox he made *The Strange Death of Adolf Hitler* (1943), *Sahara* (1943), *None Shall Escape* (1944), *Paris Underground* (1945), *The Spider* (1945) with Cara Williams (married to a Beverly Hills real estate broker), *Mademoiselle Fifi* (1944) with Simone Simon (single and living in Paris), and *The Dark Corner* (1946). He escaped being typecast as a Nazi through roles in *Sentimental Journey* (1946) and *Unfaithfully Yours* (1948).

In 1949, after a quarrel with his studio, he walked out on his contract and went to Europe, where he made quite a few German films in which he played the lead, something that always eluded him in Hollywood. After a very serious auto accident in 1955 he returned to the United States. He had become a citizen in 1944.

Kurt made *The Enemy Below* (1957), *Legion of the Doomed* (1958), *The St. Valentine's Day Massacre* (1967) and *What Did You Do in the War, Daddy?* (1966), but his career never caught fire again. One severe disappointment came when Marlon Brando got the role he wanted so much in *The Young Lions.*

He has a fine singing voice and was seriously considered for the original Broadway cast of *The Sound of Music.* The reason he wasn't used was that he didn't look old enough to be the father of seven children. He was so flattered he didn't mind at all.

Kreuger may not have become a star but he has a consolation in living like one in a beautiful Beverly Hills home on a private road and driving a Rolls-Royce. He has never married and lives with his German shepherd. Kurt follows the ski season around the world. He occasionally sees Helmut Dantine, with whom he made *Hotel Berlin* (1945) and *Escape in the Desert* (1945). Another friend from the old days is Andrea King (widowed and living in Beverly Hills).

His money is invested in Beverly Hills homes, which he rents to luminaries.

In 1981, after a successful double-bypass heart operation, Kreuger took a trip around the world, instructing his travel agent to arrange for every possible luxury.

Kurt Kreuger explained his attitude toward his career recently: "I like doing something now and then but the part must appeal to my ego or my bank account. So when you see Kreuger on the screen you can be sure he's either got a very juicy part or he's being paid a hell of a lot of money."

Michael Knowles

Kurt Kreuger today in his Beverly Hills home.

"The Ol' Professor," as Kay Kyser was called when he had his "Kollege of Musical Knowledge."

Kay Kyser

The once popular bandleader was born on June 18, 1906, in Rocky Mount, North Carolina, to the first registered woman pharmacist in the state. His father, who was almost totally blind, also practiced pharmacy. Kay's real name is James Kern Kyser.

In both high school and college Kay was class president, editor of the yearbook, and cheerleader and coach of the football team. While at the University of North Carolina he also found time to organize a band, which soon developed such a reputation that they were playing school dances in neighboring states. However, on their first play date, in 1926, Kay was so nervous he was unable to lead the group. The baton had to be taken over by his old friend, the late Johnny Mercer.

After college he had a few lean years. Then Kyser opened at Chicago's famed Black Hawk Restaurant in September 1934 with a group called "Kay Kyser's Kampus Klass." It was soon changed to "Kay Kyser's Kollege of Musical Knowledge." But by that time the group had made a big hit not only with the club's audiences but on the regional radio network that carried the bands from the Black Hawk.

The Kyser sound was much like that of his idols, Fred Waring and Guy Lombardo, but Kay's group had much more class than the Mickey Mouse bands that merely imitated the giants. His boys stayed with him year after year and had a reputation for being well dressed and groomed. They got along so well that one of the complaints most often heard was that there was too much nonsense going on during songs like "Praise the Lord and Pass the Ammunition" and "Who Wouldn't Love You?", two of their biggest hits. However, the jokes and kidding worked well for the novelty numbers, which were their specialty.

Kyser's theme from the very beginning was "Thinking of You." Some of his vocalists were Ish Kabibble, the King Sisters, Ginny Simms, Harry Babbitt, and Mike Douglas, who was then known as Michael Douglas.

He and his band appeared in such feature films as *You'll Find Out* (1940), *My Favorite Spy* (1942), and *Swing Fever* (1943). His musical-quiz radio program was popular throughout the 1940s, during which time he played at 580 U.S. military installations around the world. In March of 1950 the program moved to NBC television. Kay always wore the traditional cap and gown, as did his musicians. The show's contestants had to answer his true-or-false questions, but with an incorrect answer. If they gave the correct answer, Kay would say, "That's right. You're wrong!" Incorrect answers drew "That's wrong. You're right!" Questions that couldn't be answered were referred to the studio audience by Kyser, who would shout, "Students?"

The man whom musicologist George Simon once referred to as "a luscious ear in the field of corn" called it quits in 1954, when he turned over his TV hosting chores to Tennessee Ernie Ford.

Eleven years earlier he had married his songstress, Georgia Carroll, a former Powers model. The couple live in a 155-year-old house in Chapel Hill, North Carolina. Kay is a teacher and practitioner of Christian Science.

He has turned down interviews and very lucrative offers to return to TV with the same reply: "Those were wonderful years but they are long over. My concerns today are with my family and my faith."

A fan who brought around some of Kyser's old movies to show him said that his three daughters were not a bit interested in seeing them and that it seemed Kay and Georgia watched only out of politeness.

His lectures on Christian Science draw standing-room-only crowds around the country. The "down-home" style that was his trademark for many years on radio and in pictures is just as appealing on stage. Kay Kyser is still a star.

Jon Virzi

Kay Kyser after one of his recent lectures on Christian Science.

Arthur Lake and Penny Singleton played "Dagwood" and "Blondie" in twenty-eight feature films between 1938 and 1950. They also costarred on the Blondie radio series.

Arthur Lake

The actor who became world famous as "Dagwood Bumstead" was born in Corbin, Kentucky, on April 17, 1905. At the time, his father and uncle were touring with a circus, in an aerial act known as "The Flying Silverlakes." His mother, Edith Goodwin, was an actress. His parents later appeared in vaudeville in a skit called "Family Affair" and spent years traveling with small shows that played throughout the South and Southwest. Arthur and his sister, Florence, became part of his parents' act in 1910.

Mrs. Silverlake brought her children to Hollywood in 1917, hoping to get them into movies. Arthur had already made his screen debut in *Jack and the Beanstalk* (1917). He acted in westerns and eventually got a good part in the successful feature *Skinner's Dress Suit* (1925).

Universal Pictures signed him to a contract and changed his surname to Lake when the head of the studio, Carl Laemmle, Sr., thought that Silverlake sounded too Jewish. He was featured in their *Sweet Sixteen* comedies. First National Pictures borrowed him to play the title role in *Harold Teen* (1928), which was based on the popular comic strip character.

Arthur signed with RKO shortly after that studio was formed. There he made *Dance Hall* (1929), a hit of the time, and *Cheer Up and*

Smile (1930), a part that had originally been written for "Whispering" Jack Smith. His leading lady in it was Dixie Lee, who had not yet married Bing Crosby. Arthur was all set to play *Tol'able David,* but at the last minute his studio refused to loan him. The late Richard Cromwell got the role, and it made him a star. A few of Lake's other talkies were *Indiscreet* (1931) with Gloria Swanson, *Silver Streak* (1934), *Orchids to You* (1935), and *Topper* (1937).

Lake was free-lancing when he heard that Columbia Pictures was looking for someone to play "Dagwood Bumstead" in a series of low-budget films to be based on the *Blondie* comic strip. Although it is hard to imagine anyone else playing the character, over two dozen name actors were tested. Two who were seriously considered were Eddie Quillan and Frank Albertson. "But," Lake admits, "I had a couple of people rooting for me named Marion Davies and William Randolph Hearst."

Lake had become very friendly with the sons of the newspaper tycoon and was a frequent guest at the beach house of Marion Davies, Hearst's mistress. There he met Davies's niece Patricia Van Cleve, whom he later married at San Simeon.

Arthur Lake and Penny Singleton played "Dagwood" and "Blondie" in all twenty-eight of the features. They were also together on the radio show for the first seven years of its twelve-year run. Lake did "Dagwood" all the time the show was on the air and for a brief time on TV. He was sorry when the movie series was canceled in 1950.

Filmologist Don Miller has called Arthur Lake as "Dagwood" "the greatest piece of casting in the history of movies. He made 'Dagwood' a bit dumber than he was in the funnies and etched the characterization more broadly. He *was* 'Dagwood Bumstead.'"

Fan mail still pours in for "Dagwood" from around the world. Lake delights in being recognized and often appears at benefits, where he is invariably presented with a dagwood sandwich. Many of his friends and some of his six grandchildren call him "Dagwood." He never misses an installment of the *Blondie* comic strip, which is now drawn by Dean Young, the son of Chic Young, who created it.

The Lakes live in a house on the grounds of the Thunderbird Country Club in Palm Desert, California. They have twelve dogs, the youngest of which is named after the "Bumstead's" son, "Baby Dumpling."

Arthur Lake and Penny Singleton were among those who signed author Richard Lamparski's new walkway on September 20, 1981.

Paul Adrian

Veronica Lake was one of the most popular pinups of World War II. She often said of herself, "I never did cheesecake. I just used my hair."

Veronica Lake

The actress who became a star as the girl with the peekaboo hair was born Constance Ockelman in Brooklyn on November 14, 1919. She grew up in Lake Placid and Miami.

After coming in third in a Miami Beach beauty contest, Constance and her mother came to Hollywood. She took acting lessons and appeared in a few little-theatre productions before landing small parts in movies. The name she used at that time was Constance Keane. Her early credits were *Sorority House* (1939), *All Women Have Secrets* (1939), and *Forty Little Mothers* (1940). It was in the last, a film directed by Busby Berkeley, that her soon-to-be-famous hairdo was first seen.

The screen test she made at M-G-M failed to get her a contract, but Paramount signed her, changed her name, and put her in *I Wanted Wings* (1941). The blonde mane was kept under a boy's cap during much of *Sullivan's Travels* (1941), which Preston Sturges directed. Her height was very much in her favor when she played opposite Alan Ladd in *This Gun for Hire* (1942). Not only was she short enough to complement him, but their screen chemistry made them for a while the hottest duo in movies. They were together in *The Glass Key* (1942), *The Blue Dahlia* (1946), and *Saigon* (1948). Contrary to what fans believed, Lake and Ladd never knew each other very well.

Her dislike of Fredric March, whom she called "a pompous poseur," never showed when they costarred in *I Married a Witch* (1942).

John Russell Taylor, writing in *Sight and Sound*, once recalled her screen presence: "Ah, the tension which would build up in a film as one waited for the invitation in that strange husky voice, in the provocative swing of the sequinned box shoulder, to reach its consummation at a moment of climactic abandon when the face-obscuring mane of blonde hair would be swept aside in an embrace and reveal the full glory of the large, lustrous eyes, the slightly sunken cheeks and then heavily made-up lips which marked the apogee of 40s glamour."

She made *Out of This World* and *Hold That Blonde* in 1945, both with Eddie Bracken. The same year Veronica and the late Sonny Tufts were teamed in *Bring on the Girls* and *Miss Suzy Slagle's*. Her other credits include *Star Spangled Rhythm* (1943), *So Proudly We Hail*

(1943), *The Hour Before the Dawn* (1944), *Duffy's Tavern* (1945), and *Isn't It Romantic?* (1948). Her last major picture was *Slattery's Hurricane* (1949). By then she had left Paramount.

After that Veronica's private life was almost as well publicized as her movie roles had been. She divorced her first husband; she was sued by her mother for nonsupport; she and her second husband, director Andre De Toth, filed for bankruptcy and their Hollywood home was seized for nonpayment of taxes. After she and De Toth were divorced Veronica moved to New York City, where she became the hostess at a restaurant in the Martha Washington Hotel. Before a brief comeback in an off-Broadway revival of *Best Foot Forward* (1963) she worked as a waitress in Greenwich Village. The show was a hit and her notices were good, but all she did after it was a low-budget movie and some minor stage appearances. In the sixties Ms. Lake turned up in England, where she played opposite Ty Hardin (hosting a religious TV show and living in Prescott, Arizona) in *Streetcar Named Desire*.

Her autobiography, *Veronica* (she always called herself Connie), did quite well when it was published in 1971. By then, however, her drinking, which had long been a serious problem, had taken its toll both physically and psychologically. Both in the book and in her interviews she revealed a brutally frank Veronica Lake. That quality, as well as the great vulnerability she projected, were never captured on the screen. Her humor about herself and her undisguised contempt for falseness are traits that could only stymie a career in the movie capital.

When she died of hepatitis in July 1973 Veronica Lake was about to be divorced from her fourth husband, a retired British naval officer. She was a grandmother and had just turned fifty-two.

Veronica Lake with author Richard Lamparski in 1971.

Robert Rosinek

For many of the years she spent under contract to Universal Pictures, Laura La Plante was that studio's most popular female star.

Laura La Plante

The blue-eyed blonde who was for a number of years the top female star on the Universal lot was born in St. Louis, Missouri, on November 1, 1904. At fifteen she began playing bit parts in Christie comedies. In 1920 she was given what seemed at the time to be her big break when she won the part of the daughter in the *Bringing Up Father* series. The only trouble was that the series flopped. Laura returned to walk-ons. Not until she played with Charles Ray in *The Old Swimmin' Hole* (1921) did the producers begin to take notice of her all-American good looks and flair for light comedy.

Most of her pictures were made during her long contract with Universal. At first they cast her as Tom Mix's leading lady and opposite William Desmond in his serials *Perils of the Yukon* (1922) and *Around the World in Eighteen Days* (1923).

What makes Laura's success tale so unusual is that at the time it was more desirable to be exotic than it was to be the girl next door.

Her two most outstanding films were the spooky classic *The Cat and the Canary* (1927) and the part-talkie *Show Boat* (1929), for which she wore a dark wig to play the role of Magnolia. Other films were *Smoldering Fires* (1924) with Pauline Frederick, *Teasers* (1925), *Silk Stockings* (1927), *Scandal* (1929), *The King of Jazz* (1930) with the late Paul Whiteman, and *Lonely Wives* (1931).

Not only was Laura La Plante lovely to look at, she had a sense of fun that came across on the screen. Fans sensed that she thoroughly enjoyed what she was doing. For a long time that was true. But about the time talkies came in Laura began to be aware that she was missing out on things ordinary people took for granted. She had been married to the director William Seiter since 1926, yet they never seemed to have much time together. She longed to travel, but her schedule didn't permit it. Then she was assigned to a picture to be directed by William Wyler, who made it very clear that she was not his choice. With two years to go on her Universal contract, Laura asked for her release and left for Europe.

"Everyone had been so nice to me for such a long time and then all at once I felt unwanted," she said recently. "I was very hurt and wanted to get far away."

In Europe Laura divorced Seiter and married producer Irving Asher. They settled in London and she appeared in several plays and movies, including *The Church Mouse* (1935) with the late Ian Hunter.

After their return to Hollywood in the forties, Asher continued to produce motion pictures. The only hint of a movie comeback for Laura was in 1943, when Myrna Loy announced she wanted out of her M-G-M contract. Laura was seriously considered for the role of Nora Charles in the *Thin Man* series. But she did not make a screen appearance until 1956, when she accepted the role of Betty Hutton's mother in *Spring Reunion*. Fans and critics alike agreed that the only thing wrong with her return was that she looked too young for the part. The same year she teamed with silent star Aileen Pringle in a dramatization of a suffragist's race for the U.S. presidency at the turn of the century. Called *She Also Ran,* it was the TV debut for them both.

The Ashers retired to the California desert over ten years ago. They live in a condominium in Rancho Mirage, almost next door to silent star Billie Dove. Their son Tony is the coauthor of the Beach Boy hit "Wouldn't It Be Nice?" Both he and his sister are in advertising. Laura has one grandchild. She has remained friendly over the years with her contemporaries Patsy Ruth Miller and Ruth Taylor, who live nearby.

Musing recently about her life, Laura La Plante said: "I'm so happy now that I left when I did. Had I continued making picture after picture I'd never have had the time to really live and enjoy my family. My career was wonderful, but then, so were the years that followed. Now I sculpt in my spare time. I consider myself to be a very lucky person."

Dollie Tombers

Laura La Plante and her husband, Irving Asher, live in a condominium in Rancho Mirage, California.

Jack La Rue, the "Merchant of Menace."

Jack La Rue

The screen and stage actor known as the "Merchant of Menace" was born Gaspare Biondolillo in New York City on May 3, 1902. As a boy he hung around movie studios until he got a part as a bellboy in a Norma Talmadge film. Jack made his debut on Broadway playing a mandolin in *Blood and Sand* (1921), which starred Otis Skinner.

Director Howard Hawks saw La Rue on Broadway in *Midnight* (1930) and brought him to Hollywood to play a heavy in *Scarface*. After three days of shooting it was obvious that Jack had too much authority to be believable as Paul Muni's henchman. La Rue suggested the unknown George Raft replace him, and Raft became a star.

The mere presence of Jack La Rue on the screen could set a terrifying mood. He was the mean and sexy tough guy, and audiences loved to loathe him. Some of his hundreds of credits are *The Mouthpiece* (1932), *Good Dame* (1934), *Times Square Lady* (1935), *Captains Courageous* (1937), *Big Town Czar* (1939), *Paper Bullets* (1941), and *Murder in the Music Hall* (1946). His swan song was *Robin and the Seven Hoods* (1964).

Now and then he was cast against type, as in *A Farewell to Arms* (1932), in which he played a priest. But probably the definitive La Rue was the sadistic abductor of the late Miriam Hopkins in the shocker *The Story of Temple Drake* (1933).

One lady he never threatened was Mae West, who had him as her gigolo for three years in *Diamond Lil* (1929), on Broadway and on tour. He was also in her picture *Go West, Young Man* (1936).

He was a great favorite in London and played there in both *Golden Boy* in 1938 and in *Four Hours to Kill* in 1949. He even made an English gangster film, *No Orchids for Miss Blandish* (1951).

Jack has been married and divorced several times. One of his fiancées was Ida Lupino. The photograph she autographed and gave to him over forty years ago hangs on the wall of his Century City apartment. His only child, Jack junior, is also an actor.

In 1969 he sold the Italian restaurant he had operated in North Hollywood. During the nine years he owned it Jack had acquired $187,000 worth of bad checks and unpaid tabs signed by Hollywood's elite.

La Rue was greatly saddened by the death of his close friend Jimmy Durante in 1980. He talked frequently with George Raft and Mae West, who passed on the same year. Aside from a loss of hearing, Jack is in good health.

The guy who robbed, roughed up, and rubbed out more people than anyone else on the screen abhors violence. He strongly objects to the amount of it that is currently seen on TV. He lives quietly in an apartment he shares with his sister in a high-security building. Says La Rue, "You've got to be very careful these days. There are some terrible people out there."

Jack La Rue in the bar of his Century City apartment.

Richard Lamparski

Lash La Rue, the "King of the Bullwhip" in 1949.

Lash La Rue

The screen's "King of the Bullwhip" was born Alfred La Rue on June 14, 1917, in Gretna, Louisiana. He has said that his mother was widowed during World War I. At other times he has described his father as a real estate salesman who moved the family about a great deal.

After military school, he attended a college in Long Beach, California, where he took dramatics to correct his lisp and stammer.

La Rue was screen-tested by Warner Brothers, but they failed to sign him because it was felt that he looked too much like Humphrey Bogart. It was George Brent who suggested he try his luck at Universal. There he was tested in a scene from the Deanna Durbin movie *Christmas Holiday*. Ms. Durbin, who was then the reigning queen of the lot, put in a good word for him, and he was put under contract. He has said of their brief relationship, "She needed me and I needed someone who knew which way to go."

During his one year as a Universal contract player, he was in a serial, *The Master Key* (1945), and the Durbin vehicle *Lady on a Train* (1945).

He credits director Bob Tansey with creating Lash La Rue. Tansey hired an expert to teach him how to use the bullwhip and a double for the scenes in which he had to fight. Riding a horse is something La Rue never did learn very well.

He was introduced as the "Cheyenne Kid" in *Song of Old Wyoming* (1945), an Eddie Dean western. After stealing the show in another Dean picture, *Caravan Trail* (1946), he was teamed with the late Al "Fuzzy" St. John, who was his funny sidekick. From then on, La Rue was the star of all the westerns he made.

Among Lash's features are *The Return of the Lash* (1947), *Dead Man's Gold* (1948), *Son of Billy the Kid* (1949), *The Vanishing Outpost* (1951), and *The Black Lash* (1952).

Although generally dismissed by western-film historians, Lash La Rue pictures did very well at the box office when they were made and are thought to still draw a considerable audience when shown on TV. There were Lash La Rue comic books, too, which were published in four languages.

La Rue provided a decided change from the clean-cut singing cowboys like Gene Autry and Roy Rogers. His garb and manner were distinctive, but the real gimmick was his long black whip. It was lightning fast and loud as a bullet.

When the production of B westerns all but ended in the early fifties, Lash hit the road as the star of rodeos and carnivals. What little money he had left from picture-making went to the IRS for back taxes. La Rue made another small fortune in personal appearances. He and his wife invested in a restaurant-motel in Reno, Nevada. It was his tenth marriage, and when it broke up in 1963 his wife got the property in the settlement. Four days later, his collection of western costumes, guns, saddles, and whips was stolen. He has been on the move ever since.

The strangeness of his screen presence may have been the very thing that appealed to his many fans. Although he played good guys, he wore all black, the color usually reserved in low-budget westerns for "varmints." His character, which has been described as "hard-bitten" and "with a perpetual snarl," was that of an outlaw who has decided to go straight.

In 1956 he was arrested in Memphis for receiving stolen property. The following year his son married the granddaughter of Aimee Semple McPherson. In 1958 he took an overdose of sleeping pills when his wife at that time refused a reconciliation. In 1964 he took a large advertisement in a Hollywood trade paper apologizing for his past behavior and asking for work as an actor. In 1965 he was reported selling furniture in Atlanta. One year later he was arrested for vagrancy in Tampa, Florida.

After his Tampa arrest, Lash says, he saw the error of his ways. He became an evangelist after "The Lord opened my spiritual eyes."

When police in Georgia arrested him in September 1974 for public drunkenness, Lash had a large black whip in his car. Although the original charge was dropped, he later was tried and convicted of attempting to exchange one of his Bibles for the marijuana owned by two teenage hitchhikers he had picked up. Said the prosecuting attorney, "That was one of his better performances."

In an article, "Lash Whips It Out," published in *Oui* magazine in 1975, he told interviewer Grover Lewis about his appearance on the *Wyatt Earp* TV show in the fifties and his feelings for its star, Hugh O'Brian: "I wish the Lord had allowed me to snuff that twerp."

He claims to be an ordained minister of the Universal Christian Church but does not rule out a screen comeback. Asked recently the title of his last picture, he replied, "I haven't made it yet!" A few years ago he played a role (with his clothes on) in a hardcore porno movie, *Hard On the Trail.*

Still dressed all in black, Lash drives around Hollywood in a 1968 Cadillac hearse with his bed in the back and a bumper sticker that reads: GOD LOVES YOU. He lives on Social Security and "love offerings."

Lash La Rue today.

Paul B. Southerland of Oklahoma City, Oklahoma

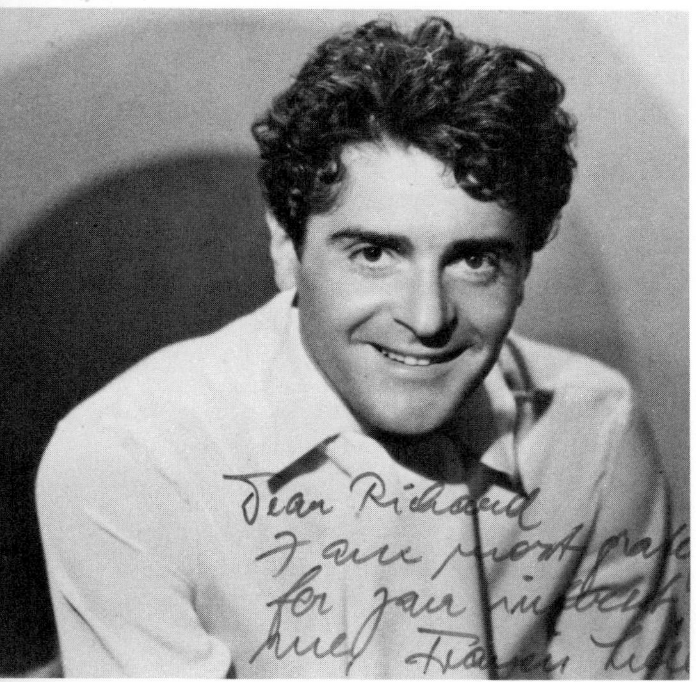

Francis Lederer was a matinee idol in the mid-thirties.

Francis Lederer

The Czech leading man of stage and screen was born Frantisek Lederer on November 6, 1906, in Prague. As a young man, he worked his way through the Prague Academy of Dramatic Arts by dressing windows for a department store, and then toured Eastern and Central Europe with a repertory company for several years. He was first leading man with the Burg Theatre in Vienna when Max Reinhardt brought him to Berlin in 1930 to play Romeo to Elisabeth Bergner's (widowed and living on East Square in London) Juliet. By then he had been seen with Louise Brooks (living in Rochester, New York) in the silent classic *Pandora's Box* (1929) and in *The Wonderful Life of Nova Petrowa* (1930), and was the rage of German and French cinema audiences.

Lederer's big success, one he was never able to equal, was *Autumn Crocus,* which he did first in London in 1931, to rave notices. He and the play were imported to Broadway, opening November 19, 1932. The production was one of the highlights of the season, and his subsequent tour with it was a triumph. Francis came to Hollywood, and everyone expected the handsome young man with the charming accent to become a major star in the United States. It never happened.

He was tested to play Romeo opposite Norma Shearer, but nothing came of it. There was serious talk of an M-G-M contract, but it was never signed.

There were rumors of temperament as the reason that his career in pictures didn't bring stardom. It seems more likely that he was poorly managed, by a relative who knew nothing about the entertainment business. After they parted company Francis was represented by Abe Lastfogel, who got him a contract with Columbia Pictures. He was set to play Frederic Chopin under Frank Capra's direction when the director left the studio. "[Harry] Cohn told me to my face that he would ruin me," said Lederer recently. "As though it was my fault that he and Capra had fallen out. He made the threat in front of Lastfogel, who never said a word. I could have sued, of course, but even as naive as I was, I knew that Hollywood was run by Harry Cohn and his ilk. It would have been professional suicide."

In Hollywood he made *Pursuit of Happiness* (1934), *My American Wife* (1936), and *The Lone Wolf in Paris* (1938). He was fine in all of them; also in *The Man I Married* (1940) with Anna Sten, and *The Diary of a Chambermaid* (1946) with Hurd Hatfield (living in Stony Brook, New York). But the only time he really registered on screen was in *Confessions of a Nazi Spy* (1939).

Lederer was set for *Break of Hearts* at RKO but at the last minute was replaced by Charles Boyer. Again the word around Hollywood was that he was hard to handle. Another theory is that for that role, as with others, he simply lacked the sex appeal that had been so evident on stage. Certainly he couldn't have been very temperamental or choosy about what he did when he appeared in *The Bridge of San Louis Rey* (1944), *The Madonna's Secret* (1946), *Million Dollar Weekend* (1949), *Captain Carey, U.S.A.* (1950), and *The Ambassador's Daughter* (1956).

During his picture-making days, Lederer returned to the stage occasionally, in 1939 taking over for Laurence Olivier in *No Time for Comedy* on Broadway, and in various road companies such as *Watch on the Rhine* and *The Diary of Anne Frank*. And he was still a big draw on European stages following the end of World War II. One of his last screen appearances was as the Count in *The Return of Dracula* (1958) with Ray Stricklyn (now a Beverly Hills public relations executive).

Francis lives with his third wife, socialite Marion Irvine, in a large home that resembles an old mission. Lederer was first married to the opera singer Ada Nejedly. His second wife was Margo (married to Eddie Albert). He owns a great deal of land in Canoga Park, California, where he lives.

Not only isn't Francis bitter over what didn't happen with his career; he seems rather disinterested in it. The money he made was well invested and provides him with the time for his pet project—the American Academy of Performing Arts, which he founded in Hollywood in 1957, and where he often lectures and teaches what he did so well—acting.

Sandy Brown Wyeth

Francis Lederer today.

Joan Leslie in 1943.

Joan Leslie

Born Joan Agnes Theresa Sadie Brodell in Pittsburgh, Pennsylvania, on January 26, 1925, Joan, along with her sister, was singing and dancing in vaudeville while still in grammar school. While they were on tour with their act in New York City, an M-G-M talent scout saw Joan and signed her to play Robert Taylor's little sister in the Greta Garbo film *Camille* (1937).

Free-lancing after *Camille,* she did *Men with Wings* (1938), in which she supported Andy Devine, *Winter Carnival* (1939), *Two Thoroughbreds* (1939) with Jimmy Lydon, *Nancy Drew, Reporter* (1940) with Bonita Granville (the wife of billionaire Jack Wrather), *Laddie* (1940), and *High School* (1940) with Jane Withers.

The picture in which she got her big break was *High Sierra* (1941) with Humphrey Bogart. Put under contract to Warner Brothers, Joan played opposite Gary Cooper in *Sergeant York* (1941) and did two films that year with Eddie Albert: *The Wagons Roll at Night* and *The Great Mr. Nobody.* From then on the studio treated her as the top ingenue on the lot. On her sixteenth birthday she posed with Jack Warner beside a new Buick, supposedly a present from him. After the photos were taken, she never again saw the car. But there was nothing chintzy about the roles she was being given.

In 1942 she was seen in two of the finest pictures produced that year: *The Male Animal* and *Yankee Doodle Dandy,* singing and dancing along with Jimmy Cagney.

In 1943 Joan had a role in the excellent drama *The Hard Way,* in which she played the kid sister of Ida Lupino. She celebrated her eighteenth birthday on the set of *The Sky's the Limit* (1943), in which she was the dancing partner of Fred Astaire. She was Ronald Reagan's girl in *This Is the Army* (1943), an Irving Berlin musical. Also in 1943, Ms. Leslie and Eddie Cantor teamed up in *Thank Your Lucky Stars.*

In 1945 she began appearing with Robert Hutton (married and living in Kingston, New York) in a series of films that were quite popular at the time: *Hollywood Canteen* (1944), *Too Young to Know* (1945), and *Janie Gets Married* (1946).

Joan made two films with Robert Alda, *Rhapsody in Blue* (1945) and *Cinderella Jones* (1946). In 1945 she was loaned to Twentieth Century–Fox for *Where Do We Go from Here?,* which had in its cast two players who were to marry years later: Fred MacMurray and June Haver.

During World War II Joan Leslie appeared

often at defense plants and army bases to entertain the workers and the boys in service. Few Hollywood stars put in as many hours as she did at the famous Hollywood Canteen. She was the "girl next door" or the "girl back home" to tens of thousands of GIs throughout the forties who sent for her photograph.

Among the pictures she made after the war were *Repeat Performance* (1947), *The Skipper Surprised His Wife* (1950), and *Born to Be Bad* (1950).

In 1950 Joan married Dr. William Caldwell, a surgeon she met indirectly through Loretta Young. The following year she gave birth to identical-twin girls. After becoming a mother she made a few movies, such as *Jubilee Trail* (1954) with Vera Hruba Ralston (married and living in Santa Barbara, California), but found that she had less time for and interest in acting. Her last feature film was *The Revolt of Mamie Stover* (1956). If she has any regret about her career, it is that she lost the part of Marilyn Miller in *Look for the Silver Lining* to her friend June Haver.

The Caldwells live in a large home in the Las Feliz section of Los Angeles. Their daughters, both of whom have Ph.D.s, teach English literature at universities in other states.

Joan is seen occasionally on TV shows, such as *The Incredible Hulk* and *Charlie's Angels*. She has appeared on television commercials for Avon products, Folger's Coffee, and American Greeting Cards. Her agent is the son of the agent she had over thirty years ago.

Her friends from the old days are Ann Blyth and Jeannie Cagney.

Much of her time is donated to St. Ann's Maternity Hospital. Joan Leslie is a devout Roman Catholic.

Mathew Tombers

Joan Leslie today in her Los Angeles home.

Noel Neill and George Reeves in a scene from one of the 104 episodes of Superman that were made for television.

"Lois Lane": Noel Neill and "Jimmy Olsen": Jack Larson

The half-hour *Superman* programs have been playing on television since they were first produced in 1952. It was and still is popular with children, science-fiction buffs, and those who just appreciate the unconscious camp of its performers.

George Reeves, who portrayed the "Man of Steel" in all 104 episodes, shot and killed himself on June 16, 1959.

Phyllis Coates played "Lois Lane" in the early *Superman* TV shows but left the series for another part. Today Ms. Coates is married to a physician and lives in Big Sur, California.

Noel Neill, who took over the role from Phyllis Coates, had never read a *Superman* comic book, nor had she ever heard the radio show or seen the movie serials (although she had played the same role in them opposite Kirk Alyn as "Superman").

The daughter of a Minneapolis newspaper editor, Noel had worked as a reporter, but only for a brief period. She acted in feature films, such as *Here Come the Waves* (1944) and *The Big Clock* (1948), before landing the role on the series.

Says Noel of the character she portrayed: "Lois Lane' was a strange type of reporter. She never carried a pencil or notebook, never wrote a thing, never saw a printing."

After the production of the *Superman* television series ended in 1957, Ms. Neill, who was married at the time, retired. She is now divorced and lives in the Santa Monica Canyon. In recent years she has toured North America with clips of the TV shows that she screens at colleges and nostalgia conventions. During the question-and-answer portion of one personal appearance, a young man told her he used to listen to the TV shows but didn't see much of them because he was under the TV set. "Why?" asked Ms. Neill. "I hoped you'd ask," said the student gleefully. "I was trying to look up 'Lois Lane's' dress!"

Although it has been a long time since Jack

Larson has done any acting, he is still frequently recognized as "Jimmy Olsen," the pubescent cub reporter.

Only lately has Larson been willing to talk about his role on the famous series. Almost all of his lines on the show were prefaced with such exclamations as "Jeepers!", "Golly!", and "Gee, whiz!" "As an actor," he says, "I felt hopelessly typecast by the part. As a human being, it seemed as though my privacy had been completely taken away from me. But now I watch the old shows and get a real kick out of them. They're funny and moral and filled with energy."

Larson had edited his high school newspaper, acted in movies, and read many *Superman* comic books when he got the part of naive, enthusiastic "Jimmy Olsen." He enjoyed making the films and has been amazed since by their continuing popularity and the compliments he has received for his role. Among those who have told him how they admired his characterization have been Sir John Gielgud and Sir Laurence Olivier.

Larson is the author of poetry, librettos, and plays that have won excellent reviews and have earned him grants from the Rockefeller, Koussevitsky, and Ford foundations. The Joffrey Ballet is currently staging a monodrama that he wrote.

Jack shares a house designed by Frank Lloyd Wright in Brentwood, California, with a puli dog.

Noel Neill is single and lives in the Santa Monica Canyon.

Richard Lamparski

George Reeves and Jack Larson.

Jack Larson has composed works that have been performed at the Hollywood Bowl and Carnegie Hall.

Michael Jacobs

Nick Lucas at the time of his engagement at the Edgewater Beach Hotel in Chicago in 1924.

Nick Lucas

The "Singing Troubador" was born Dominic Nicholas Anthony Lucanese in Newark, New Jersey, on August 22, 1897. He played the guitar in grade school and by his teens had mastered mandolin and banjo as well—and earned money locally playing for parties and weddings.

After graduation he played clubs and toured vaudeville houses for two years with the Kentucky Five, a group that featured Ted Fio Rito on piano. Then he played his guitar with the Vernon Country Club Band; many people credit him with being the first to replace the banjo with guitar. Another first attributed to him is the introduction of the six-string guitar to popular music.

After the Armistice, Lucas toured the Continent and appeared at London's Kit Kat Club and the Café de Paris. The Prince of Wales brought the Queen of Spain to hear him at the latter, and a few weeks later Nick performed for them at a private party. Upon his return to the U.S. he signed with Ted Fio Rito, who was becoming a name as the leader of the Oriole Orchestra at Chicago's Edgewater Beach Hotel. Their performances were broadcast over radio, with no payment to the musicians since at that time there were almost no commercials on radio and no way to measure the audience the then infant medium was reaching. It was at this stand that Nick began singing, and the mail poured in. Brunswick

Records got word of his popularity and signed him to a recording contract in 1925. His first record was "My Best Girl." Overnight, it began to get him top money in vaudeville houses around the country, and he followed up with "Dancing with Tears in my Eyes," "Among My Souvenirs," and "When You Wore a Tulip."

In 1929 Nick made two highly successful and historically important features for Warner Brothers. In *Gold Diggers of Broadway,* one of the first all-talkie musicals, Lucas warbled "Painting the Clouds with Sunshine," which he expected to be the big hit of the production. It was a hit all right, but nothing to compare with his other number, "Tip-Toe Thru' the Tulips with Me," which he sang while chorus girls pranced through a field of artificial tulips. The song has been associated with him ever since. Both his sequences in the film were in early Technicolor. In the all-star *Show of Shows* he sang "Li-Po-Li" to Myrna Loy, who was made up to look Chinese.

Although Lucas made only one other feature, *Disc Jockey,* a 1951 cheapie, in the early thirties he appeared in a number of shorts for Warner's and Universal. Warner's had offered him a contract after his first movie success, but Nick chose to continue in vaudeville, where he was commanding $3000 a week. The studio, therefore, signed a young man from Pittsburgh, Dick Powell.

Despite the Depression, Lucas did quite well, and had his own radio series for several seasons during the thirties. Of course, vaudeville was hit hard at this time, but he remained one of its big draws. When the famed Palace Theatre ended its stage policy in November 1932 Nick was on the closing bill, along with Hal LeRoy (widowed and living in Maywood, New Jersey).

Beginning in 1948, he was with *Ken Murray's Blackouts* in Hollywood for one hundred straight weeks. When Tiny Tim began to click in the late 1960s, Nick was back in the picture: during all his talk show appearances the new star spoke of how Lucas had inspired him. At Tim's request he came to New York from Hollywood for Tim's famous TV wedding; on December 17, 1969, Nick sang "Tip-Toe Thru' the Tulips" before the largest audience in the history of the *Tonight* show.

Nick has never stopped working and is offered far more bookings than the few he accepts, such as at Harrah's Club in Reno and at conventions. The Nick Lucas guitar, introduced in 1925, has paid him royalties ever since. The guitar pick named after him is still a top seller. Some of those who credit Nick Lucas as having greatly influenced them are Gene Autry, Merle Travis, Barry Kessel, and Roy Clark.

Lucas's wife of fifty-three years died in 1970, but he has a daughter and three grandsons. He visits them often at their ranch in Colorado. And he is close to his brothers, Anthony and Lib. Nick lives by himself in an apartment just above Hollywood Boulevard.

Howard W. Hays

Nick Lucas in Hollywood at age eight-four.

Jimmy Lydon in 1947.

Jimmy Lydon

The "Henry Aldrich" of the movies was born on May 30, 1923, in Harrington Park, New Jersey, one of nine children. His father, a heavy drinker, refused to work when Jimmy was nine years old. In a frantic effort to support the family, all of the children who were old enough took whatever jobs they could find. A friend suggested that Jimmy try getting parts in Broadway shows. "From the very beginning," says Lydon, "it was a very ugly experience."

He got bit parts in a number of plays before landing featured roles in *Western Waters* (1937), *Sing Out the News* (1938), and *The Happiest Days* (1939). He auditioned, rehearsed, and toured so much that when he was signed for his first movie, *Back Door to Heaven* (1939), he had practically no education and had never seen any kind of a show from the audience.

Freddie Bartholomew was up for the lead in *Tom Brown's School Days* (1940), but Jimmy got it. Freddie (now the vice president of a New York advertising agency) played a supporting role. Paramount signed Jimmy in 1941 for a series of B pictures based on the "Henry Aldrich" character that had proved so popular on stage and radio. Lydon sensed he would be typecast and asked the studio head, Y. Frank Freeman, to put him in other features as well. Freeman's reply: "You're getting paid. Go do your work."

Jimmy starred in nine features of the "Aldrich" series, beginning with *Henry Aldrich for President* (1941). By the time he had completed the last one, *Henry Aldrich Plays Cupid* (1944), his screen image was so firmly set that he was never able to shake it. It didn't matter that he had parts in A features: *Life With Father* (1947), *The Time of Your Life* (1948), *The Magnificent Yankee* (1950).

Jimmy's chief asset as a juvenile was a very engaging smile and a distinctive voice. But as an adult he went unnoticed in such pictures as *Island in the Sky* (1953) and *I Passed for White* (1960). Except for those in the audience who remembered him from their Saturday matinee days: "There's 'Henry Aldrich,'" they'd say when he came on the screen.

As an adult, his first real professional decision was in 1956, when he decided to work on the other side of the camera. For a year and a half he begged associates in Hollywood to give him a chance. He became a coordinating producer on TV in series such as *McHale's*

Navy and *Wagon Train;* then he was associate producer on *77 Sunset Strip* and *Temple Houston* for several seasons. To date he has produced seven features, the best of which is *Chubasco* (1968). In 1972 he worked under Bill Idelson (who used to play "Rush" on radio's *Vic and Sade)* on the *Anna and the King* TV series. Their executive producer was Gene Reynolds, another juvenile actor.

In 1981 Lydon was coproducer and codirector of *The Priceless Gift,* a compilation of Fox Movietone Newsreels.

Jimmy is still bitter about the childhood he never had and deeply resents the loss. However, he sent money to his father every month until his father's death a few years ago. Jimmy's father image and best friend from the time of his arrival in Hollywood was Robert Armstrong, star of such adventure films as *King Kong* and *Mighty Joe Young.* Armstrong died in 1973.

The one good thing to come from "Henry Aldrich" was a happy marriage. His mother-in-law was the late Olive Blakeney, who played "Mrs. Aldrich." His father-in-law was the late "patent-leather heavy" Bernard Nedell. The Lydons live in the Hollywood Hills with their two daughters. Both wanted to act as young girls, but Jimmy was firmly against it: "I don't like to see kids on stage or screen. It's unnatural."

Sandy Wyeth Brown

Today Jimmy is a partner in a production company, Nobles/Lydon, which releases through Twentieth Century–Fox.

Diana Lynn was under contract to Paramount Pictures during the 1940s.

Diana Lynn

The pert pianist-actress was born in Los Angeles on October 7, 1926. Her father was an oil-supply executive. Her mother, who was an accomplished pianist, wanted her daughter to have a career on the concert stage.

Diana was thirteen years old when she accompanied another child who was being auditioned as a violinist for the picture *They Shall Have Music* (1939). After they played the violinist was dismissed and Diana was engaged. The film was about Michigan's Interlochen Music Camp, and Diana, billed under her original name, Dolly Loehr, was featured in it as a child pianist.

Paramount Pictures signed her and cast her in *There's Magic in Music* (1941). It wasn't until *Star Spangled Rhythm* (1942) that she became Diana Lynn on the screen.

As cute and as gifted as she was, her studio didn't quite know what to do with her for a while. Years later she explained it to the *New York Times:* "By the time they had decided on a role I had grown up a little more and was too tall for it."

The Major and the Minor (1942) changed her career and her image. Diana played the sharp-tongued roommate of Ginger Rogers in the comedy, which also starred Ray Milland. Her performance brought her good notices, the attention of fans, and the part of Betty Hutton's kid sister in *The Miracle of Morgan Creek* (1944).

Paramount starred Diana and the late Gail Russell in the film adaptation of the best seller *Our Hearts Were Young and Gay* (1944). Her two life goals at that point were to become a movie star and to travel. When it was announced that she would play one of the two girls making an unchaperoned tour of Europe, she felt both of her dreams had come true. The picture did make her a star and spawned a sequel, *Our Hearts Were Growing Up* (1946), but both were shot in Hollywood.

During the early part of her career her piano playing was emphasized, especially in her publicity. She played at benefits and to entertain GIs. In 1946 Diana made a three-record album playing themes from movies as well as Mozart. But, as Diana explained it years later, "One summer I broke my arm and I just never played again."

After leaving Paramount in 1950 she made about a dozen films, but none that could sustain the career momentum that she once had at her home studio. *Rogues of Sherwood Forest* (1950), *The People Against O'Hara* (1951), and *Bedtime for Bonzo* (1951) were among them. Her last screen appearance was in *Play It as It Lays* (1972).

Diana's five-year marriage to an architect ended in divorce in 1953. Three years later she married the son of Dorothy Schiff, then the publisher of the *New York Post.* Her second husband, Mortimer Hall, wasn't enthusiastic about her having a career, and after her second child was born she stopped acting almost completely.

Diana never lost her yearning to travel. During the last few years of her life she ran the travel agency in Manhattan's Bonwit Teller.

In an interview held not long before she died Diana Lynn talked about her career: "It was great fun—at least most of it was. Boys were put off by the fact that I was famous. I didn't like that part. But I'm certainly glad I did it, although I don't miss acting or Hollywood. I still have pretty clothes and I meet celebrities. One of my children has Gore Vidal as a godfather. I think that's glamorous. I hope there's no one out there feeling sorry for me, because I love my life."

In late 1971 Diana suffered a stroke. She died soon afterward on December 19.

Sarah Richardson

Diana Lynn photographed in Bonwit Teller shortly before her death.

Ben Lyon married Bebe Daniels in 1930.

Ben Lyon

The leading man of the screen was born on February 6, 1901, in Atlanta, Georgia. His father was a successful businessman, and his mother, who was born in Germany, was renowned locally as a great beauty. When Ben was four years old the family moved to Baltimore, where he eventually attended the exclusive Park School. In 1916 he arrived in New York City, where he was enrolled in a prep school. But he soon fell in love with the movie industry, which had not yet moved its center to Hollywood. One of his close friends at the time was a pretty and ambitious hat check girl named Norma Shearer (living at the Motion Picture Country Hospital).

Against his better judgment, Ben's father subsidized him while the teenager sought out work as an extra, which paid $2.50 a day. After touring the country for two seasons, beginning in 1918, with *Seventeen,* Ben supported the legendary Jeanne Eagels in her play *The Wonderful Thing* (1920). He had small parts in such pictures as *Open Your Eyes* (1919) and *The Heart of Maryland* (1921), but he longed to be a star. Samuel Goldwyn saw him in the play *Mary the 3rd* (1923) and signed him for his film *Potash and Perlmutter* (1923). Then he got *Flaming Youth* (1923), which starred Coleen Moore, and a five-year contract with First National.

Ben worked steadily through the silent era, appearing with a dazzling array of female stars—Gloria Swanson, Anna Q. Nilsson, Blanche Sweet, Barbara LaMarr, Pola Negri (living in San Antonio, Texas), and the late Pauline Starke. His credits during the era include *So Big* (1925), *The Savage* (1926), *The Tender Hour* (1927), and *For the Love of Mike* (1927) with Claudette Colbert.

When sound came to movies he continued to remain active, doing *The Flying Marine* (1929) with the late Shirley Mason, *Indiscreet* (1931), *Hat Check Girl* (1932), *I Cover the Waterfront* (1933), and *Frisco Waterfront* (1935) with Helen Twelvetrees.

If Ben Lyon rates as a movie immortal it would be for his part in the classic *Hell's Angels* (1930). Although it was never released, the silent version starred Ben and Greta Nissen (married and living in Montecito, California); it was decided that her accent was too heavy for the sound version, and Lyon suggested Jean

Harlow, then almost an unknown, as a replacement. During the filming, he and the other players played jokes on the young producer, Howard Hughes. Eventually, Ben had regrets: "We used to pretend we were talking about him when we were actually only moving our lips. Even then his hearing was very poor. He took it very well, but it really wasn't funny when I look back on it. I never think about it that I don't feel ashamed."

In 1936, Ben and his wife, the late Bebe Daniels, left Hollywood to accept an offer from London's Palladium. They also thought they would avoid kidnap threats, so common at the time in the movie colony. They were just as popular in the British Isles, doing vaudeville tours, features films, and several highly successful radio and TV series.

For a number of years Ben was director of casting for Twentieth Century–Fox in England, and he is credited with bringing Marilyn Monroe to the studio. However, whenever the subject came up he was quick to add that he also turned down Leslie Caron ("Truthfully, I couldn't see a thing to her—then!") and Audrey Hepburn, because she took too long to respond to a note he had sent backstage.

After Ben left Fox he headed his own talent agency in London, but gave that up after Bebe Daniels died in 1971. A year later he married his costar from silent days, Marion Nixon, the widow of director William Seiter. They lived in a luxurious apartment in Westwood, California.

Ben and Marion Lyon were aboard the *Queen Elizabeth II* on a cruise of the Pacific in March 1979 when he died suddenly.

Jon Virzi

Mr. and Mrs. Ben Lyon (Marion Nixon).

May McAvoy's favorite portrait of herself from her career in silent films.

May McAvoy

The star of silents and of the first film musical was born in the family brownstone at Forty-first Street and Park Avenue in Manhattan on September 8, 1901. Her father and paternal grandfather owned and operated a huge livery stable that filled the block now occupied by the Waldorf-Astoria Hotel. "I wanted to be somebody," said May, and she tried to get her mother to allow her to become an actress. Even after an agent approached her, Mrs. McAvoy was against the idea. She was set on May's becoming a schoolteacher. But when Mrs. McAvoy realized how unhappy her daughter would be if deprived of a chance, she relented.

Armed with photos of herself, May visited the various casting offices around New York, and found them very receptive. Her first job was for a commercial for Domino Sugar, which led to modeling jobs and to movies. She looked even younger than she was, and she is short (reassuring to male leads), features then much sought after in actresses.

Her first feature was *Hate* (1917), filmed in Savannah, Georgia. Her notices were so good that she was hired for *To Hell with the Kaiser* (1918). For a couple of years she was an ingenue in vehicles for such stars as the late Norma Talmadge and Florence Reed, until studio executive J. Stuart Blackton made her a leading lady at Pathé. She wanted very much to play the lead in *Sentimental Tommy* by Sir James Barrie, but the part had been cast. However, the star Faire Binney proved inadequate, and May, who had impressed the director with her work in *The Devil's Garden* (1920), replaced her. The film was released in 1921 and made stars of May and the late Gareth Hughes.

When May arrived in Hollywood at age twenty she was already a star, but knew practically no one. She was signed to a contract with Realart and put to work in one programmer after another. She had such directors as William C. De Mille, John Robertson, George Fitzmaurice, and William Desmond Taylor. Cecil B. De Mille wanted her for one of his epics, but when she was told that she would be nearly nude, she refused. He never spoke to her again. May was doing very well and had her heart set on appearing in *The Little Minister* or *Peter Pan*. Both were owned by Paramount Pictures, the parent company of Realart. But she lost out on both, subsequently buying out her contract, which had paid her $500 a week.

In 1923 May was the Queen of the Roses at the annual Rose Parade. She is the only movie star ever to be so honored.

As a free-lance artist she made $1500 a week filming *The Enchanted Cottage* (1924), a great hit, and then did *Lady Windermere's Fan* (1925), for which she got twice that amount.

May replaced the late Gertrude Olmstead in *Ben Hur* (1926), in the role of Esther. It seemed an endless role because the Italian extras and workmen were making so much money they did not want the production to come to an end. They continually sabotaged the sets. There were even threats to kidnap May. One day, while she was talking with F. Scott Fitzgerald, a set and row of dressing rooms exploded in flames right in front of them.

In 1927 May McAvoy signed a contract with Warner Brothers. She was given the part opposite Al Jolson in the first motion picture musical, *The Jazz Singer* (1927). The film revolutionized the movie industry. Within a short period all films were talkies. Ironically, it was May's last important Hollywood feature. She made a number of pictures after *The Jazz Singer*, including *The Terror* (1928), England's first talkie.

A story has circulated for years that McAvoy retired from the screen because she had a pronounced lisp. She has no speech impediment. She stopped making movies because she married the treasurer of United Artists, who asked her not to work. She did return to pictures, but not until 1940, after her son was old enough not to require constant care. Until the mid-fifties she had a contract with M-G-M, making countless appearances in bit roles. She was unbilled and mostly unnoticed, except by her fans from the silent days.

Now widowed, May McAvoy lives in a home in Sherman Oaks filled with period furniture and memorabilia from her career. Her oldest and closest friend is Lois Wilson, with whom she attends mass every Sunday at a Catholic church.

Sandy Wyeth Brown

Today May McAvoy lives in Sherman Oaks, California.

***Sheena, Queen of the Jungle* was a program that brought fathers together with their sons in front of the family television set.**

Irish McCalla

The actress who played the first liberated woman on television was born and raised in Pawnee City, Nebraska, one of eight children. Irish's birthday was Christmas 1929. She left home for California when she was seventeen years old "to escape the cold weather."

After a succession of waitress jobs she went to work at Douglas Aircraft. She was terminated from all of these positions after slapping either a boss's face or a customer's face. "Where I come from," says Irish, "pretty girls are not overlooked, but no one mauls them. I wasn't used to it, and I did not like it. I still don't."

A friend suggested she try modeling. She was popular as a pinup right from the start. If the photographers were no more gallant than other men in Hollywood had been, at least she was being paid better. "And," adds Irish, "it was always a frontal approach, which I can handle." Ms. McCalla is 5 feet 9 inches tall.

Anita Ekberg, who had just been named Miss Sweden, was first signed for the title role of *Sheena, Queen of the Jungle,* but failed to show up to film the pilot. A photographer friend suggested Irish, who was grateful for the chance to make $365 a week. She used the money to get a divorce from her husband, an insurance man. Her two little boys announced to their playmates that "Mommy is going to work in the jungle."

The program's locale was supposed to be Africa, but it was actually filmed in Mexico. Twenty-six half hours were made over a seven-month period in 1955 and 1956. Had they not been all in black-and-white, *Sheena* would probably still be in syndication.

Like the comic strip character, the TV "Sheena" wore a leopard skin and spoke in pidgin English. She fought bravely and successfully against ivory poachers and white hunters.

The male regular on the series was Christian Drake, who was forever stumbling into trouble. The audience at home may have been relating to her as a sex object, but the scripts had "Sheena" very much in command. In a complete reversal of roles, it was "Sheena" who always came to Drake's rescue. She reserved most of her attention and affection for her constant companion, "Chim." She and the chimpanzee often held hands, making him the world's most envied ape.

Irish did a few features after *Sheena,* in which she played small parts: *She Demons* (1958), *The Beat Generation* (1959), *Five Branded Women* (1960), and *Hands of a Stranger* (1962).

She received residuals only for the last thirteen episodes of the show. For years afterward, however, she commanded large fees for personal appearances.

Irish has been divorced from her second husband, an actor, since 1966. In 1981 she married an executive of a glass manufacturing firm. The couple live in a house on the Pacific Ocean in Malibu. She keeps a studio a few miles down the beach, where she paints. Irish has been a successful artist for over ten years and has had several one-woman shows. Three of her oils were borrowed from a gallery by Pat Nixon and hung in San Clemente while it was the Western White House. Her art, which is mainly of the Old West, has been reproduced on a series of limited-edition plates.

She is delighted when she is recognized, which happens frequently.

Paul Adrian

Irish McCalla was one of nineteen Hollywood celebrities who signed their names in the new walkway in front of author Richard Lamparski's Hollywood home on September 20, 1981.

In 1937 Joel McCrea became the first actor to play the character "Dr. Kildare," in the picture Internes Can't Take Money.

Joel McCrea

The handsome leading man of the screen was born in South Pasadena, California, on November 5, 1905. His first brush with movie stars was as a newsboy delivering papers to the western star William S. Hart. Joel attended Hollywood High School and Pomona College.

By 1920 he was a stunt man, even doubling for female stars while falling off a horse. McCrea is one of the very few stars to rise from the ranks of the extras. Fans of silent films still catch a glimpse of him in such old pictures as the Garbo vehicle *Single Standard* (1929).

In 1929 things began to happen to him. He was seen in *Jazz Age* (1929) and then hired by the father of his former high school friend Cecilia B. De Mille for a featured role in *Dynamite* (1929). Joel and De Mille formed a friendship that lasted until the latter's death in 1959, although they only made one other picture together, *Union Pacific* (1939). McCrea was originally cast as the male star of De Mille's *Northwest Mounted Police,* but felt uncomfortable in the part and was replaced by Gary Cooper.

He was put under contract to RKO and appeared in such pictures as *The Silver Horde* (1930), *Kept Husbands* (1931), *Most Dangerous Game* (1932), *Private Worlds* (1935), and *These Three* (1936), the screen adaptation of Lillian Hellman's play *The Children's Hour.* His performances were low-keyed and his screen personality was likable, if not very distinctive. He became what is called in the movie industry "a dependable performer." It was his "everyman" image that made Alfred Hitchcock choose him for the male lead in the superb thriller *Foreign Correspondent* (1940). Some of his other films were *Wells Fargo* (1937), *Dead End* (1937) with the late Wendy Barrie, and, in the forties, when he really came into his own, *Sullivan's Travels* (1941), *The Great Man's Lady* (1942), *The Palm Beach Story* (1942), and *The More the Merrier* (1943). Then began his western period, which he never really left: *The Virginian* (1946), an exceptionally good one; *Ramrod* (1947); *Four Faces West* (1948); *Colorado Territory* (1949);

Cattle Drive (1951); *Wichita* (1955); *The Tall Stranger* (1957); *The Gunfight at Dodge City* (1959); *Ride the High Country* (1962); and *Mustang Country* (1976).

In 1952 McCrea and three other Hollywood actors had formed Four Star Productions, which produced some of the early money-making series on television. In 1959 he and his son Jody starred as Marshal Mike Dunbar and Deputy Ben Matheson on the television series *Wichita Town.*

Joel had close professional associations with several ladies: the late Constance Bennett, who for a time was also his constant companion, Barbara Stanwyck, and Frances Dee, whom he married in 1933. The two separated several years later but have since reconciled. They live on their huge ranch in Camarillo, California. They have three sons: David, who manages their ranch in Shandon, California; Jody, who works on their Camarillo ranch; and a considerably younger boy, who was born when the McCreas were well into middle age.

McCrea credits his astute business sense to what he learned from his old friend Will Rogers, who taught him real estate values. In the sixties Joel sold 1200 acres of ranchland near Moorpark, California, for $1,300,000. He had purchased it in 1931 for $19,500.

His wealth is not the only reason McCrea has turned down many parts in movies and on television. "Will Rogers told me years ago that if you don't stand for something you'll fall for anything," Joel often says. "I think a lot of the trash being made today comes from minds that lack that principle. I think too many movies today are just filth."

Jon Virzi

Joel and his wife, Frances Dee, live on their huge ranch in Camarillo, California.

Gisêle MacKenzie in the mid-fifties.

Gisêle MacKenzie

The songbird of the fifties and sixties was born on January 10, 1927, in Winnipeg, Canada. Her father was a physician and her mother played the piano and organ. When they realized that their two-year-old daughter was musically inclined Gisêle was taken for lessons in violin and singing. Until her violin was stolen she concentrated on playing. At that point she switched to singing.

Gisêle received her formal training at the Royal Conservatory of Music in Toronto. Shortly after graduation she landed her own radio program, which was called *Meet Gisêle.* Two executives of the Campbell Soup Company were driving through Canada on vacation when they heard her. She was brought from Toronto to Hollywood to be the songstress on the *Bob Crosby Club 15* radio show.

Gisêle MacKenzie is best known for the five years she spent singing on *Your Hit Parade* and for her professional association with Jack Benny. The latter began when Benny saw her in Las Vegas and made her a regular on his TV shows and road tours. She still glows when she speaks of how much he helped her career and of her fondness for him. She worked with him not only as a singer-violinist but as a foil for his comedy. He appreciated her musicianship. She seemed to spark him in front of an audience.

On *Your Hit Parade* she had the opportunity to sing her own hit "Hard to Get," which reached the coveted number one position for several weeks.

For a time she had her own program, *The Gisêle MacKenzie Show,* on television and guested with many others such as Dinah Shore, Jimmy Durante, and Dean Martin. For one season she played the wife of Sid Caesar on his TV series.

There was talk of Gisêle making movies, but when Jack Benny set up an interview for her with Dore Schary the meeting lasted less than fifteen seconds. "He walked in," she recalls, "took one look at me, and said I reminded him of Rosalind Russell of twenty years before and that he wasn't looking for one. I came home and cried for days!"

In the comedic exchanges she had with Benny, Gisêle proved quite effective. She wanted to do light comedy in pictures and on Broadway. The closest she got was when she was seriously considered for the title role in

Mame. She also did the lead in several dramatic shows on television, but was thought of essentially as a singer who could be amusing.

Ms. MacKenzie's career was expertly managed by Bob Shuttleworth, who was her husband until their divorce in 1966. Since then her appearances have been chiefly in touring companies of such shows as *Sound of Music, The King and I,* and *South Pacific.*

Gisêle and her daughter, a college student, live in Encino with her current husband, a banking executive. Her son is in the air force. Although she was raised a Roman Catholic, she is now a student of Science of Mind and often lectures at Religious Science churches.

She is extremely proud of the Gisêle MacKenzie orchid, white with a gold center, named for her by an ardent fan.

Gisêle was brought together with her present husband by the astrologer Carroll Righter. Six months later they were married. Since then she has turned down all offers to go on the road. That, however, is the only restriction Gisêle places on her career. She makes it very clear that she loves to work and is available. Asked recently to a gathering of celebrities, she replied, "If there's going to be a microphone or camera there, you can count on me!"

Iris Adrian and Gisêle have been close friends for many years.

Paul Adrian

Maggie McNamara was nominated in 1953 for the Academy Award as the Best Actress of the year in The Moon Is Blue.

Maggie McNamara

The pert Oscar nominee was born June 18, 1931, in New York City, one of four children. Maggie's parents were Irish immigrants who divorced when she was a child. She attended Straubenmuller Textile High School and began modeling when still in her teens.

She was twenty years old when David O. Selznick saw her picture on the cover of *Life* magazine. She was offered a screen test but declined. His interest did, however, prompt Maggie to study acting and dance. The following year she debuted on Broadway in *The King of Friday's Men.*

Barbara Bel Geddes had opened on Broadway in the role of "Patty O'Neil" in the hit play *The Moon Is Blue.* That was March of 1951. When Otto Preminger, who had produced and directed the F. Hugh Herbert play, was casting for the Chicago company, he chose Maggie McNamara.

Terry Moore and Diane Lynn were two of the stars whose names were being mentioned for the role in the movie. Preminger's announcement that Maggie, an almost total unknown, would play the plum part on the screen was the first surprise. Although the play was a bit risqué for the time, everyone assumed that Preminger would film a laundered version.

It was the time of the Legion of Decency, an organization that rated films by a Roman Catholic value system, and the Breen Office. The latter determined whether or not a feature met the standards set forth in the Motion Picture Code. Both organizations objected to the reference to the girl's seduction and the words "pregnant" and "virgin." Despite dire warnings within the industry, the picture was released without any censorship. It did not receive the much desired "Seal of Approval" and was rated "Condemned" by the Legion of Decency. *The Moon Is Blue* was denounced in Catholic churches all over America. In spite of this the film was a box-office success. Some thought that it became a hit because of Preminger's defiance. Certainly it received far more publicity than it would have, including Maggie's photo again on the cover of *Life.* Also, she was nominated as that year's Best Actress.

After *The Moon Is Blue* Maggie McNamara's name and face were familiar to the moviegoing public. Preminger sold her contract to Twentieth Century–Fox.

Like the movie that made her, Maggie proved to be quite unorthodox. She refused to do any cheesecake. She did not take up permanent residence in Hollywood. She went on suspension when she turned down a role in *King of the Khyber Rifles.* After rejecting *Loser Takes All* she was again taken off salary. The April 1954 issue of *Photoplay* explained: "Maggie McNamara, like Brando and Montgomery Clift, wants to be accepted for what's inside, rather than on the surface."

She finally took the role of one of the young women in *Three Coins in the Fountain* (1954) and had a small part in *Prince of Players* (1955). In 1955 Fox announced that her contract was being canceled "by mutual agreement."

About this time her husband, David Swift, who was one of the creators of the *Mr. Peepers* TV series, left her for a French model. Maggie entered into a relationship with another screenwriter after the divorce.

In 1962 she was back on Broadway in *Step on a Crack,* which had a brief run. Preminger used her again in a small part in *The Cardinal* (1963). That was about the last the public saw or heard of Maggie McNamara until the news of her death in March 1978. She was found in her Manhattan apartment, where she had taken her life. The official report listed the means of death as "acute chemical poisoning."

Over the years in obscurity Ms. McNamara had supported herself in various jobs, including time buyer for a small advertising agency. Near the end she worked as a typist.

Arthur Bell, writing in the *Village Voice,* quoted one of her friends as saying: "She was a volatile, delightful woman, yet possessed of demons. She spoke of death more than most of us do. She was always angry at the injustices of the system. Poverty upset her. The idea that the rich had so much, the poor so little."

Another acquaintance whom Bell spoke with said: "Whatever happened to Maggie wasn't because of rejection. It was because of her own desires. She wasn't sitting at home waiting for the phone to ring. The phone rang. She just wouldn't answer."

In 1968 Maggie McNamara was working as a time buyer at a small Manhattan advertising agency.

Jon Virzi

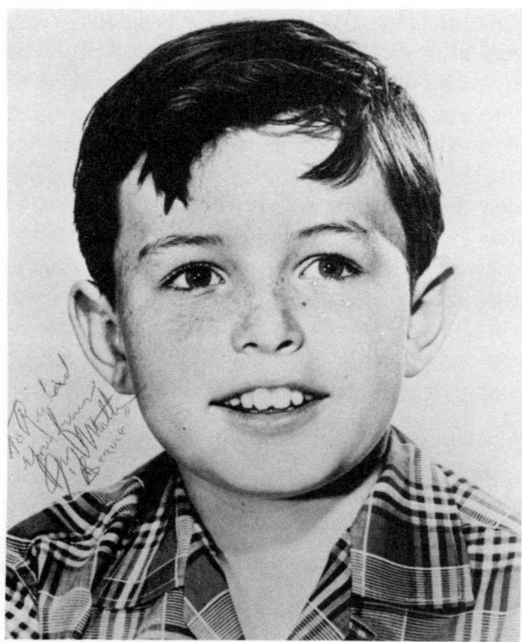

Jerry Mathers as "Beaver Cleaver."

Jerry Mathers

The star of the television series *Leave It to Beaver* was born on June 2, 1948, in Sioux City, Iowa. By the time he was two years old his family had moved to Los Angeles. One day when his mother had taken him shopping she was approached by the advertising director of the department store, who asked if Jerry could model for their Christmas calendar. The photographer who took the photos suggested to Mrs. Mathers that she take Jerry to see a particular agent who specialized in children.

At the age of two and a half Jerry debuted on the late Ed Wynn's television show, and then with his sister Susie played Faith Domergue's children in *This Is My Love* (1954). Alfred Hitchcock saw him on a Lux Video Theatre show and signed him for *The Trouble with Harry* (1955).

By the time Jerry was auditioned for the title role of "Beaver Cleaver" he had been seen with Bob Hope in *The Seven Little Foys* (1955) and *That Certain Feeling* (1956). The producers and director were impressed when Jerry told them that he hoped he could finish with the audition right away because he didn't want to be late for Cub Scout practice. That was exactly the sort of boy they conceived the character to be.

The program debuted on CBS-TV on October 4, 1957, switching to NBC and finally to ABC before it expired six years later into syndication, where it has remained ever since.

The situation comedy featured a respectful, well-meaning boy who, usually through no fault of his own, got into trouble. His "real" name on the series was Theodore, but almost everyone called him "Beaver." There was an older brother, "Wally," played by Tony Dow, and their neighbor "Eddie Haskell," who took great pains to be very courteous to "Beaver's" parents but was really the local troublemaker. That part was played by Ken Osmond.

The show was produced by George Gobel's production company, and although the cast worked five days a week turning out thirty-nine episodes a year, Jerry has admitted that his relationships with his TV family were always very businesslike and he seldom hears from them today. Barbara Billingsley played his mother, a character who seemed to respond emotionally to everything. Hugh Beaumont was "Mr. Cleaver," a man with very fixed ideas about how boys should think and behave. Jerry's own father was a high school principal, and he used to take him crow-shooting on weekends.

Jerry says he wasn't at all depressed when the show went off the networks, as by that time he had become very involved in his school sports program. Although he did a few guest appearances on such shows as *Batman* and *Lassie,* he turned down many for fear they would interfere with his football and swimming practice.

At the height of the Vietnam War, a wire service story reported that Jerry Mathers had been killed in action, and Shelly Winters repeated the news on a network talk show. Although the Matherses had a retraction out within twenty-four hours, many fans still believe Jerry is dead.

Mathers's salary, which began at $500 a week, was well invested. He doesn't feel troubled in any way for having been a TV star so young, and figures that because "Beaver" had such an all-American image he has not been typecast.

Since the series ended Jerry has done a stretch in the air force, attended college, gotten married, and been divorced. For eighteen months in 1979 and 1980 he and Tony Dow toured ten cities in the play *So Long, Stanley.* In 1981 he appeared in *The Girl, the Gold Watch and the Dynamite,* a made-for-TV movie.

Jerry Mathers is unmarried and lives in Woodland Hills, California.

Jerry is divorced and lives in the San Fernando Valley.

Peter Schaeffer

Joyce Mathews has been married seven times. She was twice married to and divorced from Milton Berle and impresario Billy Rose.

Joyce Mathews

The much-married showgirl was born Jane Mathews in New York City on December 5. Her father sold his seat on the New York Stock Exchange and retired when he was thirty-one years old. When Joyce was eleven her parents divorced and Joyce moved to Los Angeles with her mother.

Talent scout Ben Bard spotted her in a drugstore just before she was to graduate from Hollywood High School. With her mother's permission, he brought her to the late Busby Berkeley, who immediately gave her a job as a dancer in the picture he was making. Paramount put her under contract and changed her first name. She had small parts in such pictures as *$1000 a Touchdown* (1939) and *The Way of All Flesh* (1940) and posed for a lot of publicity stills.

Feeling she wasn't getting anywhere in movies, Joyce moved to New York City, where she landed a minor role in the Al Jolson show *Hold on to Your Hats* (1940). A Venezuelan colonel named Gonzalo Gomez, the son of a South American dictator, saw her in the show, and although he was over twenty years her senior, they got married. Forty-eight hours after the ceremony, Joyce left him.

"It was one of those dumb things to do," said Ms. Mathews. "When I was married to Billy Rose we ran into Gomez and I couldn't even remember who he was, but then, why should I? I hardly knew him."

She was in the Sophie Tucker–George Jessel show *High Kickers* (1941) when she became Mrs. Milton Berle. Although the comedian tried to discourage Joyce from acting, she appeared on stage in *Get Away Old Man* (1943), *Men to the Sea* (1944), and *Burlesque* (1946) during their six years together. They divorced in 1947, with Joyce retaining custody of their adopted daughter.

Joyce and Berle were remarried in 1949, but by 1950 they had again divorced. Their weddings, divorces, separations, and squabbles were reported in full in the press. It seemed as though they couldn't live with each other or without each other. "That's about it,"

Ms. Mathews admits. "But now that that's all over we get along fine."

On July 16, 1951, the big story on front pages across the country was Joyce Mathews's attempted suicide in the apartment of Billy Rose. His wife at the time was swimming champion Eleanor Holm. Rose called the police after Joyce slashed her wrists with a razor and then threatened to jump out a window. One of those to visit her in the hospital was Milton Berle, and there were rumors that they might marry for the third time.

After what columnist Jack O'Brian called "Broadway's longest running romance," Rose and Joyce were wed in 1956, with Ben Hecht acting as best man. The wedding ring had an eleven-carat diamond. In 1959 they were divorced. Two years later they remarried, only to break up again in 1963. They remained close, however, until Billy Rose died in February 1966.

Rose left Joyce a trust fund that pays her $35,000 a year. Two months after Rose's death she became the wife of a thirty-one-year-old executive. Eventually, they too were divorced.

In 1974, with her daughter as her matron of honor, Joyce married for the seventh time. Her present husband is the television actor Don Beddoe. The Beddoes live in Mission Viejo, California, near the travel agency Joyce owns and operates. The two met when Joyce booked Beddoe and his first wife on a cruise. Mrs. Beddoe died while they were on that trip.

Recently she spoke of her life today: "All those years I was around my biggest kick was knowing famous show people. Now that my close friend Jacqueline Susann is dead, the only actors I know are Milton and my present husband. And Don is retired. I don't even see movies anymore, and I used to just love them. But they aren't at all like they used to be. But then, what is? I don't want to see anything that hasn't got a real happy ending."

Donna Schaeffer

Joyce is now married to the actor Don Beddoe, but she uses the name Joyce Rose at her travel agency in Mission Viejo, California.

Kerwin Mathews was with Spencer Tracy and Frank Sinatra in The Devil at 4 O'Clock (1961).

Kerwin Mathews

The actor best known as the star of adventure films was born on January 8, 1926, in Seattle, Washington. His mother, who was a nurse, divorced his father shortly after his birth and took her son to live in Wisconsin. An only child, Kerwin grew up in a remote area. There wasn't anyone for him to play with for miles around.

He was active in plays at Beloit College, both as a student and later as an instructor. Talent scouts offered him screen tests twice before he agreed to try his luck in movies. "I told the studios as well as myself that I was more interested in the stage," he admitted recently. "The truth is my mother made me promise I'd get my teaching certificate. In case Hollywood didn't work out, I'd have a profession to fall back on."

Mathews was at the Pasadena Playhouse when an agent saw him and brought him to Harry Cohn, who headed Columbia Pictures. "I was so green I knew nothing of his reputation," says Kerwin of the mogul who was famed for his rudeness and crudeness. "Ignorance is bliss, because I was at the studio for eleven years and he was always very fatherly toward me. I became aware, of course, of how a lot of people were being treated, but I'm not temperamental and I was a very hard worker. He appreciated that and was very protective of me. I did, however, once see him talk to a woman while he was sitting on the toilet."

Mathews not only acted in Columbia pictures, he also coached other players, such as Kim Novak, dubbed foreign films, and acted in screen tests.

Cohn had *Joseph and His Brethren,* a much delayed biblical epic, in mind for Kerwin when he signed him, but the picture was never made. Instead he was cast in *Five Against the House* (1955) with Guy Madison, *The Garment Jungle* (1957), *The Last Blitzkrieg* (1959), *Man on a String* (1960), *The Warrior Empress* (1961), *The Devil at 4 O'Clock* (1961), *Maniac* (1963) with Nadia Gray (married and living in Manhattan), *The Viscount* (1967), *Battle Beneath the Earth* (1968), and *The Boy Who Cried Werewolf* (1973).

Mathews often got top billing in the films he made. He played a wide variety of roles, such as a priest, a marine sergeant, a mythical hero, and an FBI agent. He got along well with his directors and fellow actors, played all the parts assigned to him without protest, and cooperated fully with publicists. But he never became a star. His screen presence, like his real-life personality, is very likable but in no way flamboyant. He just never registered strongly with the press or public.

His real claim to lasting fame is for the three movies he made for children: *Seventh Voyage of Sinbad* (1960), which still plays to good houses at Saturday matinees, *The Three Worlds of Gulliver* (1960), and *Jack the Giant Killer* (1962).

Kerwin Mathews has lived in San Francisco since 1970. He manages Pierre Deux, a shop in the midtown area specializing in antiques and fine fabrics.

He is recognized frequently and still gets offers to appear in films and on TV, but he seems far more interested in his present profession than in acting. "I appreciate the opportunities to work in Hollywood again," he says, "but I know the nature of that business. I was wonderfully secure during those years at Columbia. Once it ended I was just another name actor waiting around for the phone to ring. The business I'm in now is enjoyable and steady. And I *love* living in San Francisco."

He is still in close touch with his former costars Kathy Crosby and Kim Novak.

Kerwin Mathews has remained a bachelor.

Today Kerwin manages Pierre Deux, a shop featuring antiques and fine fabrics, in San Francisco.

Sarah Richardson

<u>The Dick Van Dyke Show</u> ***with Larry Mathews and Mary Tyler Moore debuted over CBS-TV on October 3, 1961.***

Larry Mathews

The child star of the *Dick Van Dyke Show* was born in Burbank, California, on August 15, 1955. His father is a painting contractor.

When Larry was four years old he was sitting on his front porch singing. The mailman listened to him and, calling him a "natural entertainer," suggested to his mother that Larry be given acting lessons. Impressed by his outgoing personality, the instructors at acting school recommended him to an agency that specialized in children. Shortly afterward Carl Reiner called the firm and described the boy he was looking for to play the son of Dick Van Dyke and Mary Tyler Moore on the *Dick Van Dyke Show*.

Larry appeared in the pilot and was signed for the series. It premiered on the CBS network on October 3, 1961, and lasted for five seasons. It has been in syndication ever since.

Larry liked being on the show and felt very comfortable with each member of the cast and crew. When Van Dyke decided against continuing the show, Larry was disappointed. He recalls being the only one unhappy at the "wrap" party.

One of the few parts he played on TV aside from "Ritchie" was a guest spot on the *Dick Powell Theatre*. "There simply was no call for my services after our series ceased production," says Larry.

Used to tutors on the set, Larry attended public school for the first time when he entered the seventh grade. He found classes boring and the other kids less than friendly. But by the time he entered high school he had changed so much physically that he was no longer recognized as "Ritchie." He studied theater arts at UCLA.

Larry did some acting in little-theatre productions but eventually admitted to himself that he hated going on interviews for acting parts and was getting nowhere professionally. He would still like to act if offered a role, but he says, "They'll have to come and ask me, and I know that's not very likely."

Larry has no regrets about his part on the program. Twenty percent of his earnings was put in trust for him and he now feels well adjusted to being out of the spotlight. "At home I was always treated exactly the same as the other six kids in my family," says Mathews. "My ego was never allowed to get out of hand."

The closest relationship he made during those years that he has retained has been with Joey Bishop. Another friend from his days as "Ritchie" is Danny Thomas, a partner in the firm Larry now works for. He is now in charge of postproduction for the TV series *Soap*. Eventually Larry would like to produce and direct.

He is unmarried and lives in Venice, California. The name he uses today, both professionally and privately, is his real name, Larry Mazzeo.

Larry goes by his real name, Larry Mazzeo.

Howard W. Hays

Critics often described Una as having "the most wonderful innocence" in all her screen portrayals.

Una Merkel

The pert character actress was born on December 10, 1903, in Covington, Kentucky. Her father, a traveling salesman, took his family all over the South by horse and buggy and by train. She went to school first in Philadelphia and later in New York City, taking dancing lessons and studying dramatics with Tyrone Power's mother.

Her first jobs came as a model for magazines, usually *True Story*. She also worked as an extra in movies being made on the East Coast. Because of her resemblance to Lillian Gish, she was signed to play the star's sister in a picture, but for lack of funds it was never finished.

Producer John Golden found her candor so refreshing when she admitted her lack of experience that he gave her a one-line part in the play *Two by Two* (1925). It ran for two weeks. Next she went into *The Poor Nut* (1925) and again had but one line. That run lasted three weeks. Jed Harris cast her with Helen Hayes in *Coquette* (1927), which she did for twenty-two months on Broadway before going on the road with it.

D. W. Griffith, struck by her resemblance to Lillian Gish, cast her in *Abraham Lincoln* (1930) opposite John Houston. He originally chose her for the role of Mary Todd, but before shooting got under way decided she would be more effective as Ann Rutledge. It was the real beginning of her Hollywood career, which would eventually add up to more than ninety features, each marked by a performance of absolute genuineness.

Una Merkel was just short of beautiful, with features somewhat perky and winsome. She was typecast for comedy early in her Hollywood years after appearing in *Private Lives* (1931).

Among her other pictures are *The Bat Whispers* (1930), *Red Headed Woman* (1932), *42nd Street* (1933), *Bombshell* (1933), *Biography of a Bachelor Girl* (1935) with Ann Harding (living in the San Fernando Valley), *One New York Night* (1935) with Charles Starrett (living in Laguna Beach, California), *Riff Raff* (1935) with the late Victor Kilian, *Saratoga* (1937) with the late Frankie

Darro, *On Borrowed Time* (1939) with Bobs Watson (a Methodist minister and the father of nine children), *Sandy Gets Her Man* (1940) with Baby Sandy (a legal secretary living in Highland Park, California), *The Bank Dick* (1940), *The Road to Zanzibar* (1941) with Joan Marsh (married and living in Ojai, California), *Twin Beds* (1942) with the late George Brent, *It's a Joke, Son* (1947) with the late Douglass Dumbrille, *With a Song in My Heart* (1952), *The Kentuckian* (1955) with the late Diana Lynn, *The Parent Trap* (1961), and her last, *Spinout* (1966).

Probably she is best remembered for *Destry Rides Again* (1939), in which Una and Marlene Dietrich had a knockdown, drag-out fight on a barroom floor that ended when both were doused with water. Her best part was in *Summer and Smoke* (1961), for which she won an Academy Award nomination.

In 1944, after an absence of fifteen years, she returned to the New York stage to do *Three's a Family,* again working with John Golden. She also did *The Remarkable Mr. Pennypacker* in 1953 and *The Ponder Heart* in 1956, for which she won an Antoinette Perry Award. In 1959 she was in *Take Me Along,* the Broadway musical version of Eugene O'Neill's *Ah Wilderness!*

Una shared an apartment in the Hancock Park area of Los Angeles with her father until his death in 1977. He had been associated with Dr. Lee De Forest, the electronic genius of radio and television, in the pioneering of talkie films in 1923.

Una seems to lack any of the ego usually associated with actresses. Recently, looking at a still of herself as an adorable thirties blonde, she commented, "I really was kinda cute. I wish I'd known that then. I always thought I came over like a little hick."

She summed up her recollections of all those she has worked with: "I don't remember in all those years ever being with unpleasant people."

Una lives in an apartment in Los Angeles that is filled with antiques her father collected on his world travels.

John Oster

The late Russell Patterson, one of the most renowned commercial artists of his day, named Constance the "typical American girl."

Constance Moore

The movie actress publicized as the "typical American girl" was born on January 18, 1922, in Sioux City, Iowa. When she was six months old her family moved to Dallas, where Constance later attended several fashionable private schools.

She began singing over a local radio station while still in high school. Her salary of $5 a week was tripled when her godfather, who owned a chain of drugstores, decided to sponsor her. She was still on the staff at KRLD when talent scout Rufus LeMaire came to Dallas and offered her a screen test. Her mother refused, explaining that she was afraid Connie would only have her heart broken if the studio decided not to sign her. LeMaire relented and the young singer was given a stock contract with Universal Pictures, which began at $100 a week.

At first, she did Bs like *Border Wolves* (1938) and a "Buck Rogers" serial. But Moore soon developed a skill at studio politics. She made a friend who saw to it that she was cast opposite every young leading man the studio was considering. Executives were confronted with their starlet in each and every screen test, and in a variety of roles and costumes.

Her first A, which has become a classic because of its star, W. C. Fields, was *You Can't Cheat an Honest Man* (1939). Her personal favorite, and a great hit at the time, was *I Wanted Wings* (1941). Her others include *Argentine Nights* (1940), *Take a Letter, Darling* (1942), *In Old Sacramento* (1946), *Hats Off to Rhythm* (1948), and *The 13th Letter* (1951).

Her appearance in 1942 on Broadway in the Rodgers and Hart show *By Jupiter* brought Connie some excellent personal notices. In the 1940s she co-starred on radio with Joseph Cotten in *Ceiling Unlimited,* a series.

Constance Moore developed a very rewarding friendship with the late Louella Parsons.

The columnist gave her as much space as many major stars received.

During the fifties she concentrated on nightclubs, where she did rather well. Her voice was pleasing and she was certainly pretty enough. For eight consecutive years Constance opened the season at New York's swank Maisonette Room in the St. Regis Hotel.

On TV she was Robert Young's leading lady in *Windows on Main Street* during the season of 1961–62 and then replaced Irene Hervey (the divorced wife of Allan Jones and mother of singer Jack Jones lives in Los Angeles) in *The Young Marrieds,* a thirty-minute daytime series, during the season of 1965–66.

The uncomplicated, effervescent image she had on the screen differs drastically from the picture the late Veronica Lake went out of her way to paint in her autobiography. She told one interviewer, "Even in that town of phonies, Connie is a standout."

Ms. Moore is very much in evidence on the Beverly Hills–Palm Springs social circuit. She has maintained close friendships over the years with many of her contemporaries. Connie was a staunch supporter of George Murphy in both of his campaigns for the U.S. Senate. She and Murphy appeared together in *Show Business* (1944).

When she was still in her teens, Constance married Johnny Maschio, who was then a theatrical agent. He is now in the real estate business. The couple live in a house atop a mountain in Beverly Hills that commands a panoramic view of the San Fernando Valley. They have a son and a daughter. The Maschios have been grandparents since 1961.

Jon Virzi

Constance Moore today with one of her granddaughters.

She does not rule out acting again. Almost all of her free time, however, is spent working with the Braille Institute, of which she is an officer.

Dickie Moore in the early thirties.

Dickie Moore

The cute little boy from the 1930s movies was born in Los Angeles in 1925 of French-Irish parentage. According to Dick, as he is now known, a family friend—then secretary to Fox Pictures' president Joe Schenck—had to be picked up at Dickie's house one day when her car stalled, and the studio's casting director came to get her. Dick, who was playing in his crib, was seen by the director, who thought he bore a close resemblance, at eighteen months, to John Barrymore. That was the beginning of his career. "Frankly," Dick admits, "it just sounds too pat to be completely true." Whatever the facts, Dick made his screen debut playing Barrymore as a baby in *The Beloved Rogue* (1926). But his earliest recollections are of making *Passion Flower* (1930) with the late Kay Francis and *Squaw Man* (1931).

Contrary to what most people think, adult actors, Dick claims, were always very nice to him. He has unpleasant memories only of a few directors and teachers who tutored him at studio schools. Although he was allowed to see his films, he had little interest in them and felt no personal ambition until his late teens. In his early adolescence he was quite withdrawn and self-conscious, and in his acting then he could not bring himself to exhibit any of the charm or cuteness he had projected so strongly as a little boy. He says: "I knew what was wanted of me and I knew how to do it, but simply was unavailable to myself and too inhibited to execute technically that which I knew the character must do." Later he became very interested in his art, and after a stint in the army during World War II, covering United States Pacific operations for *Stars and Stripes,* the army newspaper, even acted in, co-directed, and coproduced a two-reel 35mm short subject called *The Boy and the Eagle,* which was nominated for an Academy Award in 1949.

During his movie-making days Dick was starred or featured in over two hundred films, including *Blonde Venus* (1932), in which he played Marlene Dietrich's little boy, *Oliver Twist* (1933), *Peter Ibbetson* (1935) with Ann Harding (retired and living in Westport, Connecticut), *Sergeant York* (1941) with Gary Cooper, and *Miss Annie Rooney* (1942), in which he gave Shirley Temple her first screen kiss. Many of his films, including his string of *Our Gang* comedies, are entertaining a new generation of movie buffs on television. As an adult he added radio, television, summer stock, Broadway, and off-Broadway to his credits, as both actor and director. His last film was *Member of the Wedding* (1952), and in 1956 he appeared on Broadway with Siobhan McKenna in George Bernard Shaw's *Saint Joan.* He has produced and directed USO-sponsored overseas tours, was a member of the acting faculty of the American Academy of Dramatic Arts, and has lectured extensively on the theater. In addition, Dick is the author of the book *Opportunities in Acting Careers* and coauthor of *Relationship of Amateur to Professional in the American Theatre,* commissioned by the Rockefeller Fund, and his television writing credits include *The Jewel Box,* presented by NBC.

Today Dick is president of the New York-based public relations firm that bears his name and lists among its clients prominent performing arts organizations and national and international labor unions.

Dick no longer minds being kidded about "Dickie." He is the father of two sons and lives in Manhattan.

Asked if he has any regrets about his acting career, he says: "I enjoy my life. I would never go back and redo a moment of it. There were difficult times; there are always difficult times, but I think there are difficult times even for people who don't have my background."

Recently he had dinner with Gloria Jean. The two hadn't seen each other since they made *The Under Pup* (1939) together. "She was my first big crush," says Dick. "We had a great time together." Dick is also back in touch with Sybil Jason and Edith Fellows through a club they have formed called "The Survivors." He is also a frequent date of Jane Powell.

Paul Schaeffer

Dick Moore is the head of his own public relations firm in New York City.

Natalie Moorehead with her first husband, Alan Crosland, the director of Three Weeks, Don Juan, and The Jazz Singer. They were divorced shortly before he was killed in a car crash in 1936.

Natalie Moorehead

The stylish menace of the early talkies was born Nathalia Messner in Pittsburgh, Pennsylvania, on July 27, 1901.

She acted in stock companies before coming to New York City, where she appeared in several flops. Then George M. Cohan gave her the lead in his play *The Baby Cyclone* (1927). In it she played opposite Spencer Tracy.

Natalie came to Hollywood just as sound was changing picture-making. Even before she arrived word reached her that Lilyan Tashman was threatening to "run her out of town." "I never met her," Ms. Moorehead said recently, "but in the first picture I did, *Thru Different Eyes* (1929), I played with her husband, Edmund Lowe. We got along fine." Ms. Tashman may have been worried because Natalie and she would certainly be up for the same parts. There was an obvious similarity in their hairstyles as well as their manners, although Natalie says that she had her mannish bob first. "It was called the 'Baby Cyclone' cut," she maintains, "and it caused a mild sensation when audiences saw it in the play. I'm sorry Miss Tashman was upset by me or my coiffure or whatever it was, because I loved her in pictures."

She married Alan Crosland, who had directed her in *The Furies* (1930) and *Captain Thunder* (1930).

During the decade in which she made pictures Ms. Moorehead was seen in over forty features. Always free-lancing, she worked not only at all the major studios but for independent producers and even poverty-row units like Chesterfield and Invincible. Among her credits are *The Girl from Havana* (1929) with the late Lola Lane, *Shadow of the Law* (1930) with Regis Toomey (widowed and living in Brentwood, California), *Parlour, Bedroom and Bath* (1931) with the late Charlotte Greenwood, *The King Murder* (1932) with Dorothy Revier (widowed and living in West Hollywood), *The Menace* (1932) with Bette Davis in a small role, *Private Detective 62* (1933) with the late Margaret Lindsay, *Heart of Arizona* (1938) with the late Russell Hayden, *Adventurous Blonde* (1937), and *Lady of the Tropics* (1939). Her last was *Flight Angels* (1940). Natalie had the distinction of playing the first person killed in the first of the *Thin Man* features, in 1934. More often than not she was either killed or arrested before her movies ended.

In 1942, divorced from Crosland, she married a wealthy Chicagoan, and she has not lived in Hollywood since. Ten years after her second husband died she married Juan Torena, the international soccer champion and star of Spanish-language films. The two had met during the thirties at the home of the late silent star Doris Kenyon. The Torenas lived in Europe for several years before settling in Montecito, California. Her close friend there is Virginia Cherrill.

"I first came to Hollywood because I wanted to try my luck in pictures," she said during a recent interview. "I liked them and the people I played with, but I never felt I had the makings of a first-rate actress. When I felt it was over I left. Juan and I seldom even visit Hollywood. This may be hard to understand, but in the years we've been married I don't think the subject of our careers has ever come up. We're not trying to avoid it but we live in the present. Fortunately, we have a lovely present."

Ms. Moorehead has no children. She and her husband are Roman Catholics.

Natalie Moorehead and Juan Torena recently in their home in Montecito, California.

Richard Lamparski

Dennis Morgan was under contract to Warner Brothers throughout the forties.

Dennis Morgan

The Hollywood leading man of the 1940s was born on December 20, 1910, in Prentis, Wisconsin, of Swedish parents. He acted in Marshfield High School plays and sang in the glee club. While attending Carroll College in Waukesha, Wisconsin, he was a member of the football team. At both the Wisconsin Conservatory of Music in Milwaukee and the American Conservatory in Chicago he studied voice. During his Chicago days he shared his room and his vocal coach with another hopeful, the late John Carroll.

Morgan's first break came when he got a job singing at the Palmer House Hotel in Chicago. After that he was a radio announcer on station WTMJ and did a couple of seasons in stock. While traveling with an operatic group, for which he sang in *Faust* and *Carmen,* he came to the attention of the late Mary Garden, who arranged for him to have a screen test at Metro-Goldwyn-Mayer. He was put under contract and sent to the Culver City lot.

For two years he did absolutely nothing but draw a very good salary. Finally, it was decided to have him sing "A Pretty Girl Is Like a Melody" in the now famous finale of *The Great Ziegfeld* (1936). At the premiere, Dennis was amazed to see himself on the screen mouthing words that another voice was singing. Without his knowledge, the studio had dubbed in the voice of Allan Jones.

Morgan left M-G-M and went to Paramount, where he was usually cast as a heavy, wearing a mustache. He then moved to Warner Brothers, where he fared no better, although they did drop his real name, Stanley Morner, for Dennis Morgan. Some of his films were made under the name Richard Stanley. The Burbank studio put him in one B film after another until Sam Wood took a chance on him for *Kitty Foyle.*

Dennis had heard that the director was looking for someone to play the part of a society snob. When he went to see Wood at RKO, he was offered the role of the young intern but flatly refused anything but the rich boy. Finally he got the part, and Warner's agreed to loan him out for the picture. It was a tremendous success and a great boost to his career. His costar Ginger Rogers won an Academy Award for her performance in the title role in 1940.

He returned to his home lot in triumph and was rewarded with some plum roles in such movies as *God Is My Co-Pilot* (1945) and *My Wild Irish Rose* (1947) with Andrea King (widowed and living in Beverly Hills). When he was not working on a picture he was making personal-appearance tours, in which he sang the songs from some of his films. His screen credits include *Waterfront* (1939), *Three Cheers for the Irish* (1940), *The Hard Way* (1943), *Christmas in Connecticut* (1945), *One Sunday Afternoon* (1948), and *Painting the Clouds with Sunshine* (1951).

He was teamed with Jack Carson in several films, notably *Two Guys from Milwaukee* (1946). They were close friends off the screen and remained so until Carson died in 1963. Morgan had tried to join the comedian's vaudeville act during his period in Chicago.

When his movie career seemed over in the 1950s, Morgan did quite a bit of television work. He was seen on NBC's *Star Stage,* CBS's *Stage 7,* and ABC's *Crossroads.* He played a prominent role in the TV version of *Stage Door.* In 1960 Dennis had his own series for a short time, *21 Beacon Street.* From time to time he has turned up in low-budget features such as *Uranium Boom* (1956) and *Rogue's Gallery* (1967).

Dennis Morgan and his wife, who was his sweetheart in high school, have three children. They live a few miles from the entrance to Yosemite National Park in Awahnee, California. He considers himself retired from business and performing. Always astute in money matters, Morgan had his last Warner Brothers contract written so that he received a salary of $25,000 a year until 1966, rather than pay huge taxes during the few years of his heyday. His time is spent playing golf and working for the American Cancer Society. Each Sunday he reads the scripture in his local church.

Jon Virzi

Dennis Morgan snapped during a recent visit to Hollywood.

Ella Mae Morse, the "Cow-Cow Boogie Girl," in 1944.

Ella Mae Morse

The "Cow-Cow Boogie Girl" was born in Mansfield, Texas, on September 12, 1926. By the time she was nine years old, Ella, with her mother at the piano, was singing with her father's small band, appearing at lodge parties and school dances.

By 1939 her parents had separated, Ella had quit school, and her mother was working for $17 a week in an underwear factory. In 1939, just a few days before her thirteenth birthday, Ella married Dick Showalter, who led a small group under the name Dick Walters. Ella hung around the Adolphus Hotel, in Dallas, and tried to get a job with Phil Harris. He turned her down because of her age. The late Rudolf Friml also said no, as did Tommy Dorsey. But when Tommy's brother Jimmy came to town, Ella decided to say she was nineteen; her mother promised to back her up. She was hired at $100 a week and went with the Dorsey band to their New Yorker Hotel engagement.

She had an excellent musical sense, but was quite unprofessional and seemed to have no feeling at all about what could or should be done on radio. She sang risqué lyrics and would announce on a coast-to-coast hookup that she had forgotten the words of a song.

Within a few weeks Dorsey found out about her age and she was replaced by Helen O'Connell. Thereafter Ella sang with Freddie Slack, Dorsey's former pianist. Slack's newly formed band had a long engagement at the Pacific Square Ballroom in San Diego.

But Ella didn't make it until she cut "Cow-Cow Boogie," one of the first records produced by the new company Capitol Records in 1942. The song had been done first by Ella Fitzgerald in a movie, but it landed on the cutting-room floor. Backed by Slack, Ella did it in one take, and although her contract called for a flat $35 fee, Johnny Mercer later authorized that she be paid royalties on the million-plus seller. She followed it up with such hits as "Mister Five by Five," "House of Blue Lights," "Shoo Shoo, Baby," "No Love, No Nothin'," and "Milkman Keep Those Bottles Quiet."

Ella was one of the nation's top vocalists during the big band era. She appeared with Charlie Barnett at the Strand Theatre in New York City and was seen in four movies: *Reveille with Beverly* (1943), *Ghost Catchers* (1944) with the late Lon Chaney, Jr., and Martha O'Driscoll (Mrs. Arthur Appleton of Chicago), *South of Dixie* (1944), and *How Do*

You Do (1945) with Harry Von Zell (living in Los Angeles) and the late Bert Gordon, the "Mad Russian."

In 1944, two years after her divorce from Showalter, she married a doctor, a union that lasted until 1953. Five years later she married her present husband, Jack Bradford, a carpenter. In 1959 she recorded her last album, *The Morse Code,* with Billy May, but nothing much happened with it. Her sound was out during the fifties and sixties, and she underwent a period of serious illness. In 1964 she was dealing 21 in Reno.

Ella and her family live in a small house in Hermosa Beach, California. All six of her children are out on their own and she feels that she can now afford to spend the time to pursue a career. In 1980 she played the Rainbow Room in Manhattan with Sy Oliver's band, and she headlines the show at Disneyland at least once a year. "The public never forget you," she says. "I believe they'd love to see me back, and I want to be back." She is very encouraged by the recent surge of interest in music of her period among people in their late teens and early twenties.

Ella Mae Morse and her husband live in Hermosa Beach, California.

Howard W. Hays

U.P.I.

"Mad Man" Muntz in 1952 with his Muntz television set.

"Mad Man" Muntz

The used-car king who became a household name was born Earl Muntz in Elgin, Illinois, in 1914. By the time he was ten years old he was building single-tube radio receivers, which he sold for a dollar apiece, and was wheeling and dealing among the neighborhood kids. By 1928 he had quit school and had his own business installing car radios, a rare accessory in those days.

In 1934 he bought twenty-eight old cars for $360 and opened his first used-car lot, which he later moved to Chicago. In 1941 he opened up in Los Angeles. At the suggestion of his friend Lionel Sternburger, the man who reputedly invented the cheeseburger, Muntz hired publicity man Mike Shore to make his lot at Eleventh Street and Figueroa the best-known in town. Shore hired the artists who created Bugs Bunny to do a caricature of a man wearing long red flannels and a Napoleon hat, and "Mad Man" Muntz was born.

Jingles proclaiming Muntz the "automotive mad man" were heard on thirteen radio stations 176 times a day. Skywriting and billboards informed Los Angeles that if it weren't for his wife, the Mad Man would simply give his cars away. The message was, he bought them retail and sold them wholesale because "it's more fun that way." Not only did his huge ad budget of between $30,000 and $50,000 a month pay off handsomely, but his image lent itself so easily to comedy that there was hardly a comic who didn't have at least one Mad Man Muntz joke in his routine. Jack Benny, Bob Hope, Red Skelton, and Abbott and Costello made him a national joke on their radio shows. In one season alone, out of his thirty-nine programs Bob Hope made thirty-two references to Muntz, every one heard from coast to coast.

After the war Earl took on the Kaiser-Frazer dealerships in New York and Los Angeles, selling $72 million worth in 1947 alone, with a personal profit (before taxes) of $1.25 million. Next came Muntz TV, a surprisingly good set with a built-in antenna and one-knob picture control. Its low price did much to bring down the cost of TV sets nationally. Working with seventy-two stores nationwide, Muntz sold $20 million worth by 1950. His sets were pitched as flamboyantly as were his used cars, and he even named his new baby girl Tee Vee. By then he was also selling his Muntz Jet, an automobile that retailed for $5,500 and at the time was the only sports car made in the United States. On this venture Muntz really lived up to his reputation: the car cost him $6,500 to manufacture. His Jet business collapsed when he was forced out of the TV company during the 1953–54 recession, but the car is still rated by automotive experts as one of the best of its kind ever assembled domestically.

After a hiatus that lasted until 1958, Muntz was back in Hollywood with a big promotion campaign for Muntz Stereo, the first company to offer stereo tape decks for cars, including a four-track cartridge. In 1960 Muntz Stereo grossed over $30 million.

Earl now operates out of a low-rent area of Van Nuys where he sells home video recorders, earth stations, and the Muntz projection TV screens. He does almost no advertising and yet his sales are second in the nation only to a large chain. "I've always had a reputation for high quality and standing behind my products," says Muntz. "Now I underprice everyone and let word of mouth do the rest."

Vivienne Segal, who recently bought a Muntz projection TV screen, said: "It was delivered exactly when it was promised for. They installed it perfectly and no one even asked me for a deposit."

He lives close to his business in a huge white-on-white house, complete with tons of electronic equipment and a doorbell that plays one of his thirty-year-old jingles. The famous caricature is on almost everything in sight, including his shirts. His present wife is his seventh and is thirty years his junior.

Muntz, who has lost as well as made millions, likes to entertain people with the story of how he turned down the national dealership for the Volkswagen in 1951. "It was never just the money with me," he says. "I only sell things I'd want myself and I only work with people I like."

Parked outside his business is a 1951 Muntz Jet, his personal car.

Peter Schaeffer

"Mad Man" Muntz today alongside his 1951 Muntz Jet.

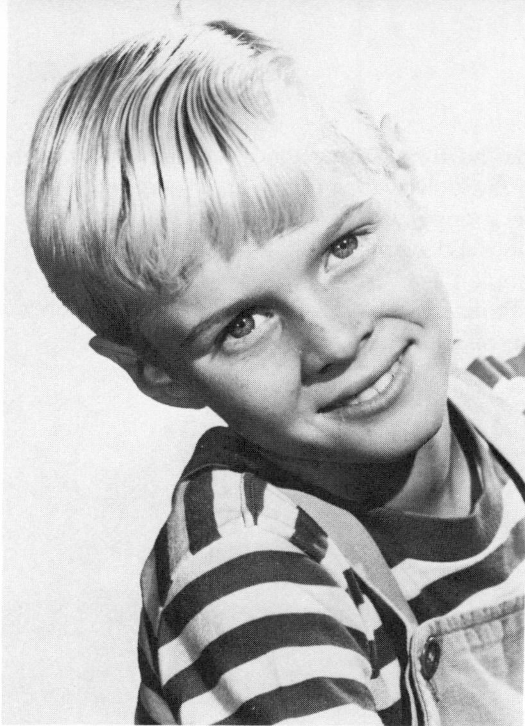

Jay North as "Dennis the Menace" in the mid-fifties.

Jay North: "Dennis the Menace"

The TV series based on Hank Ketcham's famous cartoon character premiered on CBS-TV in August 1959. It continued on the network for four seasons and is still in syndication.

The character was inspired by Ketcham's son, Dennis. The blond, impish Jay was three years old when the comic strip began in 1955. Today he is a guard at a state prison in Columbus, Ohio.

Jay North was the personal choice of Hank Ketcham, who selected him from the five hundred boys who tried out for the part. Gloria Henry and Herbert Anderson played the mischievous little boy's parents, "Alice" and "Henry Mitchell."

North, who was born August 3, 1952, is the only child of divorced parents. His mother was the secretary to the West Coast director of AFTRA, the theatrical union. Jay's first appearance on television was on *Queen for a Day*. Some of his other TV credits of the time were *Wanted—Dead or Alive, 77 Sunset Strip,* and *Desilu Playhouse.*

Jay was paid $600 for each of the 146 *Dennis the Menace* episodes he made and received residuals right up until the last few years. Almost all of his earnings were invested in Los Angeles real estate.

After production of the show ended, North starred in the film *Zebra in the Kitchen* (1965) and guested on a number of TV shows. He costarred with Sajid Kahn in *Maya* (1966), a color feature about the adventures of two boys in the jungles of India. It was made into a series of eighteen hour-long episodes that ran on NBC-TV during the 1967–68 season. By then his salary had risen to $1,100 a week.

Since then Jay North has made an R-rated feature film, *The Teacher* (1974), and toured in such plays as *Butterflies Are Free* and *Norman, Is That You?* He was married briefly to a Playboy bunny.

In the last few years Jay has grown increasingly discouraged about his professional life. "My career just sort of dried up," he told one reporter in 1977, when he became Seaman Recruit Jay North of the U.S. Navy. After being sworn into the Navy by Reservist Captain Jackie Cooper, Jay said, "I'm not going to sit around Hollywood for the rest of my life waiting for a part."

"Dennis" made North financially independent, but he would still like to act. But the only work he has done since being discharged from the service was a cameo role in the TV movie *Scout's Honor* in 1980. In it with him were Lauren Chapin from the cast of *Father Knows*

Best, Paul Peterson of the *Donna Reed Show,* and Angela Cartwright of *Make Room for Daddy.* The navy, too, was a disappointment. In spite of its promises, Jay was never trained for law enforcement work in the service. He is a strong advocate of the death penalty, not only for murder but for drug dealing as well.

North is very friendly with Herbert Anderson. "I'm much more comfortable with people of his generation than I am with my own," he explained recently. "And the younger generation—forget it!" He refers to himself as "a real conservative in every way, a square." He dislikes long hair on males, drugs of any kind (although he both drinks and smokes cigarettes), rock 'n' roll music, and young women who do not "dress and act like real ladies."

Jay North lives by himself in a condominium in Sherman Oaks and frequents jazz clubs in the area.

Jay North, Angela Cartwright, Paul Peterson, and Lauren Chapin together for an ABC-TV movie, Scout's Honor.

In The Harvey Girls (1946), as in all her films, Virginia seemed stricken by facial atrophy.

Virginia O'Brien

The deadpan singer-comedienne was born April 18, 1921. Her father was captain of detectives of the Los Angeles police department for twenty-two years before spending fifteen years as prosecuting attorney. Although she never had any professional aspirations, she began taking dancing lessons after seeing Eleanor Powell in several movies. But since she was frail, her family prevailed upon her to switch to singing.

One of the producers of *Meet the People* heard her practice and suggested she audition for the show, which was about to open in Los Angeles; the director liked her imitation of Ethel Merman. She was cast in the production, but when she went on stage opening night she froze. Though she remembered every word of her song, she was unable to move a muscle. The audience was convulsed, but Virginia was in tears when she reached her dressing room. The producers consoled her with the news that though she didn't turn out the way anyone had planned, it was fine as far as they and the audience were concerned—and Louis B. Mayer. He had seen her number, and after a test she was signed to an M-G-M contract.

Because of her uncle, the director Lloyd Bacon, Virginia wasn't as impressed with the stars she met at the Culver City lot as most teenage girls might have been. But she did want to date some of the young men there—Robert Sterling, for one. However, word was passed that Mayer was a personal friend of her father's and that he took a personal interest in her well-being. John Raitt was the only one who ever asked her out.

Virginia married Kirk Alyn (single and living in Quail Valley, California), who played "Superman" in the first movie serials. She is a grandmother by their son John.

The tall gal with the deadpan face went over big with audiences in the 1940s, and she could command as much as $5000 a week for personal appearances in presentation houses.

Some of her songs were "Rock-a-Bye, Baby" in *The Big Store* (1941), "Salome" in *Du Barry Was a Lady* (1943), "Take It Easy" in *Two Girls and a Sailor* (1944), and "Life Upon the Wicked Stage" in *Till the Clouds Roll By* (1946). All were done with the stiff gestures and flat voice. The only time she remembers smiling was at the conclusion of her number in *Thousands Cheer* (1943). She was also in *Lady Be Good* (1941), *Ship Ahoy* (1943), and *Meet the People* (1944).

Virginia was very happy at Metro, but in only a few of her sixteen features did she ever do much more than her famous comedy songs. Her pleading with the front office for other roles was ignored. By 1949, when M-G-M failed to pick up her option, she was hopelessly typecast. The only movie work she was able to find thereafter was *Francis in the Navy* (1955), made the year of her divorce from Alyn. Virginia has worked off and on over the years in small clubs, and although she has tried everything from country to Latin music, audiences want most to see her old routines. However, when her movies are shown on TV, her bits, which sometimes had been shot and added after completion of a picture, are regarded as unessential to the plot and are often cut.

Virginia, who speaks with an unaccountable Texas drawl, travels a great deal with her third husband, a contractor, in their small plane. They live in Sylmar, California.

Touring in *The Big Broadcast of 1928* from 1972 to 1974 reawakened Virginia's interest in a career. She appears in shows at the Masquers and the Motion Picture Country House.

Howard W. Hays

Virginia O'Brien today with her daughter Gale, who is by her second husband.

In 1944 Michael O'Shea starred in Man from Frisco, a Republic picture.

Michael O'Shea

The actor with the big Irish face was born on St. Patrick's Day, 1906. His full name was Edward Francis Michael O'Shea. His father shoed horses for Long Island socialites and had five brothers who were policemen. He teased his son constantly, telling him that he would never grow tall enough to qualify as a cop.

O'Shea quit school before he turned twelve and began hanging around a gymnasium. There he met his idol, Jack Johnson, the former world heavyweight champion. Eventually the two worked out a comedy routine, which they took to the Apollo Theatre in Harlem before embarking on a thirty-week tour of vaudeville houses.

O'Shea earned a living as a stand-up comic in small speakeasies during Prohibition. Eventually he formed his own dance band, which played what was then called the "laundry circuit" (Chinese restaurants). With twenty-two sidemen, the group was called "O'Shea and His Stationary Gypsies."

Tiring of the music business, O'Shea became an actor. After several years of finding work only in stock companies and bit parts, he turned to radio. He specialized in playing tough guys and smart-alecks. On many days he made appearances on several soap operas in the morning and afternoon and then several dramas and adventure programs on the same evening. He was so adept at changing voices and characters that when he was approached to audition for a part on Broadway he turned it down. "I was making over eight hundred dollars some weeks on radio," he explained in a 1973 interview. "When I was offered a plum role on stage I just couldn't see giving up that kind of money." The play was *The Eve of St. Mark* (1942), and it took the man who wrote it, Maxwell Anderson, to talk O'Shea into doing it.

He opened in the play billed as Eddie O'Shea, the name he had used up until then. It was a hit and most critics singled him out for special praise. Shortly thereafter Twentieth Century–Fox offered him a screen contract. At first he was adamant in his refusal. "I thought movies were junk," he said. "And most of them are." But Aline MacMahon persuaded him to accept the offer. He returned to Broadway only once after that, for a successful run in *The Red Mill* (1945).

His first two movies were his best: *Lady of Burlesque* (1943) and *Jack London* (1944). While playing Jack London he and costar Virginia Mayo fell in love. They were married in 1947.

O'Shea had several things working against him. He was a bit too mature for a leading man, and he wasn't really good-looking enough by Hollywood standards. When he had signed his Fox contract most of the best young leading men were in service. After they returned at the end of World War II Michael was given only supporting player roles.

O'Shea described the rest of his screen roles as "mediocre." Among the pictures were *It's a Pleasure* (1945), *Mr. District Attorney* (1947), *The Threat* (1949), *Captain China* (1950), *The Model and the Marriage Broker* (1952), and *It Should Happen to You* (1954).

Michael worked as an actor less and less after appearing in the TV series *It's a Great Life* from 1954 to 1956. He and Virginia Mayo seldom socialized with people in show business, so when he changed professions the film industry was barely aware of it. As a member of the Ventura County Sheriff's Office O'Shea worked with the FBI as an undercover man infiltrating organized crime. In the late sixties he began spending a lot of time at the Friars Club in Beverly Hills. By observing, eavesdropping, and at times watching card games through a peep hole in the ceiling, he and his colleagues were able to expose a crooked gambling racket. The case made headlines when it broke, but Michael's involvement was purposely kept quiet.

A few months before he died Michael O'Shea talked about his move from entertainment into law enforcement. "One of my earliest memories is my dad talking about cops. To him, if you weren't a police officer you were almost a bum. He was long dead when I went with the Sheriff's Office, but I made my peace with my dad in my own mind. I'm a cop—and not a bum!"

The O'Sheas, their daughter, and her husband lived together in a modern house in Thousand Oaks until he died in December 1973 of a heart condition.

Michael O'Shea photographed in his home shortly before he died in December 1973.

Richard Lamparski

Cecilia Parker in 1937.

Cecilia Parker

Andy Hardy's sister, as she was known from her part in twelve of the famous series, was born in Fort William, Ontario, Canada, on April 26, 1914. She was brought up in Hollywood, where as a teenager she began working as an extra and doing bit parts in movies such as *The King of Jazz* (1930).

She and her sister Linda played Siamese twins in the talkie version of the Lon Chaney movie *The Unholy Three* (1930) and repeated their act in Grace Moore's *A Lady's Morals* (1930).

Cecilia got a Fox contract in 1931 and made twenty westerns and two serials in one year, after which she was dropped.

She liked making westerns, such as *The Rainbow Trail* (1932) with George O'Brien, but found the late Ken Maynard "quite impossible."

In 1934 she made *Here Is My Heart* with Bing Crosby and *The Lost Jungle* with the late Clyde Beatty, and then signed an M-G-M stock contract. There was an attempt to create a screen love team of Cecilia with Eric Linden (the father of three, living in Laguna Beach, California), and they were paired in several features, such as *Ah, Wilderness!* (1935) and *Sweetheart of the Navy* (1937). But once she made the first of the highly successful Hardy series, *A Family Affair* (1937) with Julie Haydon (teaching at the College of St. Teresa in Winona, Minnesota), her professional fate was sealed. She did other roles, such as Garbo's sister in *The Painted Veil* (1934), but in the public's mind she was "Marian Hardy," daughter of Judge Hardy and sister of Mickey Rooney. She even tested for Melanie in *Gone With the Wind*, but no plum roles came her way. Directors and producers thought that she was simply too closely identified with the part not to be distracting in important roles. She knows for a fact that she lost a Harold Lloyd feature because of that reasoning.

In 1945 Mickey Rooney was drafted, the

series ended, and Cecilia retired. In 1937 she married Dick Baldwin, who costarred with her in *Gambling Daughters* (1941). The two have been wheeling and dealing in real estate ever since.

For the past fifteen years the Baldwins have lived in Ventura County in California. They now share a mobile home in Oxnard when Cecilia is not baby-sitting with one or more of her five grandchildren. The Baldwins have two sons and a daughter.

Her only return to her profession was when Mickey Rooney talked her into making *Andy Hardy Comes Home* (1958), which was a complete disappointment. In spite of the effect it had on her career Cecilia liked doing the Hardy series, but has admitted that the sequel was a mistake. "The experience only proved to me what I've heard all my life," said Cecilia Parker. "But I had to learn it for myself—you just can't go home again."

Cecilia Parker and her husband, Dick Baldwin, share a mobile home in Oxnard, California.

Michael Knowles

The cast of the original Lassie TV series: Tommy Rettig as "Jeff," Lassie, the late George Cleveland as "Gramps," Donald Keeler as "Porkey Brockway," his dog Pokey, and Jan Clayton as "Ellen Miller."

"Porkey": Donald Keeler

The child actor of television was born Joey Vieira in Los Angeles on April 8, 1944. His brother is Ken Wetherwax, who played "Pugsley" on *The Addams Family.*

Joey was playing basketball with other members of his third-grade class when he was approached to be an extra in a scene for an episode of *Meet Mr. McNutley*, a TV series of the 1953–54 season that starred Ray Milland. Joey came over so well that a part was written in for him. During that same season he was seen regularly on another show, *Pride of the Family*. Joey played the next door neighbor.

Joey's name changed when the producers of the first program thought he should use his mother's maiden name, Keeler (Joey's aunt is Ruby Keeler). For the first name Joey picked his middle name, Douglas. But when the credits ran at the end of the first appearance they read, "Donald Keeler." He kept that as his professional name until recently.

Joey is probably best remembered for *Lassie*. He was on it for four years playing "Porkey," best friend of the show's star, Tommy Rettig. It would be inaccurate to call him the sidekick, because "Porkey" was usually some distance behind "Jeff" and Lassie. The shows often ended with the chubby "Porkey" huffing and puffing as he ran, trying to catch up with his friend. According to Joey, however, he never lagged behind in popularity with the audience. He insists that he received as much fan mail as Tommy Rettig.

After *Lassie* Joey played very similar parts on *My Three Sons* and *The Many Loves of Dobie Gillis*. "I can't tell you how tired I got saying those same lines over and over again," he said recently. "Finally I decided that I'd had it with the tennis shoes and the beanie. I went to England."

Vieira spent a year abroad, during which time he produced an English rock group. He returned when he was twenty-one years old, with the intention of taking the money he had made acting and going into business. To his great surprise, his family had spent almost all of it.

He had made a vow that he would never again play a fat person. To make certain, he lost more than fifty pounds. But the amount of money offered him to play a running part on *Hank* was too tempting. He signed the contract and put the weight back on. It was touted as the series that would run "on and on and on." The show, which starred Dick Kallman in the title role, was canceled after eleven episodes. *Hank* was one of the most expensive failures of the TV season of 1965–66. Dick Kallman, who became a dealer of fine antiques, was murdered in New York in February 1980. The crime has never been solved.

The *Starsky and Hutch* episode Keeler appeared on in 1977 was his first acting job since *Hank*.

Today he is known as Joey Vieira again. He has his own firm, which produces TV shows, commercials, and recordings. The album he produced, *Drum Drops,* is the top-selling record among aspiring drummers, who practice with it.

"Porkey" is a divorced father of two. His home and office are in the San Fernando Valley. He and Tom Rettig still see each other. His lawyer is Bobby Diamond.

"Porkey" is now known by his real name, Joey Vieira.

Eleanor Powell always choreographed her own dance numbers for both stage and screen.

Eleanor Powell

The girl who was crowned the World's Greatest Female Tap Dancer in 1930 by the Dancing Masters of America was born in Springfield, Massachusetts, on November 21, 1912. She was an only child. Her mother, thinking that dancing lessons might help her daughter gain some poise and overcome her shyness, enrolled her in a ballet class.

When she was only thirteen, Gus Edwards saw her do acrobatics on the beach in Atlantic City and asked her mother's permission to put her into the show he was producing at the Ritz Grill. In her late teens she went to New York, determined to get into a Broadway show, but found that all of the jobs went to those who could tap. After only ten lessons from Jack Donahue and a lot of private practice, she landed a spot in *Follow Through* in 1929. In 1931 she was in *Fine and Dandy,* and the following year Flo Ziegfeld gave her a part in *Hot Cha,* which starred Buddy Rogers, Bert Lahr, and Lupe Velez.

When she was signed by Metro-Goldwyn-Mayer from her Casino de Paree engagement in 1935, Eleanor was still rather shy and not pretty by Hollywood standards. M-G-M made her undergo extensive dental work, gave her voice lessons, and unleashed its beauticians on the new contract player. It was a very glamorized Eleanor who tested for a featured role in *Broadway Melody of 1936.* The late Louis B. Mayer saw the test and gave her the lead. Playing a dual role, Eleanor did an imitation of Katharine Hepburn as well as a couple of dazzling dance numbers, and emerged a brand-new and very big star. The studio rushed her into *Born to Dance* (1936), with James Stewart as her leading man and what looked like five hundred chorus boys to back her up in the finale. The next year they put her with the late Ilona Massey and Nelson Eddy in *Rosalie* and with Robert Young in *Honolulu.* Some other pictures she brightened were *Broadway Melody of 1938, Broadway Melody of 1940, Lady Be Good* (1941), *Ship Ahoy* (1942), *As Thousands Cheer* (1944), and *Sensations of 1945.*

At the height of her career Eleanor made as much as $125,000 a picture, plus huge sums for personal appearances.

While appearing in *At Home Abroad* with Bea Lillie and Ethel Waters at the Winter Garden Theatre, the film *Broadway Melody of*

1936 was playing across the street at the Capitol. At the same time she was starring on *The Red Horse Tavern,* a weekly radio program aired coast-to-coast in front of a studio audience.

Eleanor retired shortly after her marriage to Glenn Ford in 1943. The only work she did after that was a TV series entitled *Faith of Our Children,* which ran from 1955 to 1958. The religious series won five Emmys and many other awards. In 1959 the Fords were divorced, and Eleanor has not remarried.

In 1961, when she was forty-eight, her only child, Peter, talked her into a comeback. It was the kind that most performers only dream about. She looked great, and her dancing brought the house down at Las Vegas' Sahara and Manhattan's Latin Quarter. The act ran fifty-five minutes, during which she was assisted by four young men. She did this act from 1961 to 1964.

Friends and fans urged her to dance professionally again, but her answer was always: "I was born in Springfield, Mass., and played my first theatre in the round there in 1964. I consider this to be my farewell performance. If I were an actress only, I could go on with plays, as so many of the stars of my era are doing, but when it comes to dancing, *you can't go back.* It's much nicer for the public to remember."

Eleanor Powell died in February, 1982.

Jon Virzi

Eleanor photographed at a recent function at the Academy of Motion Picture Arts and Sciences.

The googly-eyed actor in 1943.

Eddie Quillan

The googly-eyed comedian and character actor was born in Philadelphia on March 31, 1907. By the time he was seven years old Eddie was performing in vaudeville with his sister and three brothers in an act called "The Rising Generation." The Quillan kids did well on stage, but they loved the movies and begged their father-manager to get them work in motion pictures. The elder Quillan knew Nick Harris of the famous detective agency. Harris happened to know Mack Sennett. When the kids were in Los Angeles, booked at the Orpheum Theatre in 1925, they approached the producer and were given a screen test. It was run a few days later, but it so discouraged them that they walked out of the projection room before it was over. Sennett, however, was very impressed—but only with Eddie, whom he signed to a contract.

Quillan made eighteen two-reelers, beginning with *A Love Sundae* (1926). But he balked at doing a blue bit in one of the scripts and walked off the lot forever. He free-lanced for a while, getting good parts in such silent features as *Show Folks* (1928) with Lina Basquette (single and living in Wheeling, West Virginia; she is one of the country's leading handlers of pedigreed dogs and a frequent judge at dog shows). Cecil B. De Mille offered him a small role in *The Godless Girl* (1929), but he turned it down. That impressed the director so much he gave Eddie the comedy lead. After that he played the lead in Leo McCarey's first feature, *The Sophomore* (1929).

Eddie's double take, which he had developed on the stage and mastered in silents, combined with his youthful enthusiasm, got him lots of work in talkies. He thinks his best was *Big Money* (1930). His other credits include *Girl Crazy* (1932), *Strictly Personal* (1933), *Mutiny on the Bounty* (1935), *Big City* (1937), *Young Mr. Lincoln* (1939), *The Grapes of Wrath* (1940), and *The Kid Glove Killer* (1942). In *Mutiny* and *Grapes* he was surrounded by some of the top talent in Hollywood. In his small parts in them he turned in performances so natural and touching that he was singled out for praise by critics and fellow actors. But producers continued to cast him as a bellhop, an elevator man, and a soda jerk. Although he worked constantly, it was in B pictures like *It Ain't Hay* (1943) and *This Is the Life* (1944).

In the mid-forties Eddie tried his luck at owning a bowling alley in nearby El Monte. He enjoyed it and it prospered, but when he was cast in *Brigadoon* (1954) he was glad to be back in the movie business.

A few years ago he sold the big house he had bought during his peak years. He now lives with his sister in a smaller one in North Hollywood. Their youngest brother, the late Joe Quillan, penned many shows on radio and

TV for Eddie Cantor and Joan Davis, as well as nearly all the *Our Miss Brooks* series. The Quillans are devout Roman Catholics, and religious objects are displayed throughout the house; a large statue of the Blessed Virgin rests in the backyard.

Never really a part of the Hollywood social scene, Quillan, who has never married, has one close friend in the profession: Lloyd Nolan.

For a number of years Eddie got very little work on TV. "Casting directors are so young these days they haven't a clue as to who I am or what I've done," he said in 1972. "How do you tell someone you've been in over one hundred movies?" Since then, probably because of the popularity of his old pictures with the younger generation, he has been rediscovered. After appearing several times on *Mannix* and *Lucas Tanner,* he did a few *Police Story* shows. Michael Landon used him six times on *Little House on the Prairie.* Robert Blake thinks highly of Eddie's work and has had him on both of his series.

"Funny how things work out," said Quillan recently. "I guess I missed becoming a star, but I always made a good living and still do. I wonder if I had hit it big would I still have my wonderful family and the many good friends I have. Somehow I doubt it."

Eddie Quillan recently in the den of his North Hollywood home.

Mathew Tombers

Hollywood's suave tough guy in the 1930s.

George Raft

Hollywood's suave tough guy was born on September 26, 1895, in Manhattan's Hell's Kitchen, of German, Italian, and Dutch ancestry. The family was desperately poor. He was at various times a mover's helper, a driver for gangster Owney Madden, a prizefighter, and a dancer. George left home at twelve and had very little education. Hanging around speakeasies, he became an excellent ballroom dancer and what was then called a "ladies' man." For a while Raft worked for "Texas" Guinan at her El Fey Club.

Little is known about his marriage in 1916 to actress Grayce Mulrooney, except that she was older than George. Although it didn't last long, they were never divorced. The most influential woman in his life was Virginia Peine, who divorced her wealthy husband to live with Raft. Virginia polished him in the areas of clothes and behavior. When he left her it was for Norma Shearer (living at the Motion Picture Country House). After that it was Betty Grable. All Hollywood assumed that George and Betty would marry. During their five-year courtship they were considered one of Hollywood's hottest couples, although her biographer, Doug Warren, doubts that they ever slept together. The relationship ended in 1943, when she married Harry James. Raft admitted many times over the years that he regretted not marrying her.

After appearing on Broadway in such shows as *Gay Paree* (1925) and *Palm Beach Nights* (1926), he went to Hollywood, where at first he was cast in small roles, such as in *Quick Millions* (1931). It was with Paul Muni in *Scarface* (1932) that he really clicked, projecting the epitome of "cool" by repetitiously flipping a coin. Twenty-eight years later he parodied himself by repeating the performance with Jerry Lewis in *The Bellboy* (1960). In later years he said that his only professional regret was not keeping the fifty-cent piece he flipped in *Scarface.*

George's roles were not restricted to sinister types. He was, however, always in command, even as a convict. Among his pictures were *Night After Night* (1932), which introduced Mae West to movies, *Bolero* (1934), in which he and Carole Lombard started a national tango craze, *Rhumba* (1935), *Each Dawn I Die*

(1939), *The House Across the Bay* (1940), *Manpower* (1941), *Broadway* (1942), *Nob Hill* (1945), *Johnny Allegro* (1949), *Around the World in 80 Days* (1956), *Some Like It Hot* (1959), and *Rififi in Panama* (1966).

At his height, George Raft made over $200,000 a year, but he was very generous and was a compulsive gambler. Beginning in 1955, George suffered a long string of misfortunes. Because of his known association with gamblers and racketeers, the New York Tax Commission refused him permission to buy an interest in the Flamingo Hotel in Las Vegas. That year he lost $100,000 on his ill-fated television series, *I Am the Law,* in which he played a cop. In 1959 his Havana gambling casino (he was a partner) was closed by Fidel Castro, without compensation, and five years later *The George Raft Story,* which starred Ray Danton, flopped. The following year he appeared before a federal judge for sentencing on income tax evasion. Pleas for clemency from Frank Sinatra, Bob Hope, Red Skelton, Bing Crosby, Jimmy Durante, and Lucille Ball moved the judge to limit the sentence to a fine of $25,000 and a suspended sentence. But as the tears rolled and he sobbed out his public apology for the television cameras, the tough-guy image was gone forever.

Several months later he was the front man and manager of a posh London gambling club in Berkeley Square. By 1968, though, British authorities left no doubt that George and his associates were unwanted. He returned to Hollywood to file for Social Security benefits. His Beverly Hills home and furnishings were auctioned for $63,400, most of it going to his creditors.

During the seventies Raft was seen nightly playing a convict who starts a riot in a prison mess hall on an Alka-Seltzer commercial.

Near the end of his life he used to startle tourists who came into the Las Vegas Riviera Hotel reservations office in Beverly Hills. George worked there part time, booking rooms.

Long after he was no longer "hot" George Raft was considered "cool." Hollywood is noted for shunning its has-beens, yet he was well liked and looked after right to the end of his life. Old friends saw to it that he always had a decent address, a recent-model car, and a natty wardrobe. If he was no longer good copy, he remained good company. It all agreed with him, because as late as 1979 he told an interviewer, "I don't feel like an old man and I don't feel like a poor man."

Raft was in Mae West's first film and in her last, *Sextette* (1978). He died on November 25, 1980, two days after she did.

Jon Virzi

George Raft in a photo taken shortly before he died in the autumn of 1980.

Esther Ralston, the "American Venus," was under contract to Paramount Pictures in the late twenties.

Esther Ralston

The movie actress known as the "American Venus" was born in Bar Harbor, Maine, on September 17, 1902. When she was two years old her parents worked her into their act, playing vaudeville, the Chautauqua circuit, carnivals, burlesque, and repertory companies. They were billed as "The Ralston Family with Baby Esther, America's Youngest Juliet."

By 1917 the Ralstons had arrived in Hollywood, where Esther became a bit player in films starring Lew Cody and Viola Dana. In 1920 she got a tiny part in *The Kid,* the film that made Jackie Coogan a star. Signed to a contract by Universal, she made *Oliver Twist* (1922) with Coogan and Lon Chaney. After working in pictures with Conway Tearle and Jack Dempsey, Esther was cast as "Mrs. Darling" in the silent classic *Peter Pan* (1925) and signed to a contract with Paramount Pictures.

She got her title, the "American Venus," from the 1925 picture of the same name, in which she starred. That same year she married George Webb, a director-actor. In *A Kiss for Cinderella* (1926) she played a fairy godmother. She then appeared in the critical and box-office success *Old Ironsides* (1926) with Charles Farrell (retired and living in Palm Springs). Esther and Clara Bow had the leads in *Children of Divorce* (1927).

Josef von Sternberg presented her for the first time as a dramatic star in *The Case of Lena Smith* (1928), which he directed.

Richard Dix and Esther made their talkie debut together in *Wheel of Life* (1929). In 1931 she was Lawrence Tibbett's leading lady in *The Prodigal.* She played London's Palladium and toured the provinces for a year after that. Then she made *After the Ball* (1933) with Basil Rathbone and *Rome Express* (1933) with Conrad Veidt.

In 1933 Esther returned to Hollywood, where she and Webb were divorced. She was put under contract to M-G-M, but after she rejected Louis B. Mayer's advances she was loaned out for pictures that were hardly calculated to help further her career. Her only important film for Metro during that contract was the Joan Crawford movie *Sadie McKee* (1934). That year she married Will Morgan, a singer.

In 1936 she appeared in *Reunion* with the Dionne quintuplets. Returning to her old lot, Paramount, she did *Hollywood Blvd.* (1936), which included cameo performances by her contemporaries from silent days. Esther's other movies in the late thirties were either undistinguished or just bad. Examples are *Girl from Mandalay* (1936) with the late Conrad Nagel and *Shadows of the Orient* (1937) with

Regis Toomey (living in Brentwood, California).

Esther Ralston's last film of consequence was *Tin Pan Alley* (1940), an Alice Faye musical in which she played the great vaudevillian Nora Bayes.

Her second marriage ended in divorce in 1938, and the following year she married a newspaperman. In 1941 and 1942 Esther played the title role in the radio soap opera *Woman of Courage*. She went into retirement through the forties to raise her children. From 1950 until 1952 she toured the straw hat circuit. Esther was divorced again in 1954 and has not remarried.

In 1956 she went to work at B. Altman's department store on Long Island and became head of the boys' shop. Esther left in 1961 for a running part on NBC-TV in *Our Five Daughters*, a soap opera that lasted a year. There were also appearances on *Kraft Theatre* and *Texaco Playhouse* on television. From 1965 to 1967 she was a partner in a talent agency in Manhattan. Then she spent ten years working in an electrical supply store in Glens Falls, New York.

The "American Venus" now lives by herself near one of her children in Ventura, California. She commutes to Los Angeles to appear in TV commercials and see old friends.

Jon Virzi

Esther Ralston lives by herself in Ventura, California.

Vera was billed for a time as "The Most Beautiful Woman in the World."

Vera Hruba Ralston

The former "Queen of Republic Pictures" was born Vera Hruba in Prague on June 12, 1921. When she was twelve her brother Rudy convinced her to concentrate her considerable energies on ice skating rather than on classical ballet, which she had been studying since she was four. One year later Vera was the skating champion of Prague.

In the Berlin Olympics of 1936 she finished second to Sonja Henie. According to Vera, Adolf Hitler asked her how she would like to skate for the swastika and she replied, "I'd rather skate on it!" The Führer, she says, was livid. She was on the last plane to fly out of Prague when the Nazis marched into the Sudetenland. She arrived in New York City with $30 and landed a job with an ice revue at the Hotel New Yorker. Then came a two-year tour with *Ice Vanities* before she was signed as a principal with Ice Capades.

Vera was taking acting lessons from Josephine Dillon, the first wife of Clark Gable, when she was signed to a long-term contract with Republic Pictures. This was after making appearances in *Ice Capades* (1941) and *Ice Capades Revue* (1942).

Billed as Vera Hruba Ralston, who "skated out of Czechoslovakia into the hearts of America," she appeared in *The Lady and the Monster* (1944) and *Lake Placid Serenade* (1944). The latter had a plot not unlike her own story. Her billing for *The Lady and the Plainsman* (1946) was minus the Hruba (the "H" is silent). Among her other films are *Wyoming* (1947); *Angel on the Amazon* (1948), in which she played a woman who had been frightened by a panther and could never age; *I, Jane Doe* (1948), her personal favorite; *Fair Wind to Java* (1953); *Spoilers of the Forest* (1957) with Hillary Brooke (Mrs. Ray Klune of San Luis Rey Downs, California); and her swan song, *The Man Who Died Twice* (1958).

All of Vera's features were made at Republic, a lot never known for an A product. However, the studio's president, Herbert J. Yates, took a personal interest in her career from the beginning, and veteran employees were amazed at just how much he was willing to spend on his star. Republic stockholders were somewhat differently impressed, and in 1956 their objections took the form of a lawsuit that claimed that Sterling Hayden was hired "at an improvident and excessive salary to induce him to appear with Miss Ralston" in *Timberjack* (1955). It was alleged that John Wayne refused to work with her after their two costarring vehicles bombed at the box office.

In fact, said the suit, only two of Vera's twenty features had even made back their negative costs.

Yates and Vera, who was forty years his junior, were married in March 1952. Until he was deposed at Republic in a 1958 proxy fight, he continued to indulge her with production values usually found only in lavish movies made on major lots. Until he died in 1966, he saw to it that she had a life-style on a par with those of Hollywood's reigning queens. Her large collection of his expensive gifts includes a diamond bracelet she discovered one night inside her broiled trout.

The former star lives in Santa Barbara's exclusive Hope Ranch in a mansion complete with full-time help, watchdogs, and a $5,000 whirlpool bath. She inherited half of Yates's estate, which was valued at over $10 million.

Always popular on the Republic lot, Vera sees many of those who worked on her twenty-eight films. For several years she was so ill she could not even walk. She attributes her complete recovery to faith healer Oral Roberts.

For a time the woman whose name exhibitors once refused to put on their marquees contemplated a comeback. In 1972 she said that she did not believe she was ever properly used in pictures. Her heavy accent, which was one of the reasons that caused her to be dubbed the "Queen of the Clinkers," is considerably lighter. She felt that her real forte would be light comedy.

Since then, however, Vera Hruba Ralston has become the wife of Charles Alva, a somewhat younger man who was in the fine foods business when they met. Said a friend and neighbor recently, "To him she's still a big star, and Vera has really blossomed since the marriage. She looks and acts twenty years younger."

Doug Coder for City of Hope

Vera Hruba Ralston on a recent return visit to the facility that was once Republic Pictures.

Joyce Randolph originated the role of "Trixie Norton" on The Honeymooners and played it for six years. Art Carney was "Ed Norton," a sewer worker.

Joyce Randolph

The original "Trixie" of television's *The Honeymooners* was born Joyce Sirola in Detroit, Michigan, on October 21, 1925. She is of Finnish descent.

Joyce acted in a number of plays presented by the Wayne State University Workshop. She was picked from one of their productions for a role in a road company tour of *Stage Door* in 1944. When that tour ended, she began another, a revival of *Abie's Irish Rose,* which took her on the road for a year.

The first actress to play Gleason's wife, "Alice," was the late Pert Kelton. *Red Channels,* a right-wing publication that flourished during the McCarthy era, named her in one of its issues as having once been sympathetic to Communist causes. Ms. Kelton, whose career until then had included both motion pictures and the Broadway stage, was dropped immediately and replaced by Audrey Meadows.

Joyce Randolph performed on TV as early as 1946 at General Electric's experimental laboratory in Schenectady, New York. In 1948 she began working fairly regularly on television, mostly in the mystery dramas that were so popular at the time. She ended up as a corpse so often that a newspaper critic gave her the title of "the most murdered girl on television."

Gradually she managed to get some exposure in comedy. Casting director Joe Cates saw one of her appearances on the *Colgate Comedy Hour* and auditioned her for a skit opposite Jackie Gleason.

The first time Joyce and Gleason worked together was in late 1950. His TV show then was a local one, done live on New York's Channel 5. The sketch they did was a dramatic one. Two weeks later, at Gleason's request, she was hired again.

Joyce continued in the role of "Trixie" until 1957, when Gleason moved his home and production company to Florida. Ms. Randolph did some commercials after that but has devoted most of her time and energies to being a wife and mother. She married in 1955.

Mostly likely, her years as "Trixie Norton" would have remained only a happy memory had it not been for the *25th Anniversary Salute to the Honeymooners* in 1975. The idea for the TV special was born at a dinner party in Las Vegas attended by Gleason, Art Carney, Audrey Meadows, and Jane Kean. Ms. Kean played "Trixie" beginning in 1966, when the series was reactivated. It was she who was signed for the special.

Joyce let it be known through an interview in the *New York Daily News* how annoyed and hurt she was not to have been asked to play the part she had created. The *News,* owner of New York's Channel 11, which carried *The Honeymooners* reruns, hired Ms. Randolph to host a special of their own immediately preceding Gleason's show. Ads proclaiming the program to be "The Real Original Honeymooners Special" were run. Joyce's participation was emphasized with copy reading: *JOYCE RANDOLPH WHO WILL NOT BE SEEN ON THE ABC* HONEYMOONERS *SPECIAL TONIGHT. . . .*

Joyce Randolph lives in Manhattan. She occasionally is seen on television commercials.

Hosting her own show made Ms. Randolph feel a bit better about what she sees now as an awkward situation. "I don't blame Jackie or Jane Kean," she has said. "I'm sure that had I been at the dinner he'd have asked me. Of course, I wasn't invited to that dinner, either. It wasn't for the money that I wanted to appear on that show. I never had an agent when I played 'Trixie,' so I didn't make much from it ever, and the residuals stopped long ago. My husband is the executive vice-president of an advertising agency and can well afford to support me. But 'Trixie' was the highlight of my career, and I really thought I deserved to play her one last time." So did most viewers.

Joyce's son, Randy, is a student at Yale. Joyce and her husband live in a large apartment overlooking Central Park in Manhattan.

During 1941, <u>Inner Sanctum Mystery</u>'s first year on the air, Boris Karloff* (left) *was a frequent guest. Later Raymond played host to other Hollywood stars, such as Peter Lorre, Claude Rains, and Raymond Massey.

"Raymond, Your Host"

Raymond Edward Johnson was born in Kenosha, Wisconsin, on July 24, 1911. He feels his resonant voice, which became famous over the radio in the forties, was inherited from his father, a steelworker who was known for his oratory at labor meetings. Johnson's sister, Dora, who is again living in Kenosha, was "Evie," the daughter of radio's "Ma Perkins."

After studying drama at Chicago's Goodman Theatre he taught at a small college for a while. One of his students, he says, "had the acting bug but wasn't sure he had the gift. His name was Malden Sekulovich." He later became known as Karl Malden.

Raymond began on radio in Chicago, playing on such shows as *Lights Out, Today's*

Children, and *The Story of Mary Marlin.* When the last program moved to New York City, Johnson was sent for to continue his running part.

Inner Sanctum Mysteries began over the Blue Network on January 7, 1941, sponsored by Carters Little Liver Pills. It was Johnson's idea that he be referred to only as "Raymond, your host." Although his full name was not generally known to the public, the macabre character he portrayed became nationally famous almost at once. The scripts provided him with grim jokes that were always followed by Raymond's chuckle, a sound of ghoulish glee. His appearance was prefaced and concluded with the sound of an unevenly hung door opening and closing very slowly on rusty hinges. *Inner Sanctum*'s squeaking door was as famous in those years as "Fibber McGee's" closet. At the end of each show, as Raymond closed the door he said, "Good niii-iight . . . pleasant dreeeaammss."

Recently Johnson talked about *Inner Sanctum Mysteries* and how it changed the course of his career: "I was a leading man on *Mary Marlin.* That was my category as an actor until I became the host of *Inner Sanctum.* I used to act on as many as five shows a day, but *Inner Sanctum* wasn't on the air very long before those jobs were no longer available to me. But the pay was very good, and I continued playing 'Raymond, your host' until I went into the service during World War II. After I was discharged I refused to resume the role. I was determined not to be typecasted in horror parts."

In 1945 he was about to leave for Hollywood to make a movie with Evelyn Keyes when he realized that he was physically unable. Multiple sclerosis, the disease he had been fighting, had reached the stage where his walking was impaired.

Johnson and his wife, actress Betty Kane, moved to Vermont. When they divorced in 1971 Raymond took an apartment by himself in Wallingford, Connecticut. His degenerative condition has not affected his famous voice and he still makes recordings.

During the heyday of his career Johnson's opinion of radio was considerably different than it is today. He felt that acting so much before a microphone kept him from his real goal, which was the theatre. "Like a lot of actors," he says, "I had my nose in the air about radio. It's funny how things work out, because I know now that I wouldn't be remembered at all had it not been for *Inner Sanctum.* I had no idea that those radio plays we did so long ago meant so much to so many people. It is very gratifying to know that."

Raymond Edward Johnson, who spends all his waking hours in a motorized wheelchair, says of his present circumstances, "These are the richest days of my life."

Peter Schaeffer

Although he is confined to a wheelchair, Raymond lives by himself in Wallingford, Connecticut. He says of his present circumstances, "These are the richest days of my life."

Duncan Renaldo as the "Cisco Kid."

Duncan Renaldo

The star of silents and early talkies, known to television audiences as the "Cisco Kid," was born in Spain on April 23, 1904, and named Renaldo Duncan. He arrived in the United States in 1921, when the ship on which he was a seaman caught fire in port in Baltimore. While waiting for the vessel to be repaired Renaldo met a movie director who showed him the drawings for a set to be made of Havana's docks. Renaldo, who had sketched since childhood, told him that the artist's renderings were incorrect. He offered to draw the set as it should be, and was hired at $15 a week.

He became interested in movies and talked himself into a part in *Bright Shawl* (1923), which starred William Powell (married and living in Palm Springs), Jetta Goudal (married to interior designer Howard Grieve and living in Los Angeles), and Richard Barthelmess. After that Duncan appeared in the title roles in a number of shorts on Beethoven, Schubert, and Schumann. He continued to act in films but was also assistant director, director, assistant producer, and writer. *Down to the Sea in Ships* (1923), which first brought attention to Clara Bow, had him as assistant director. The year before he had traveled with his friend Robert Flaherty as Flaherty's assistant on the famous documentary *Nanook of the North.*

Renaldo had a lead role in Thornton Wilder's *Bridge of San Luis Rey* (1929). He had been impressed with the book, but could not interest a studio or producer in its merits. Finally Renaldo optioned the property and then sold it to Charles Brabin, the director-husband of Theda Bara, who sold it to Metro for $50,000. Renaldo got $5000 and was promised the part. His performance won him his role in the same studio's first all-talkie, *Trader Horn* (1931). M-G-M spent over $3 million and shot 5.5 million feet of film throughout Africa to make the classic, in which the only other white performers were the late Harry Carey and the beautiful Edwina Booth, who became seriously ill during the shooting. Although it is widely believed that she died shortly after the picture was made, she lives in Los Angeles. She still suffers from the disease she contracted in Africa fifty years ago.

Louis B. Mayer was attracted to Edwina Booth but had been rejected by her. He believed Renaldo and his leading lady were having an affair. Through Mayer's connivance, Duncan was arrested and charged with entering the U.S. illegally. He served eighteen months in federal prison before he was pardoned by President Roosevelt. After his release Mayer sought to have him blacklisted. Renaldo told his story after Mayer's death, but never with even a trace of bitterness. Although he suffered the breakup of his first marriage and the loss of every cent he had, Duncan always referred to the episode as "an interesting time for me as a human being, a time of great personal growth."

The last episode of the *Cisco Kid* series was filmed in 1956, but the series is still playing on television around the world. It was as the "Cisco Kid," in both features and television shows, that Renaldo made his comeback. His last movie was *Satan's Cradle* (1949).

Duncan died of heart failure on September 3, 1980. He had been living in the hills of Santa Barbara with his wife, whom he married in 1956. The Renaldos had two sons and a daughter. He was active to the end of his life as a director of Santa Barbara's annual fiesta, and traveled widely making personal appearances as the "Cisco Kid." He had remained in touch through the years with Edwina Booth and Racquel Torres (living in Malibu), his leading lady in *Bridge of San Luis Rey*.

Richard Lamparski

Duncan Renaldo in his home in Santa Barbara, California, in 1978.

Tommy Rettig played Lassie's master on Lassie for four seasons in the fifties.

Tommy Rettig

Lassie's master was born Thomas Noel Rettig on December 10, 1941, in Jackson Heights, New York. A drama teacher who lived in his building wanted Tommy in her classes, but his parents were reluctant to spend money on what they thought was a very chancy profession. When he was five and a half years old, the teacher asked permission to take him to an audition for the part of "Little Jake" in the road company of *Annie Get Your Gun,* with Mary Martin in the starring role. Tommy toured forty-two cities. His salary was $60 a week.

From his role in that Irving Berlin musical, Tommy got work in such feature films as *Panic in the Streets* (1950), *Two Weeks with Love* (1950), *The Strip* (1951), and *Gobs and Gals* (1952). In 1953 he began playing "Jeff" on the first of television's *Lassie* series. When he was signed at a beginning salary of $500 a week, he had never seen any of the Lassie movies, nor had he read the books about the famous collie. But he spent the next four years on *Lassie,* working about thirty weeks a year. For the last season he was paid $2500 a week. He was replaced by Jon Provost.

Lassie was both good and bad for Rettig, professionally and personally. Viewed by millions of Americans every Sunday evening, the show made Rettig one of Hollywood's hottest boy actors. He commanded top money for his roles in such movies as *So Big* (1953), *The 5,000 Fingers of Dr. T* (1953), and *The Egyptian* (1954) with Edmund Purdom (living in Rome). But he also soon realized that he was hopelessly typecast as an actor. After he was no longer a big TV star, parts were few and far between. Being 5 feet 5 inches tall didn't help either. His personal life was hurt by *Lassie*'s six-day-a-week shooting schedule. It restricted dating. "When I found that it was my last season I was ecstatic," he said. "I had gotten to the point where I really resented not being able to go out except on Saturday nights. Of course, when I did date girls their parents always trusted me more because of my goody-goody TV image. The fools!" But he did develop close personal ties with Jan Clayton, who played his mother, and Rudd

Weatherwax, Lassie's owner and trainer, and has remained friendly with both.

When he made *River of No Return* (1954) with Marilyn Monroe, Joe DiMaggio autographed a baseball for him. His last movie was *The Last Wagon* (1956). The two parts that he wanted very much to play were the lead in the Broadway company of *The Member of the Wedding* and the film *Blue Denim.* Both went to the late Brandon de Wilde.

In 1959 Tommy married fifteen-year-old Darlene Portwood, whom he met while she was waiting for a bus. Tommy had been her big crush in grammar school. Both of their sons are music majors at the University of California at San Diego. The Rettigs were divorced in 1976.

By 1966 Tommy had to face the fact that he simply could not make a living as an actor. His agent couldn't even get him bit parts, and Tommy tried selling men's wear and working in an electronics shop and a real estate office, but all of it bored him.

Tom, as he now prefers to be called, is a resident of Los Angeles. He currently conducts Alternativity, a personal-growth workshop that he designed to help people learn the successful management of recreational drugs. He has been arrested twice on misdemeanor marijuana charges, in 1972 and 1975. He pleaded guilty to possession for personal use, and served a total of three years probation on both charges, which were dismissed at the end of his probation. He has also been arrested twice on felony charges, in 1975 and 1980. The 1975 charge was dropped; the other was not filed, and he has never been incarcerated.

Tom has been quoted a number of times as saying that he was handicapped by a very poor education in the studio schools. He never made such a statement, nor is that his belief. He was a precocious reader, has considerable expertise in a variety of subjects, and is a very literate writer and public speaker.

"Today," he says, "it looks to some people like my life is a tragedy. They aren't seeing the whole picture. From my perspective, it's been absolutely terrific."

Richard Lamparski

Tom Rettig and Jan Clayton, who played his mother on <u>Lassie,</u> have remained close friends over the years. Both live in Los Angeles.

The Ritz Brothers in the late thirties

The Ritz Brothers

The zany trio were all born in Newark, New Jersey. Their mother was from Poland and their father, who was a saloonkeeper, was born in Austria-Hungary. Their original family name was Joachim.

Al was born on August 27, 1901, Jimmy on October 23, 1904, and Harry on May 28, 1907. They were brought up in the Williamsburg section of Brooklyn.

Al was in his teens when he began dancing in amateur contests. Soon he was winning prizes of $5 and $10. While he was developing into an accomplished ballroom dancer his younger brothers, who were still in school, began entertaining on street corners around Coney Island. Al entered an important dance contest at Jazzland on Broadway that was judged by Sophie Tucker and the famed stuttering comic Joe Frisco. Ms. Tucker was a close friend of Mrs. Joachim and the godmother of Jimmy. Al and his partner, Annette Nelson, won first prize and eventually got married.

ATER Harry won first prize in a dance competition at Coney Island the boys decided to team up. Their agent, Lou Irwin, suggested they get a different name. Al took Ritz from a passing laundry truck, and they started appearing in an act modeled after the popular comic strip *Harold Teen*. Wearing pants with very wide legs, large bow ties, and little caps, they were a success right from the start at the Fox Theatre in Brooklyn in 1926. Their theme song, which they introduced, was "Collegiate."

The Ritz Brothers were brought to the attention of Earl Carroll, who featured them in his *Vanities of 1932*. They were also on the bill at the Palace Theatre and in *Continental Varieties* (1934).

The Ritzes were a smash hit at their engagement at the Clover Club, a famed gambling spot on the Sunset Strip. Darryl F. Zanuck, who was merging his new studio with Fox Films at the time, signed them to a contract. Their best pictures were the early ones they made at Twentieth Century–Fox: *Sing, Baby, Sing* (1937), *One in a Million* (1937), *On the*

Avenue (1937), in which Harry donned drag to mimic their costar Alice Faye, *You Can't Have Everything* (1937), *Life Begins at College* (1937) with Joan Marsh (married and living in Ojai, California), and *The Three Musketeers* (1939) with Pauline Moore (working with Christian women's groups in Los Angeles). But after B-unit producer Sol M. Wurtzel was put in charge of their films the boys balked. When they left a sneak preview of *Pack Up Your Troubles* (1939) Harry quipped, "We've gone from bad to Wurtzel!"

The Ritz Brothers took their high-energy nonsense to Universal Pictures, where they were paired with the Andrews Sisters in *Argentine Nights* (1940). They made a few more—*Behind the Eight Ball* (1942) with Carol Bruce (playing "Mama Carlson" on *WKRP Cincinnati)* and Johnny Downs and *Hi 'Ya Chum* (1943)—but were unhappy with the quality of their vehicles.

The nightclub business was booming in the forties and Al, Jimmy, and Harry were one of the top-salaried acts in the profession. They were among the first of the big names to play Las Vegas. In 1950 the Ritzes debuted on television in a Thanksgiving special produced by the late Max Liebman. They continued working in nightclubs right up until Al died during an engagement at the Roosevelt Hotel in New Orleans in December 1965. Since then, when Jimmy and Harry take their bows at the conclusion of their act there is a silhouette Al alongside them as they say, "The three of us thank you very much." They maintain that in all their years of living, working, and traveling together they never quarreled.

Although they say their individual contributions were about equal, most professionals think Harry was the most creative. Sid Caesar calls him "The funniest man of his time." Mel Brooks agrees. Jerry Lewis has stated that "We all borrowed and stole from him."

The Ritzes are often compared to the Marx Brothers, although their comedy differed greatly. The big put-down, which was Groucho's trademark, was never their style. The Ritzes did takeoffs. They parodied "Dr. Jekyll and Mr. Hyde," "Frankenstein," "Captain Bligh," and "Snow White and the Seven Dwarfs." Because they are thought of only as comedians, few recall that early in their careers the Ritzes were among the best precision dancers in show business.

Jimmy and Harry still make occasional appearances on talk shows and at one-night stands for substantial fees. They were on the screen for only about a minute in *Won Ton Ton, the Dog Who Saved Hollywood* (1976), but were well paid.

Harry, who has six children, lives with his wife in Las Vegas but spends much time visiting his brother in West Los Angeles. Their sister is Jimmy's next-door neighbor. They love to be recognized and still receive fan mail from all over the world. Together they are at work on the story of their lives, which they are calling *From Rags to Ritzes.*

Gawain Beirne-Keyt

Harry (mugging) and Jimmy Ritz recently in Hollywood.

Jean Rogers is remembered chiefly as "Dale Arden," the damsel in the rocket ship in two of the Flash Gordon serials.

Jean Rogers

"Flash Gordon's" girlfriend was born on March 25, 1916, in Watertown, Massachusetts. Both of her parents were Swedish immigrants. Her original name was Eleanor Dorothy Lovegren.

Jean had just graduated from high school and was planning to study art when she was chosen by the local newspaper as the entrant in a beauty contest being conducted by Paramount Pictures. She was the eventual winner of the first prize—a trip to Hollywood for an appearance in the feature *Eight Girls in a Boat* (1933).

Remaining in Hollywood, Jean spent a short time under contract to Warner Brothers before moving to Universal. There she was cast opposite Buster Crabbe in the serial *Flash Gordon* (1936). "We had fun doing it," she said recently. "But I certainly never thought that forty years later it would still be being shown. I was less than enthusiastic about making the sequel, and when I heard they were doing a third one I asked to be excluded." The last of the series, *Flash Gordon Conquers the Universe* (1940), had Carol Hughes (married to Frank Faylen and living in Hollywood) playing "Dale Arden."

Jean appeared in other serials: *The Adventures of Frank Merriwell* (1936), *Ace Drummond* (1936), *Secret Agent X-9* (1937), and *The Great Adventures of Wild Bill Hickock* (1938). Among her feature credits were *Stormy* (1935), *My Man Godfrey* (1936), *Reported Missing* (1937), *Time Out for Murder* (1938) with the late Michael Whalen, *Tail Spin* (1939) with Edward Norris, and *Pacific Rendezvous* (1942) with Lee Bowman. Her personal favorites are *Design for Scandal* (1941), in which she played a flip manicurist, and *Whistling in Brooklyn* (1943) with Red Skelton.

Jean Rogers was tested for the title role of *Rebecca,* which was played by Joan Fontaine, and for the part in *The Rains Came* that went to Brenda Joyce.

She was leading lady to John Wayne in *Conflict* (1936), Boris Karloff in *Night Key* (1937), and Glenn Ford in *Heaven with a Barbed Wire Fence* (1940), Ford's first picture.

Her only unpleasant memories are of the two films she made under the direction of the late Ricardo Cortez. Ms. Rogers has described him as "absolutely impossible—to me and everyone else on the set. No wonder he wasn't a success as a director."

Acting in movies was never anything more to Jean Rogers than a way to make a good living for herself and her ailing mother. Her last was *Second Woman* (1951) with Robert Young.

Jean has a daughter by her late husband, who was a literary agent. She lives by herself in one of the two houses she owns in Sherman Oaks, California. Until quite recently she did marketing surveys for two newspapers.

Jean Rogers and Buster Crabbe were brought together again at a nostalgia convention in Texas in 1977. "It was only the second time I'd seen Buster since we made those serials," she says. "I don't know what those kids expected when they flew us down there, but what they got was 'Flash' and 'Dale' as a couple of senior citizens."

Peter Schaeffer

Jean Rogers is the widow of a Hollywood literary agent. She lives by herself in Sherman Oaks, California.

Julie Stevens took over the title role in The Romance of Helen Trent in 1944.

"The Romance of Helen Trent"

"Time now for *The Romance of Helen Trent* . . . the real-life drama of Helen Trent, who—when life mocks her, breaks her hopes, dashes her against the rocks of despair—fights back bravely, successfully, to prove what so many women long to prove: that because a woman is thirty-five or more, romance in life need not be over; that the romance of youth can extend into middle life, and even beyond. . . ."

Thus began the trials and tribulations of the middle-aged Hollywood fashion designer who was listened to over the CBS Radio Network from 1933 until 1960. As many as four million listeners turned in to the fifteen-minute program five days each week. The show opened and closed with "Juanita," hummed by Stanley Davis, who accompanied himself on the guitar.

"Helen's" admirers included a millionaire, a gangster, a movie star, a hypnotist, and even a psychotic, but her fans knew that her real love was the handsome lawyer "Gil Whitney," played by David Gothard. Many times they nearly married; the postponements became one of radio's running gags. The series began in Chicago with Virginia Clarke in the lead role. "Helen's" husband had disappeared at sea, and she lived with her companion, a maiden lady named "Agatha Anthony," who was played by the now deceased Bess McCammon.

"Helen" became so popular and her image so fixed that when, following the script, she once ventured into the stateroom of a male fellow-passenger while on a pleasure cruise, the network was flooded with mail demanding a proper explanation. Despite her established chic dress and manner, her creators had welded a fictional character of spotless reputation.

Julie Stevens took over the part when the series moved to New York in 1944, the same year she married Charles Underhill, an executive with U.S. Steel, between broadcasts. Auditions for the "New York" "Helen" had been held on a rainy day that coincided with the last broadcast of *Kitty Foyle,* a radio soap opera featuring Julie Stevens in the title role. Julie had walked across the street and, soaking wet and depressed, been greeted in the CBS lobby by an actress who had just finished auditioning for the part. "Julie," she said, "why on earth did you come over on a day like this for this part? Dear, you are far too young to play the role." Ms. Stevens played the role for the next sixteen years. Nearly as famous as "Helen," but never enjoying her popularity, was "Cynthia Swanson," the millionaire widow who managed to marry "Gil" for a time. Her part was written and played for a heavy, and was acted by Mary Jane Higy, at the time the star of radio's *When a Girl Marries.* In her autobiography, *Tune in Tomorrow* (1968), Mary Jane recounted her life as daytime radio's most hated character; most of her mail those days was unsigned and decidedly unflattering.

Unlike radio's *Ma Perkins* or *Just Plain Bill, Helen Trent* was not sought out by fans for advice. Instead, she was inundated with suggestions about her love life. If she took her listeners' counsel to heart, it must have been some of the worst advice ever given: she was constantly involved with suicides, murders, divorces, and assorted squabbles. According to Julie, "Helen was only sophisticated on the surface. Basically she was a very naïve girl."

Despite its continued high ratings, CBS decided to cancel the series. When the show went off the air, *Time* magazine ran an obituary giving it the title of the oldest of all soap operas, outlasting *Ma Perkins* by three weeks. The show had ended with "Helen" about to marry "Gil," just short of the minister pronouncing them man and wife—in case it ever went back on the air. The Hummerts, the senior producers, were taking no chances. After all, the husband who disappeared at sea could always come through the church door in the nick of time.

When, after those decades of dates, engagements, estrangements, and postponements, the two finally did go to the altar, it was because "Helen" had asked "Gil" to marry her. Perhaps from sheer exhaustion, he responded, "You bet!"

The late David Gothard ("Gil Whitney"), photographed in 1975.

Julie Stevens lives on Cape Cod and operates Weasie's Boutique in Orleans, Massachusetts.

Betty Rowland got star billing in burlesque houses from coast to coast as the "Ball of Fire."

Betty Rowland

Burlesque's "Ball of Fire" was born Betty Jane Rowland in Columbus, Ohio, on January 23. Betty and her two sisters, Diann and Rozelle, took dancing lessons from a very early age. After appearing locally in talent shows, Diann and Betty began touring in vaudeville as a sister act.

When the Depression hit, the Rowlands were out of a job for several months until an agent got them into the chorus line of the famous Old Howard Theatre in Boston. The year was 1932. At first they did their specialty act and kept their clothes on. But after a short time they went on as singles and both became strippers.

For their parents it seemed the end of the world. Their father was a probation officer, who was so strict that he refused to allow his wife to wear a bathing suit on a public beach. "But he soon came around," said Betty recently. "Dad ended up keeping scrapbooks on all three of us girls."

Her older sister, Diann, was appearing in a Detroit nightclub when she died of a heart condition in 1945. The youngest Rowland, Rozelle, became a burlesque star in her own right and was billed as the "Golden Girl." She is now married to a titled Belgian and is known as the Baroness Empain. She and her wealthy husband have homes in Paris and New York.

Betty was shorter than most of the queens of the runway and found that moving her body in 6/8 time made her seem taller. A less accomplished dancer would have been simply vulgar, but Betty moved not only quickly but very gracefully, and her clothes fell by the wayside very slowly. Her musical theme was "In the Mood." Reviewers compared her to a whirling dervish. Not only were her features very pretty and her proportions generous, but she had skin like satin.

Orson Welles, whom she used to date, offered her a dramatic role in the stage production *Five Kings,* but Betty passed it up. She loved burlesque and has no regrets. At the time she was making $2000 a week peeling.

Betty gave it all up in 1951 for marriage to a wealthy lumberman. They shared a Bel-Air mansion until their divorce in 1964.

Of late Betty has been visiting with Rozelle in Paris for lengthy stays. The Rowlands are working on their combined memoirs, to be entitled *A Tale of Two Sisters.*

The "Ball of Fire" lives by herself in a garden apartment of a luxury building in Brentwood. She still sees her contemporary Margie Hart (living in Beverly Hills) and many of her old fans. They drop in to see her at Mr. B's, a bar in Santa Monica. She works there several nights a week as a bartender. She doesn't need the money but admits that the attention paid her is pleasing. "I don't miss burlesque the way it is now, but I think about the good old days a lot. The kids stripping today don't know what a wonderful business it was," she says. If the management of Mr. B's requests it and she is in the mood, Betty Rowland will still strip.

Betty Rowland can be found behind the bar at Mr. B's in Santa Monica, California.

Paul Schaeffer

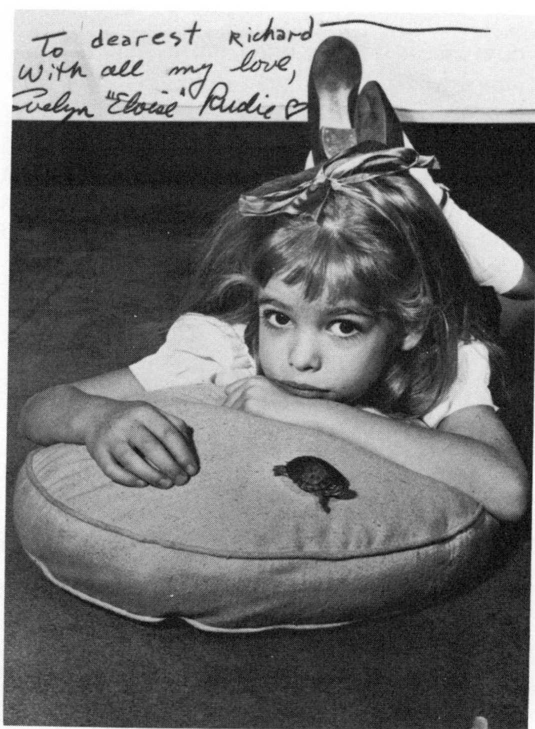

Evelyn Rudie as she appeared on the Playhouse 90 dramatization of Kay Thompson's Eloise in 1956.

Evelyn Rudie

The child actor who became a household name playing the title role in *Eloise* was born in Los Angeles on March 28.

Evelyn's parents had no plans for her to enter show business when her uncle took her with him on a visit to Henry Koster's home. The director thought she looked right to play Leslie Caron as a child in the film musical *Daddy Long Legs* (1955). Koster sent her to the picture's director, Jean Negulesco, who gave her the part.

"Eloise," the character created by Kay Thompson, was a rich little girl who lived at the Plaza Hotel in Manhattan. The original idea had been for the author to speak the lines, but two days before the production was telecast it was decided that Evelyn as "Eloise" would deliver her own dialogue. She did, going through the ninety-minute live show without a single mistake. She was eight years old at the time.

Evelyn got splendid notices for *Eloise.* Through sheer force of personality and an incredible sense of publicity she emerged more famous than the fictional child. Her press conferences from then on were better attended than those of top stars. It had been many years since Hollywood had had a child star, and the press put her on at every opportunity, encouraging her to speak out on every conceivable ill in the world. A precocious little girl, Evelyn needed little prompting.

During the rest of the fifties she appeared more in the newspapers and magazines than in television and movies. Her personality and image were so strong that it was difficult to cast her, though she appeared as a guest on many TV shows, more times than not playing herself, and just about every interviewer around had her on to say something cute.

The only two outstanding bits of work she did at that time were her appearance in the television special *The Red Mill* and a movie, *The Gift of Love,* in which she costarred with

Lauren Bacall. Both of these were in 1958.

The demise of Evelyn Rudie as a child star and public personality came one year later, when the Hollywood police, the Federal Bureau of Investigation, and all the news services were alerted that Evelyn was missing. Hours later she was "found" aboard a plane bound for Washington, D. C. Once, during a casual meeting with Mamie Eisenhower, Evelyn had been invited to visit the White House. On the spur of the moment, without informing anyone, the girl took money from her piggy bank and went off to visit the First Lady.

Almost nothing has been heard of Evelyn Rudie since. Her parents were adamant that she get a good education before accepting any more roles. She attended Hollywood High School and studied dance, piano, and acting privately. Her marriage to actor Tim O'Kelly ended in an annulment after four months.

Today Evelyn and her husband of eleven years, Chris De Carlo, are directors of the Santa Monica Playhouse in Santa Monica, California. Evelyn and De Carlo act in some of the productions and direct many of them. It is an eight-member repertory company that functions independent of grants.

She is still recognized frequently, although her hair, which was bleached blonde for *Eloise*, has been its natural brunette for many years. She says the TV and movie roles that have been offered to her have never been ones that even tempted her.

Evelyn Rudie had what she calls "a fantastic time" during her brief time in the spotlight. "I had famous friends, a stand-in, and acquaintances all over the country. It was a really great childhood."

Evelyn acts and directs at the Santa Monica Playhouse.

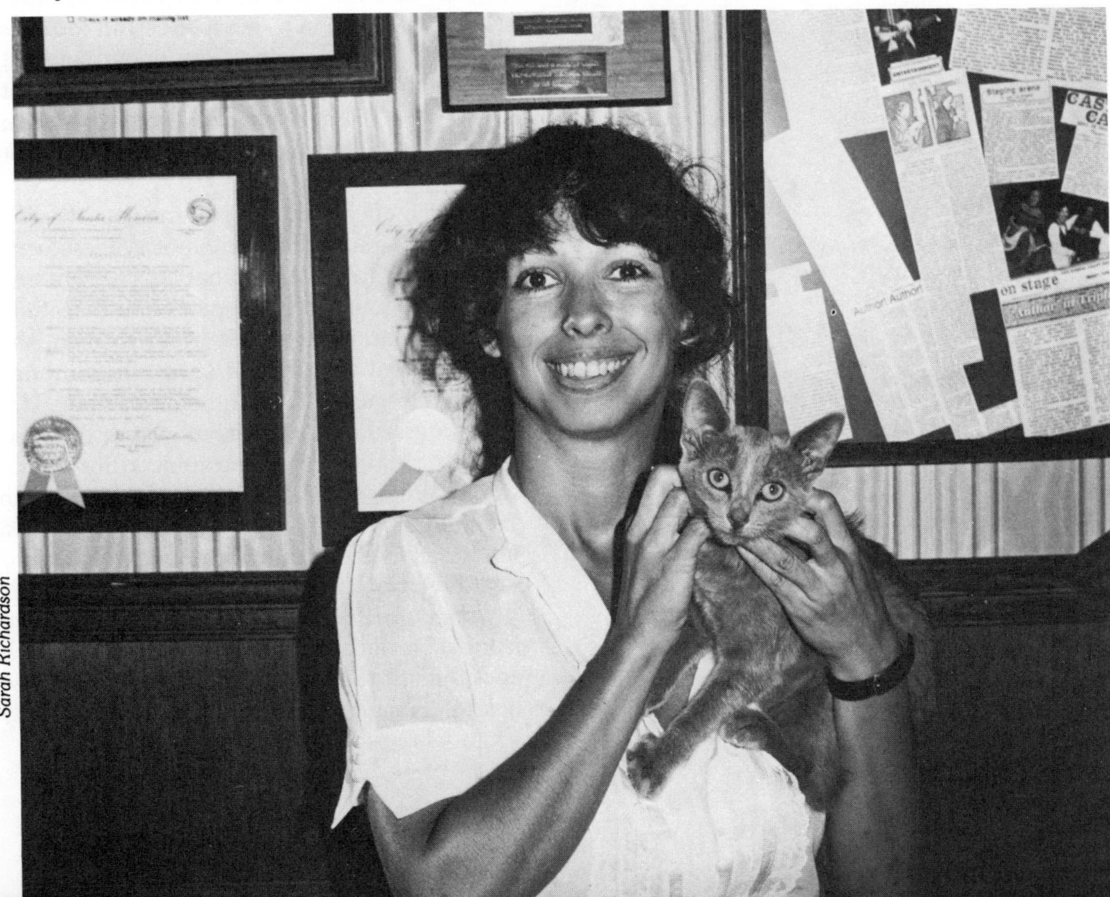

Sarah Richardson

In Whistling in Dixie (1942) with Red Skelton.

Ann Rutherford

The actress best remembered for playing Andy Hardy's girlfriend was born in Toronto, Canada, on November 2, 1920. Her father was a tenor with the Metropolitan Opera. Her mother, Lucille Mansfield, had played second lead in the Pearl White serials. Thérèse Ann Rutherford was in the first grade when her family moved to San Francisco. She performed in a number of plays there, and when she was eleven the family settled in Los Angeles.

One day, after being reprimanded by a teacher for reading Edna St. Vincent Millay in class instead of doing her assignment, Ann decided on a change of pace. She roller-skated to KFAC and auditioned for and got one of the title roles in the radio series *Nancy and Dick in the Spirit of '76*. It was sponsored by the DAR. Richard Quine (now a movie director) was featured in the role of "Dick." She had been on the radio for several years when an agent saw Ann's photo in a newspaper and took her to Mascot Films. She was put under contract, and debuted in *Waterfront Lady* (1935). Ann was Gene Autry's leading lady in several features and played opposite John Wayne in six westerns.

Shortly after Ann began making movies, Jack La Rue and the late Grant Withers were pointed out to her. Both had been stars and were now doing featured parts in a B picture. When she asked how that could happen, she was told that they hadn't saved their money and had to take whatever they could get. This so impressed her that even when she was making $500 a week, she took a bus to the studio. When M-G-M, which had signed her in 1937, threatened to drop her option if she did not forfeit the raise due her, she merely waved a fat bankbook at them and called their bluff.

Although she has been in seventy-three features, including *Gone With the Wind* (1939) and *Orchestra Wives* (1942), most fans know her for playing "Polly" in the famed *Hardy* series. She is pleased with the way it turned out, but originally she did not want the role. She remembers having to stand in a hole in scenes with Mickey Rooney, so she wouldn't look much taller than he.

Her other movies included *Dancing Co-Ed* (1939) with the late Richard Carlson, *Happy Land* (1943) with Dickie Moore, and *Whistling in Brooklyn* (1944). After she left M-G-M in 1942, her only film of any importance was *The Secret Life of Walter Mitty* (1947). When Metro called her back for a role in *They Only Kill Their Masters* (1972), it was her first picture in twenty-two years. Much of it was shot on the old *Andy Hardy* set, just before it was razed to make way for a shopping center.

Ann did some TV during the 1950s, such as *Playhouse 90* and *Studio One,* but now has very little interest in working. Her second husband, William Dozier, whom she married in 1953, asked her to guest on his *Batman* TV series, but she wouldn't. Her first marriage, for eleven years, was to department store heir David May.

Ann lives in a big white colonial house in Beverly Hills. Weekends are spent at the Dozier's Malibu beach house. She and her husband, who was previously married to Joan Fontaine, are very much a part of the Hollywood social scene. Ann likes to make paper flowers and refinishes furniture, which she enjoys more than movie-making. "I don't miss my profession because I'm married to a producer," she says. "I read all the trade papers and hear all the gossip, but now I'm more of it than in it, and that's fine with me."

Jon Virzi

On her way to a recent social function in Beverly Hills.

Randolph Scott in 1938.

Randolph Scott

The "strong, silent type" star was born on his father's country etate in Orange County, Virginia, on January 23, 1903. His grandfather at fourteen fought with Stonewall Jackson. Scott's family were among the earliest settlers of Virginia. He was educated at Woodberry Forest Prep School, where he excelled in sports. He attended Georgia Tech and played on the football team until he seriously hurt his knee. After that he took a degree from the University of North Carolina.

Shortly after Randolph came to Hollywood he was introduced to Howard Hughes, who brought him to the attention of Cecil B. De Mille. The director considered him for a part in *Dynamite* but felt he needed some training as an actor. Instead of returning home to work as an engineer for his father, Scott cashed in his return train ticket and enrolled at the Pasadena Playhouse.

Randy's earliest screen credit was for *The Far Call* (1929), a feature with music and sound effects but no dialogue. Scott was billed last. He was with Sally Blane in *Women Men Marry* (1931). He supported George Arliss in *A Successful Calamity* (1932), Nancy Carroll in *Hot Saturday* (1932), and Kate Smith in *Hello, Everybody* (1933). *She* (1935) had him leading man to the late Helen Gahagan Douglas, and in *The Last of the Mohicans* (1936) he played with Heather Angel (widowed and living in Montecito, California). *Roberta* (1935) and *Follow the Fleet* (1936) both gave his career a big boost. Mae West chose him for *Go West, Young Man* (1936). Then he made *High, Wide and Handsome* (1937), *Road to Reno* (1938), and *Jesse James* (1939). Cary Grant, with whom he shared a beach house for some time, costarred with Randy and Irene Dunne in *My Favorite Wife* (1940). He was leading man to Elizabeth Bergner (widowed and living in London) in *Paris Calling* (1942). *The Spoilers* (1942) and *Pittsburgh* (1943) followed, both with Marlene Dietrich.

From then on, Randolph Scott made practically nothing but westerns. Some of the latter, especially those he produced in conjunction with the late Harry Joe Brown for Columbia, are regarded as minor classics by cowboy cognoscenti. The first such was *Gunfighters* (1947); the last was *Comanche Station* (1960). Among his other westerns were *Union Pacific* (1939), *Abilene Town* (1946) and *Canadian Pacific* (1949). Until his swan song, *Ride the High Country* (1961) with his close friend Joel McCrea, Scott remained one of the top male box-office draws in the world. He has since then turned down a fortune in offers to star in television.

Randy, whose private life was never featured much in his publicity, lives with his second wife across the street from Dorothy McGuire in Beverly Hills. They were married in 1944 after he divorced his childhood sweetheart, who was a member of Du Pont family.

He spends much of his time playing golf at the snobby Los Angeles Country Club, where he is one of the handful of movie people ever admitted to membership. Asked why he was allowed in, one of the club's directors replied, "Because we think of Randy as a gentleman who for a time acted."

He keeps a close watch on his interests in oil and natural gas, which have made him many millions of dollars. The Scotts are often seen at Sunday services at the Beverly Hills Presbyterian Church, sometimes accompanied by their son and daughter.

He was friendly with Richard Arlen until the latter's death in 1976, and was pallbearer at the funeral of western character actor Edgar Buchanan in 1979. One of the few Randy still sees from his movie days is Steffi Duna, the widow of Dennis O'Keefe.

Jon Virzi

Randolph Scott lives quietly with his family in Beverly Hills.

To those who contact Randolph Scott from all over the world seeking interviews and photos, his response is always the same—a very polite but firm "Thanks for asking but that is no longer a part of my life."

Vivienne Segal was making musicals in Hollywood in 1930.

Vivienne Segal

The singing star of Broadway and early movie musicals was born in Philadelphia on April 19, 1897. Her father was a physician, Dr. Bernhard Segal, who strongly disapproved of girls going on the stage. He had an extensive collection of operatic recordings. Her mother, however, was very ambitious for the exceptionally pretty Vivienne.

She studied dancing from an early age and imitated the voices she heard on Dr. Segal's phonograph. In grammar school she began playing in amateur theatricals, usually taking a leading role. After several appearances in musicals Vivienne sang the title role of *Carmen* at the Philadelphia Academy of Music. On the strength of her notices she was called to New York City to audition for J. J. Shubert and Sigmund Romberg, who needed a last-minute replacement for the leading lady in *The Blue Paradise.* Taking over on four days' notice, Vivienne got excellent reviews, most of which mentioned her extreme youth. By the end of its one-year run she was a star and her father had come around.

In 1922 she was in *The Yankee Princess,* and was seen on the stage of the Palace Theatre the following year. Then came *Adrienne* (1923), *Ziegfeld Follies of 1924, Florida Girl* (1925), and *Castles in the Air* (1926).

The real triumph of her early years was heading the cast of the original production of *The Desert Song* (1926). Two years later Flo Ziegfeld starred her as "Lady Constantine" in his successful musical adaptation of *The Three Musketeers.*

Warner Brothers brought her to Hollywood and starred her in *Song of the West* (1930), *Bride of the Regiment* (1930), *Viennese Nights* (1930), and *Golden Dawn* (1930). These early talkies offered music and two-strip color photography but were only moderately successful at the box office. She returned to Broadway for *The Chocolate Soldier* (1931) and then made another movie musical, *The Cat and the Fiddle* (1934) with Jeanette MacDonald and Ramon Novarro. But she remained essentially a stage star.

Vivienne lost nearly every cent she had when the stock market crashed in 1929. Her radio work during the thirties literally kept a roof over her head and enabled her to support her widowed mother, who lived with her.

When she opened in 1938 in *I Married an Angel* it was the first time Broadway audiences had seen her in eight years. She returned in one of the hits of that season.

Two years later *Pal Joey,* which had been written for her by John O'Hara, changed the course of the American musical theatre. Audiences saw her playing a somewhat older, still very beautiful woman who is keeping a young man. "What really shocked people," says Vivienne, "is that he was a heel."

Brooks Atkinson concluded his review in the *New York Times* with the question "Can you draw sweet water from a foul well?"

Twelve years later the revival of *Pal Joey* starring Vivienne Segal was a big hit all over again and seemed much less daring. Harold Lang (teaching choreography and dance at California State University, Chico) played the title role, which had been originated by Gene Kelly. She brought to the highly sophisticated role her own warmth and vulnerability. Singing "Bewitched, Bothered and Bewildered," which she had introduced in 1940, she was for the second time in the same show the toast of Broadway.

After *Pal Joey* closed Vivienne let it be known that she was no longer interested in performing. "Like a damn fool I thought I would just be Mrs. Hubbell Robinson, Jr.", she explained recently. "He was head of production for CBS Television at the time. I thought a busy, powerful man would want a wife to come home to. By the time I figured out that he'd have preferred to see his wife's name in lights, the marriage was over." In the mid-twenties Vivienne had been married to and divorced from Hollywood and Broadway leading man Robert Ames. She had been legally separated from Robinson for over a decade when he died.

In the living room of her Los Angeles home are photos signed to her by some of the composers whose songs she sang: Richard Rogers, Oscar Hammerstein, and Noel Coward. Most of her friends are people she has known for many years. Because of a heart condition Ms. Segal lives quietly, watching documentaries and game shows on TV. Asked how she would describe her present life style, Ms. Segal replied, "Stagnation. Luxurious stagnation."

Bobby Downey

Vivienne Segal at age eighty-four.

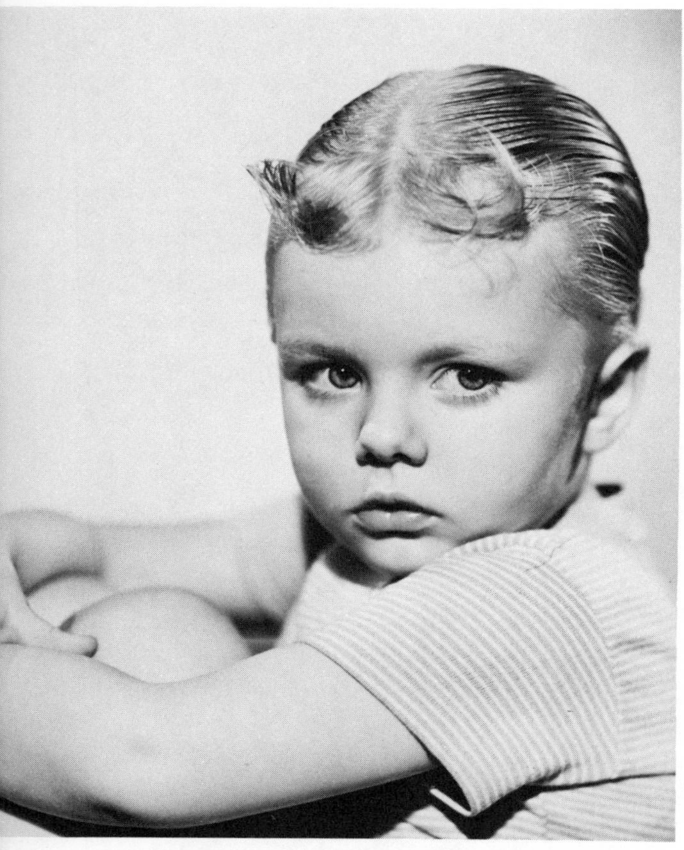

Larry played "Baby Dumpling," or "Alexander Bumstead," in twenty-eight Blondie movies.

Larry Simms: "Baby Dumpling"

The boy who became world famous playing the son of Arthur Lake and Penny Singleton in the *Blondie* movies was born in Santa Monica on October 1, 1934. His mother sang under the name Margaret Lawrence with Jimmy Greer's band at the Coconut Grove.

When Larry was three years old he modeled for the cover of the *Saturday Evening Post.* Someone at Columbia Pictures spotted his picture and suggested him for the part of "Baby Dumpling," a character in the Bumstead family. The studio was about to make films of the highly popular *Blondie* comic strip, created by the late Chic Young. The day they finished shooting the first of the features, *Blondie* (1938), the cast presented Larry with a big cake and a tricycle. It was his fourth birthday.

The pictures were always considered Bs but were very popular, due chiefly to the casting. As Larry matured "Blondie" and "Dagwood" began calling him "Alexander Bumstead." Simms has explained what the change meant to him: "There was never anything about picture-making that turned me on or off. It was just something I did. But when 'Baby Dumpling' changed to 'Alexander,' that was the high point of the whole experience for me. It meant that I got to wear long pants."

Larry made a few pictures besides the twenty-eight *Blondie* films: *Mr. Smith Goes to Washington* (1939), *The Gay Sisters* (1942), *Golden Earrings* (1947), and *Madame Bovary* (1949).

He had no particular interest in movies and saw only a few of his own. Larry spent all of his spare time with studio technicians. He wasn't a bit disappointed when the series came to an end with *Beware of Blondie* in 1950. He did not consider himself a natural actor, and no effort was made to get him other roles.

Larry made no close friends among the actors he worked with, but when he was married at age eighteen, Penny Singleton, who played his mother, "Blondie," came to the wedding. He hasn't seen or heard from his other screen parent, Arthur Lake, in many years. "Everyone at the studio was nice to me," says Larry. "But they were all adults. When there were parties on the lot I got to stir the cocktails and eat an occasional maraschino cherry."

When he was six years old his father and mother divorced. His salary, which reached as high as $750 a week, went to educate and support him and his younger brother. Says Larry, "Michael never complained but I know there must have been times when he felt left out. I was always the one who got the attention. It used to worry me."

After getting out of the navy he studied aeronautical engineering at California Polytechnic. When he was only twenty-two Larry was in charge of one of the three overseas tracking stations for *Explorer I.* He was an engineer at the Jet Propulsion Lab in Pasadena from 1956 until he retired in 1974.

Larry has been divorced twice and is the father of three.

"Baby Dumpling" now lives on his boat in the waters off Hawaii.

Jon Virzi

Larry Simms is a retired aeronautical engineer. He lives on his boat in the waters off Hawaii.

***Howdy Doody Time* debuted on NBC-TV on December 27, 1947.**

Buffalo Bob Smith

The man who was to become the first—and the most popular—kiddy entertainer ever on television got his nickname from his home town in New York.

His first job in show business was as a member of a singing trio known as the "Hi-Hatters." In 1933, the year of Repeal, they were heard on a local radio program sponsored by a brewery. The following year Ted Collins (deceased) brought them to New York City, where they were featured on the *Hudson Terraplane Show,* which starred Kate Smith. Six months later Smith was back in Buffalo as a staff pianist and musical arranger at WBEN. He held various jobs in local radio until 1946, when the New York City NBC station, then called WEAF, hired him to do their morning show Monday through Saturday from 7 A.M. to 9 A.M.

For two years Smith pestered the network brass to try him on the technically primitive medium of television, without success. He developed the Howdy Doody character on his Saturday morning radio program, which was called *Triple B Ranch.* It was basically a quiz show for children.

Howdy Doody Time finally made TV on December 27, 1947, the day after New York's famous blizzard. Its time slot was 5:30 to 6:00 P.M., Monday through Friday. It was the first offering of the day on TV at that time and was preceded by the well-remembered test pattern of one geometric design or another. This was before coaxial cable had linked the East and West Coasts, and therefore it was seen only in six eastern cities.

A few weeks after the premiere Smith suggested to the sales department that he offer a free Howdy Doody pin to any boy or girl writing in. The mail pull would be an indication of his listenership, since rating services had not at that point been developed for the new medium. All the National Broadcasting Company knew was that there were approximately forty thousand television sets in the viewing area. In three days, eighty thousand requests were received. These were the days when a family with a TV set, its seven-inch screen made larger by a thick glass bubble in front of it, was watched by as many neighbors on the block as the living room could accommodate.

Still, no one had guessed that the red-haired puppet and his friends—John J. Fadoozle, America's Number-one *(Boing!)* private eye; Cornelius J. Cobb, storekeeper in the town of Doodyville; and Flub-a-Dub, Howdy's pet—had gained such popularity in so short a time. It was a success that was to continue and even increase until Smith suffered a heart attack in 1957 and switched to one show a week on Saturday mornings from 10:00 to 10:30 A.M.

The same year he completely sold out his interest in Howdy Doody items—T-shirts, dolls, spoons, dishes, and comic books—to NBC and took a whopping capital gains profit.

The Saturday show went off the air on September 30, 1960. The original "Clarabell," a clown who never spoke but was handy with a seltzer bottle, was played by Bob Keeshan, who became CBS's "Captain Kangaroo." Judy Tyler played "Princess Summerfallwinterspring" until she was killed in an automobile accident on July 4, 1956.

Howdy Doody's chief competitor was "Mr. I. Magination" ("the man with the magic reputation"), created and played by Paul Tripp. Tripp is now living in Manhattan with his wife. Both are actors.

Since 1960 Buffalo Bob has devoted most of his time to his family. Smith has been married to his first-grade classmate since 1940. The Smiths' oldest, Robin, is a urologist. Their youngest, Chris, just received a doctorate in psychology. The middle son, Ronnie, is a bond trader on Wall Street. Bob has four grandchildren.

Smith sold out his three radio stations and a liquor store some time ago and is living very quietly, per doctor's orders, after a serious operation in 1981. He plays golf and fishes at his homes in Maine and Lauderdale-by-the-Sea, Florida. The puppet Howdy Doody, which had three heads available, was returned to Buffalo Bob Smith after the death of Rufus Rose, the show's chief puppeteer.

Buffalo Bob Smith today with the original Howdy Doody puppet.

Charles Starrett was named by Motion Picture Herald for seven straight years as one of the top ten money-making western stars in the world.

Charles Starrett

The handsome star of over 130 westerns was born in Athol, Massachusetts, on March 28, 1903. At his preparatory school, Worcester Academy, Charles was the president of the dramatic club. He attended Dartmouth and made quite a name for himself as an athlete, as well as winning a scholarship to the American Academy of Dramatic Arts. He appeared as an extra in *The Quarterback* (1926), which only whetted his appetite to become an actor.

Charles spent two years with the Stuart Walker Stock Company and then tried his luck in New York City. He was in several flops, such as *Claire Adams* (1929). Then he got the lead in several low-budget pictures. One was *Damaged Love* (1931) with the late June Collyer. He had a very showy part in *The Mask of Fu Manchu* (1932) and was seen in *So Red the Rose* (1935). But still he was not much of a name. Then Columbia Pictures chose him to take over for the late Colonel Tim McCoy and Buck Jones in westerns.

His career as a cowboy began with *Gallant Defender* (1935) with Len Slye, who later became Roy Rogers, and ended with *The Kid from Broken Gun* (1952). He made between six and eight features a year, wearing a white hat and riding his horse "Raider." In most of them he was looked to for protection by the late Iris Meredith, whose dad was usually Ed Le Saint. About the most womenfolk could expect from Starrett was a big polite smile. Lurking somewhere was Dick Curtis, who played hulking brutes for all he was worth. There was sometimes a song or two from the "Sons of the Pioneers."

Starrett was an excellent horseman and a very pleasant man to work with. He was also the best-looking good guy in westerns, but not in the way that was thought of at the time as being sissified.

In 1940 Charles played the masked do-gooder in the title role of *The Durango Kid* (1945). It was so well received that it fathered *The Return of the Durango Kid* (1945). Starrett still signs most autographs "Charles 'Durango' Starrett."

Schedules on Starrett oaters were always tight. Because of this he sometimes found himself with as much as nine months a year in which he was free to pursue his hobbies of hunting and fishing while still drawing a very nice salary. When he left Columbia Pictures after seventeen years his producer, Samuel Briskin, objected to Starrett's keeping his six-gun and holster without paying for them. He found no difficulty in adjusting to retirement thirty years ago. For the first twenty-two years he wintered in a cabin he owned in the High Sierras, but because of a heart condition Starrett sold the cabin, concentrating on fishing. When he isn't traveling he lives in a large house a few steps from the Pacific Ocean in Laguna Beach, California. Wynne Gibson, who played his mother in *Lady and Gent* (1932), shares a house in nearby Laguna Niguel with Beverly Roberts.

Charles is especially proud of being one of the founding members of the Screen Actors Guild and holds the tenth membership card ever issued in the union.

The only evidence of his career around his home is his stationary bicycle, which he has named "Raider."

The loss of income from acting was no hardship, since his grandfather, who founded a large tool manufacturing company, left Starrett a block of stock in the firm.

He married his childhood sweetheart in 1927. They have twin sons and two grandchildren.

He has admitted that while his career as a cowpoke provided a very good life, he never realized his goal, which was to become a serious actor. He is delighted with the fan mail he receives from around the world. "It's a consolation prize for my old age," says Charlie with a laugh. "My family isn't a bit impressed with my career, and my neighbors think I'm one of them—a retired businessman."

Richard Lamparski

Charles Starrett and his wife of more than fifty years live a few steps from the Pacific Ocean in Laguna Beach, California.

Gale's first TV series, My Little Margie, premiered over the CBS network on June 16, 1952.

Gale Storm

The TV star of the 1950s was born Josephine Owaissa Cottle on April 5, 1921, in Bloomington, Texas. Her father died when she was seventeen months old.

In 1939 Gale was the winner of producer Jesse Lasky's "Gateway to Hollywood" talent search. She was put under contract to RKO Pictures but was dropped after only six months. Next she went to Monogram and then to Universal.

Gale Storm made very little impact in movies. In addition to appearing in several westerns as Roy Rogers's leading lady, she made *Tom Brown's School Days* (1940) with Freddie Bartholomew (the vice-president of a New York advertising agency), *Where Are Your Children?* (1943) with Patricia Morison (single and living in Los Angeles), *It Happened on Fifth Avenue* (1947) with the late Ann Harding, *Stampede* (1949) with Rod Cameron (living in Gainesville, Georgia), *The Underworld Story* (1950) with Dan Duryea, *The Kid from Texas* (1950) with Audie Murphy, *The Texas Rangers* (1951) with George Montgomery, and *Woman of the North Country* (1952) with Ruth Hussey (married and living in Carlsbad, California).

Gale's first television series, *My Little Margie,* was one of the most popular situation comedies on the air from 1952 to 1955. It is still being syndicated around the world. Her costar was Charles Farrell (living in Palm Springs), who played her father. After filming 126 of the thirty-minute episodes, she had her second hit with *Oh, Susanna.* It survived for three seasons in prime-time beginning in 1956. Slapstick and improbable situations were the mainstays of the plots of both. Occasionally Gale would sing.

In 1955 her record of "I Hear You Knocking" was for a while the second most popular disk in the nation. The same year the Gale Storm rendition of "Teen-Age Prayer" was on the hit charts for fifteen weeks straight. Two years later her "Dark Moon" was on *Billboard*'s "Top 100" list for twenty-three weeks. She has sold over four million records.

Since 1941 Gale has been married to Lee Bonnell, who for a time acted under the name Terry Belmont. He now owns an insurance agency near the Bonnells' home in Encino, California. They have three sons and a daughter. Gale's youngest, Susanna, was named for her television show. The Bonnells have been grandparents for several years.

Her appearances on TV since her shows went off have been very scarce. Because of reruns seen around the country, she can still command a sizable fee for dinner theatre productions of such shows as *Cactus Flower* and *The Unsinkable Molly Brown*. Although she has no financial need to work again, Gale by no means considers herself retired.

During the past couple of years the public has seen a new Gale Storm. She has been talking openly about her alcoholism. Although it never seemed to interfere with her career, the star had been a problem drinker for years before she committed herself to a program offered by the Raleigh Hills Hospital. Ms. Storm felt she had such positive results from the treatment that she has discussed it freely on talk shows and has appeared on TV commercials recommending it to others. If she startled many of her old fans, she also made a few new ones with her honesty.

Jon Virzi

Gale Storm and her husband live in Encino, California.

Matthew "Stymie" Beard made forty Our Gang comedies. They are now referred to on television as The Little Rascals.

"Stymie": Matthew Beard, Jr.

"Stymie" of *Our Gang* (now seen on television as *The Little Rascals)* was born Matthew Beard, Jr., in Los Angeles on New Year's Day 1925. His father was a minister of the Church of God in Christ. Throughout most of his childhood Matthew's parents were separated.

His mother got him a part in *Uncle Tom's Cabin* (1927) when he was only seventeen months old. When he was five his father heard that Hal Roach Studios needed a replacement for "Farina." Matthew flashed a dazzling smile and won the part over five hundred others. He appeared in eight two-reelers a year over the next five years.

Although he had not seen any of the other children from the shorts except "Buckwheat" for many years, he had fond memories of both the work and the play on the Roach lot. Among his friends were Patsy Kelly, Charlie Chase, and Laurel and Hardy. The role he played, however, embarrasses him still. "We knew even then that 'Stymie' was an insult to our race," he said in 1974, "but it was the Depression and I had seven sisters and six brothers at home."

Matthew's salary, which began at $100 a week in 1930, had been raised to $500 by the time he outgrew the role and was let go in 1935. The life that he had come to love and thought would go on forever had ended, and the ten-year-old boy was devastated.

He managed to get work in movies from time to time, in features such as *Captain Blood* (1935), *Jezebel* (1938), and *Stormy Weather* (1943), but not being under contract, he then had to attend public school. His tutoring on the Roach lot had put him two grades ahead of boys his age, and he was promptly demoted. The other children in the ghetto school envied his fame and taunted him constantly. "It wasn't *my* fault I was a star," he said laughingly years later.

Beard was using drugs even before graduating from high school. Being "Stymie" didn't matter a bit in the dives and prisons he spent so many of his adult years in. "I was just another junkie doing time," he said. Even after his release in 1963 after serving part of a twenty-year sentence for heroin, he returned to narcotics. But during a thirty-day stretch for petty theft he took a long, hard look at his prospects and went to Synanon, the drug rehabilitation center in Santa Monica where he lived for seven years.

"Stymie" was especially fond of children, although he never had any. During the last years of his life he toured grammar schools, showing his films and talking to the kids about the thirty-year drug nightmare he lived through.

His career was beginning to catch fire as he appeared on such TV shows as *Sanford and Son, East of Eden,* and *Backstairs at the White House.*

"Stymie" Beard and "Buckwheat" Thomas had remained close friends since the day they met on the Hal Roach lot. Both were saddened by the passing of Allen "Farina" Hoskins in August 1980. Two months later Beard attended the funeral of "Buckwheat." He was greatly surprised and disturbed that the services for "Buckwheat" were not better attended.

In early January 1981 Beard's brother found him on the floor of his Los Angeles apartment, the victim of a stroke. "Stymie" and his wife were divorced and he had lived by himself. He died on January 8.

"The director of those shorts, Robert McGowen, gave him the name 'Stymie,'" said his brother René recently. "Because he was always getting into things and would stymie the shooting. Poor guy, he was stymied himself all of his life. He had talent and everyone liked him, but he really never got his act together."

The funeral of Matthew "Stymie" Beard drew overflow crowds. He is buried at the Evergreen Cemetery in East Los Angeles.

"Stymie," Darla Hood, and William Thomas, Jr., the son of "Buckwheat," photographed in November 1976.

Richard Stanley

Blanche Sweet in 1928.

Blanche Sweet

Blanche Sweet was the name given to a beautiful child born on June 18, 1895, in Chicago, Illinois. She was to become one of the first important motion picture stars.

Ms. Sweet was a protégée of the great director D. W. Griffith, and was with him from 1909, on at the Biograph Studios on Manhattan's Fourteenth Street, until 1913, when she starred in the four-reeler *Judith of Bethulia.* She appeared in shorter photoplays such as *Smile of a Child* (1911) and *Eternal Mother* (1912). Mae Marsh and the Gish sisters, always thought of as very early players in silents, had only small roles in Blanche's first important feature.

Her screen image was one of courage and resilience at a time when most of her contemporaries were child-women or vamps. In a number of her early pictures, such as *Goddess of Sagebrush Gulch, The Last Drop of Water,* and *Fighting Blood* (1916), she was the Pioneer Woman. When all the others had fallen by the wayside, Blanche was still in there whipping the oxen. Her most famous film of this type was *The Lonedale Operator* (1911).

In 1922 she married Marshall "Mickey" Neilan, director of such silent classics as *Rebecca of Sunnybrook Farm* (1917) with Mary Pickford and *Tess of the D'Urbervilles* (1923), one of Ms. Sweet's best remembered efforts. She and Neilan were divorced in 1929.

Her competition in *In the Palace of the King* (1923) was Aileen Pringle (living in retirement in Manhattan). She costarred with Neil Hamilton (married and living in Escondido, California) in *Diplomacy* (1926). The late Ben Lyon was her leading man in *Bluebeard's Seven Wives* (1926).

Blanche Sweet made only three talkies, all of them in 1930. In *Woman Racket* she was directed by Paul Bern, and not only spoke on the screen but sang. *Show Girl in Hollywood* gave her another chance to sing, but neither film gave her career the boost it needed. Her last appearance on the screen was in Rex Beach's *The Silver Horde.*

When a talkie career failed to materialize, Blanche became a vaudeville entertainer and achieved considerable success. She toured the United States in the early thirties with an act called "Sweet and Lovely." She proved to be a good draw for both the Fanchon Marco and Orpheum circuits. She sang, did comedy skits, and acted a scene from one of her most popular silents, *Anna Christie* (1923).

Her second husband was Raymond Hackett, whom she had met on the Metro-Goldwyn-Mayer lot several years before they were both offered parts in the road company of a play called *The Party's Over.* She admits that the main reason she took the role was to get to know the handsome young man better. They were married in 1936 and lived together until he died in California in 1963. Throughout the thirties the husband-and-wife team did road shows of plays that had been hits on Broadway. Hackett, who had the advantage of stage experience, was of great help to cinema-oriented Blanche.

After he died in 1958 she moved back to New York City. Blanche Sweet is often glimpsed by fans at the Forty-second-Street Library. She lives nearby and is an avid reader. She maintains, however, that she will never write her autobiography.

Blanche likes to tell people that she was often referred to in Hollywood as "Miss McBlunt." "I'm very frank, and they just couldn't get used to it," she said once. In that respect Blanche Sweet hasn't changed a bit.

Jon Virzi

Blanche Sweet photographed recently in Manhattan.

courtesy of Greg and Jeff Lenburg collection

The Three Stooges—Larry Fine, Moe Howard, and Curly Howard—in a scene from their 1941 short In the Sweet Pie and Pie.

The Three Stooges

The comic trio of the screen were Moe Harry Howard, born June 19, 1897, in Brooklyn; Larry Fine, born in Philadelphia on October 5, 1902; and Moe's brother, Curly Howard, born in 1903.

Moe, who had been a bit player in early silent films, performed on a riverboat, and acted in Shakespeare, joined vaudeville headliner Ted Healy in 1922. Moe's brother Sam, known as Shemp, heckled Moe and Healy from the audience—until Healy hired him about a year later, when Shemp walked on stage during a performance, mashed a pear in Healy's face, and brought the house down. Larry, who was part of a dance act in vaudeville, made it a threesome in 1925. They were billed variously as "Ted Healy and His Three Southern Gentlemen," "Ted Healy and His Gang," and "Ted Healy and His Racketeers." Healy went on as a single when the Stooges began making pictures.

They made their movie debut in a 1930 Rube Goldberg feature, *Soup to Nuts,* and then went to M-G-M, where they made a brief appearance in several features, including *Dancing Lady* (1933), and five shorts. By this time Shemp had decided to work as a single, and was replaced by the third and youngest brother, Jerry, whom the family called Babe. He's the one movie fans know as Curly, and he was without a doubt the star of the act until illness caused his departure in 1946. Shemp returned to replace Curly, who died in 1952.

The Stooges were brought to Columbia Pictures by Jules White, who directed many of their two-reelers, beginning with *Woman Haters* (1934). Two others who guided their nonsense were Del Lord and the comic star of silents, Charlie Chase.

They looked ridiculous. Grown men: Curly, who was fat, dumb, and completely bald; Moe bossing everyone around while wearing a Buster Brown haircut; and Larry, a ball of hair behind each ear adding to his look of annoyance and confusion. Kids loved the Stooges, and on matinee day in low-income neighborhoods in the thirties and forties their shorts were advertised on the marquees right along with the features.

The Stooges remained on the Gower Street through 190 starring shorts, finishing their last on December 31, 1957—but without Shemp. He had died suddenly in 1955, and been replaced by Joe Besser; when he left, after two years, Joe De Rita took over. But the chemistry worked with neither one, and although the trio continued to make personal appearances and an occasional feature, including *Snow White and the Three Stooges* (1961) and *The Three Stooges Meet Hercules* (1963), the humor seemed forced.

The Stooges' shorts, however, were always consistent money-makers for their studio, whose chief, Harry Cohn, was one of their biggest fans. Although the sound effects and customary incongruous situations were missing at their in-person dates at presentation houses during their heyday, Stooges fans were convulsed anyway when the three sang songs like "She Was Bred in Old Kentucky, but She's Just a Crumb Up Here."

Larry Fine had been living at the Motion Picture Country House for four years when he died in January 1975. Moe Howard survived him by four months. He lived with his wife, whose cousin was the legendary Houdini, above the Sunset Strip. Larry and Moe were delighted that their pictures became even more popular on television than they had been when they were made.

Joe Besser and his wife of over fifty years live quietly in the San Fernando Valley.

The Three Stooges' shorts play in many countries around the world, but not in the Soviet Union. The Russians requested the films to show in their film schools but were turned down when it was learned that they intended to use them to show how Americans had been brutalized by eye-gouging, kicks in the shin, and twisted noses presented in the name of fun.

Jon Virzi

Larry Fine photographed in June 1973.

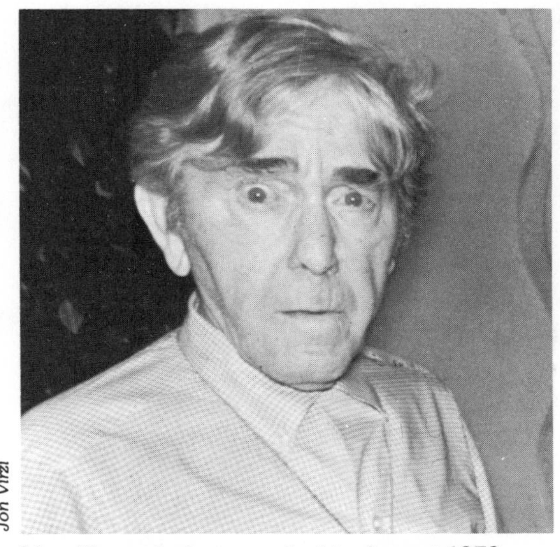
Jon Virzi

Moe Howard photographed in August 1970.

Joe Besser and his wife live in North Hollywood.

Richard Lamparski

"Gene Tierney was as sleek and as beautiful as a lynx—a shade warmer, but nowhere near as agile" was David Shipman's (author of The Great Movie Stars) assessment of the star.

Gene Tierney

The serene movie beauty was born to wealthy parents in Brooklyn on November 20, 1920. She was educated in private schools in Connecticut and Switzerland.

After turning down a contract with Warner Brothers, Gene debuted on Broadway in *Mrs. O'Brien Entertains* (1938). She was with Columbia Pictures for a short time but left before they could put her in a film. After playing the ingenue in *The Male Animal* (1940) on Broadway, she was signed by M-G-M. When that studio couldn't find a property for her, Twentieth Century–Fox signed her. She finally made her movie debut in *The Return of Frank James* (1940). The next year she registered in a showy part in *Tobacco Road.*

Even some of those who consider her an important star with a unique screen presence do not believe she ever really matured as an actress. Others, who nominated Gene for the Best Actress Oscar for *Leave Her to Heaven* (1945), thought differently. She was always so beautiful that much of the public was prepared to go to her pictures even when they were obviously unsuitable for her.

Her screen credits include *The Shanghai Gesture* (1941), *Heaven Can Wait* (1943), *A Bell for Adano* (1945), *The Razor's Edge* (1946), *Dragonwyck* (1946), *The Ghost and Mrs. Muir* (1947), *Close to My Heart* (1951), *Black Widow* (1954), and *Advise and Consent* (1962).

She was only twenty-one when she married the sophisticated fashion designer Oleg Cassini. During her first pregnancy Gene contracted German measles from a woman in the military who broke quarantine to see her at the Hollywood canteen. She gave birth to a retarded daughter. When her marriage came apart she entered into a well-publicized affair with the late Ali Kahn. Many felt their breakup was the last straw. She returned to the United States in 1955 and sought psychiatric help. The next the public heard, Gene Tierney had committed herself to the Menninger Clinic, where she experienced a series of shock treatments.

An earlier relationship that had left Gene despondent was first revealed by Otto Preminger. According to the director, she would have become Mrs. John F. Kennedy if the future president's family had not disapproved of her because she was "unsuitable."

During her affair with Howard Hughes, the tycoon brought in specialists in a vain attempt to help her daughter Daria. Gene's other daughter is the mother of two.

Twice Ms. Tierney has been signed for "comeback" pictures, and twice she had to beg off at the last minute when she did not feel up to the strain of a lengthy production.

The picture that really put Gene Tierney over was *Laura* (1944), a role she got after Hedy Lamarr turned it down. In July 1960, just as soon as his divorce from Ms. Lamarr was final, Texas oilman Howard Lee and Gene were married.

Although she does not rule out a resumption of her career, she seems to have found herself doing charity work. She has been active raising funds for cancer research, mental health, and the care of retarded children. For a while after moving to Texas she wrote a column in a local newspaper in which she reminisced about her Hollywood days.

In 1980, shortly after her autobiography, *Self Portrait,* was published, she played a lesbian gossip columnist on *Scruples,* a television mini-series.

Friends hoped Gene might return to Hollywood after the death of her husband, shortly after their twentieth wedding anniversary. She has chosen to remain in Houston.

Jon Virzi

Gene Tierney during a recent visit to Hollywood.

Pinky Tomlin was a hot show-business property in the late thirties.

Pinky Tomlin

The bumptious bumpkin whose 1935 hit song made him an overnight sensation was born on September 9, 1907, in Eros, Arkansas.

He was brought up in Durant, Oklahoma, and attended the University of Oklahoma, majoring in music and geology. His classmates dubbed him "Pinky" because of his florid complexion and red hair. It was the depths of the Depression, and Pinky worked his way through school with his own dance band. Before graduating in 1935, he wrote a song, "The Object of My Affection," for his girl, who had been Miss Oklahoma of 1933. She and other students liked it, but it wasn't until he arrived in Los Angeles that the song and Pinky took off.

He got a job singing with Jimmy Grier's orchestra at the Biltmore Bowl. The very first night that he sang his own song, it was clear he had a winner. The tune's tempo was faster than that of other songs of the period—enough to seem quite different to the dancers, who were used to crooning. On the strength of his Biltmore success, he was booked into the Paramount Theatre, where he stayed for sixteen weeks. After the fourth week, he had his name in lights.

Tomlin signed an M-G-M contract at $1000 a week. The studio saw him as a multiple talent: actor-comic-songwriter-singer. He became a regular on Eddie Cantor's radio show. *Time* profiled him, referring to his "jack-ass laughter and owlish solemnity."

Pinky wrote "Love Is All," which Deanna Durbin sang in her movie *It's a Date* (1940). He also scored his own pictures: *Paddy O'Day* (1936), *Thanks for Listening* (1937) with Aileen Pringle (single and living in Manhattan), and *Down in "Arkansaw"* (1938).

Hit songs stayed popular much longer in the 1930s than they do today, and "The Object of My Affection" was a supersmash. Recently, ASCAP, the organization responsible for tabulating royalties for composers and lyricists, named the tune as one of the most frequently played songs in its forty-year history. Among his other hits were "What's the Reason I'm Not Pleasing You?" and "The Love Bug Will Get You (If You Don't Watch Out)."

Pinky had his own radio program, a summer replacement, in 1937. With his band, he headlined New York's Roxy Theatre and toured presentation houses all over the country. He cut over a hundred records in his heyday.

Tomlin was often compared to Kay Kyser. There were similarities in their looks and personalities, but Pinky never made the money Kyser did. By 1950, he had to admit that it was all over for him. "I'm afraid," he said recently, "that my fame exceeded my income." He now has his own business developing and selling oil properties. Tomlin readily admits, however, that he would love to do a one-nighter now and then.

At the height of his fame, he was reported to be engaged to the luscious blonde Toby Wing. "It never went that far," he says, "but it did go pretty far." They still exchange Christmas cards.

Pinky and Mrs. Tomlin live in a home in West Los Angeles furnished with fine antiques. She is the former Joanne Alcorn, the same girl who was crowned Miss Oklahoma in 1933 and inspired him to write his biggest hit, "The Object of My Affection." That is also the title of his autobiography, which was published in 1981.

Pinky today in his West Los Angeles home with Mrs. Tomlin. She was Miss Oklahoma in 1933, and the inspiration for his hit song "The Object of My Affection."

Lorenzo Tucker played the title role in The Black King (1931), an Oscar Micheaux movie based loosely on the career of Marcus Garvey.

Lorenzo Tucker: "The Black Valentino"

"The Black Valentino" was born on June 27, 1900, in Philadelphia, Pennsylvania. Tucker's father was an employee of the city of Philadelphia and a close friend of the grandfather of Grace Kelly, a prominent contractor. Lorenzo's father died when he was four years old.

After two years at Temple University Lorenzo took a job for the summer in an Atlantic City hotel. There he entered into an affair with a girl who was in show business. She taught him to dance and the pair became an adagio team. Tucker never went back to college.

Evelyn Nesbit, "the Girl in the Red Velvet Swing," hired him for her act for a short time when she played the Steel Pier. Tucker found himself in demand as an emcee–straight man. In that capacity he worked with Bessie Smith. Another blues singer, Mamie Smith, featured him in her show, "Black Diamond Express." He worked with many top comics of the day, including Tim Moore, who years later became nationally famous on TV as "Kingfish Stevens" on *Amos 'n' Andy.*

Tucker did not work exclusively in black show business. Many of the productions he was in were racially mixed. He played straight man to Jimmy Savo, a white and an established Broadway star.

Lorenzo's real fame came when he returned to Philadelphia to join the cast of *Rang Tang.* The show had closed by the time he arrived, but while he was sitting in the lobby of a hotel, Oscar Michaeux, who is now considered the dean of black film, introduced himself and suggested he drop by his New York office. Michaeux made movies with all-black casts that were shown in ghetto theaters only.

Tucker had been referred to as "the Black Valentino" before he went into pictures, but it was Micheaux who publicized the title. Many thought he looked more like John Gilbert, but the movies he made were usually promoted by the producer as "starring Lorenzo Tucker, the Black Valentino." He became so popular that Micheaux used to finance his productions by promising theater owners that Lorenzo would star in them.

Some of them were *Wages of Sin* (1928), *A Daughter of the Congo* (1930), *Easy Street* (1930), *The Black King* (1931), and *Temptation* (1936).

Lorenzo spent years touring under the auspices of TOAB (The circuit of black theatres was known officially as Theatrical Owners and Bookers Association, but was referred to within the profession as "Tough on Black Asses.")

He also acted in the white theatre. He was with silent star Greta Nissen when she toured in the play *Queen of Sheba* in the late twenties. In 1931 he went on the road with Mae West in *The Constant Sinner*. In the play he portrayed a pimp to her prostitute. When the show opened in Washington, D.C., city officials demanded that a scene in which he and the star kissed be removed. Rather than comply Ms. West closed the production.

In 1961 Lorenzo became the assistant to the New York City coroner, a job he held for thirteen years. When his superior retired he attempted to reactivate his career but found that light-skinned blacks were no longer being cast in films or on TV. When he signed with an agent for commercials he was advised to tell casting directors that he was Armenian. In a scene that was edited from *Saturday Night Fever* he played an Italian.

"I've lived long enough to see that everything goes in cycles," he said recently. "Light-skinned blacks will be acceptable again. Really, it's all so silly and just shows the ignorance that is always the basis of racial discrimination."

Tucker has been married four times but is now single. He lives by himself in an apartment in the heart of Hollywood. He has no children.

He is still in touch with Bee Freeman, "the Sepia Mae West," who lives in Greenwich Village. The two worked together in *Harlem After Midnight* (1934). His close friend "Slick" Chester, "the Colored Cagney," died in 1978.

A role he would especially have liked to play was suggested by the late Hazel Scott. She felt he would be perfect to portray her husband, the Reverend Adam Clayton Powell, in the film she hoped would be made from her forthcoming autobiography.

"The Black Valentino" today in his Hollywood apartment.

Chris Albertson

"Vampira" was nominated for an Emmy as the Most Outstanding Female Personality in 1954.

"Vampira": Maila Nurmi

The glamour ghoul of the 1950s was born Maila Nurmi on December 11, 1921, in Petsamo, Finland. Her uncle was the late Olympic champion Paavo Nurmi. She was brought to the U.S. as an infant and moved about for years with her father, a writer who lectured on temperance.

Howard Hawks found her in New York playing in Mike Todd's Grand Guignol midnight show *Spook Scandals.* The director brought her to Hollywood with the intention of launching her as "the new Lauren Bacall." Her debut was to be the film version of the Russian novel *Dreadful Hollow.* William Faulkner was engaged to write the screenplay. When the project was postponed again and again, Maila walked out on her contract.

She danced for several years for Earl Carroll and at the Florentine Gardens. At the latter, she was a chorine alongside Lili St. Cyr (single and living in Los Angeles).

Maila was married to screenwriter Dean Riesner (who acted in silent films with Charlie Chaplin as Dinky Dean, the "Boy's Boy") when she conceived the idea for "Vampira." She was at a costume ball when producer Hunt Stromberg, Jr., spotted her gotten up in a torn black train with shredded sleeves and bloody scratches just above her plunging neckline. Her waist, at the time, measured seventeen inches.

She was put under contract to Channel 7 in Hollywood to host its 11 P.M. horror movies. The films were of such poor quality that Stromberg thought a weird and sexy lady would perk up viewers' interest. She talked of her pet spider, "Rollo," whom she could never seem to find, and encouraged fans to write in "for epitaphs—not autographs." In the 1950s, a time of almost enforced blandness and conformity, she wandered through mist and cobwebs and made a sensation.

Life photographed her being driven around Hollywood by a chauffeur in an old, open Packard. She carried a large black umbrella, which she would put up on sunny days, "hoping for gloom." "Vampira" was never more macabre than when she walked past a panel of appalled but applauding celebrity judges as an entrant in the Miss Rheingold contest. She was part of Liberace's Las Vegas act and made many guest appearances on TV shows. Orson Welles was one of her most enthusiastic fans.

Her act was unique and well done, but by the late 1950s she was no longer "hot." It all ended with her appearances in a few movies: *The Beat Generation* (1959) and *Sex Kittens Go to College* (1960). She believes that she is still a victim of an unspoken blacklist within the television industry because of her quarrels with the network.

Maila's star never set among Hollywood's underground, to which she is a legend. Her reputation for having known Jack Nicholson, Sally Kellerman, and Dennis Hopper before they became famous is well founded. Her friendship with Marlon Brando goes back many years. But she has never exploited or capitalized on any of these relationships. She was very close to James Dean and has assisted several of his biographers. Maila denies that Dean was homosexual, but she confirms the rumors of his strong masochistic leanings.

Maila Nurmi, now divorced, lives in a cottage in East Hollywood, which she shares with three dogs. She is deeply involved in several organizations concerned with the welfare of stray animals.

An actor whom she befriended when he first arrived in Hollywood over twenty years ago said of her not long ago: "Maila dyed her blonde hair black and wore half-inch fingernails. She used to smoke with a foot-long holder. But she was good-hearted and very real." Those may have been the very qualities that worked most against her.

Maila Nurmi recently in one of her favorite haunts, the Heliotrope House restaurant in East Hollywood.

Richard Lamparski

John Vivyan as "Mr. Lucky" in 1960.

John Vivyan

The star of television's *Mr. Lucky* was born in Chicago, Illinois, on May 31, 1923. He was wounded in battle while fighting on Guadalcanal. When he left the army at the end of World War II he had won the Bronze Star and Purple Heart.

Vivyan studied acting at the American Academy of Dramatic Arts. He had featured roles in three Broadway-bound plays that closed in out-of-town tryouts. He played in the road company of *A Tree Grows in Brooklyn,* which starred Joan Blondell.

John came to Hollywood as Eva Gabor's leading man in *Sailor's Delight.* A column by Louella Parsons brought him to the attention of producers Blake Edwards and Don Sharpe, who were looking for an actor to play the title role in *Mr. Lucky,* a TV series based on the 1943 Cary Grant movie of the same title.

Vivyan was cast as "Joe Adams," alias "Mr. Lucky," proprietor of the *Fortuna,* a luxury gambling yacht and supper club. CBS premiered the series on October 24, 1959, a time when macho adventure shows were riding high in the public favor. *TV Guide* gave the new program a cover story, which it shared with NBC's *Peter Gunn* series.

John played the lead with great cool. He was supported by the late Ross Martin as his partner, "Andamo," and Pippa Scott as his lady friend, "Maggie."

According to the rating services, *Mr. Lucky* was among the top ten shows in the nation when it was canceled after thirty-four half-hour programs were telecast. "There was no official announcement as to the reason we went off," says Vivyan, "but the story that filtered down to me was that the network had received a lot of mail complaining that they had made a national hero of a gambler. There's great irony here because the scripts stressed 'Mr. Lucky's' honesty and integrity."

His most prominent movie role was in *Imitation of Life* (1959).

For several years afterward John guested on TV shows and appeared in stock. Then, five days after he gave up his two-pack-a-day cigarette habit, he suffered a severe heart attack. It turned his hair completely white and sent him into a long recuperation, from which he is just now emerging.

He enjoys acting on stage but says that his leading ladies were jealous of his reviews and the attention he got. "Patricia Morison was the one exception," says Vivyan. "She's a real pleasure to work with. The worst of all of them was Ruth Roman." John was also in a play with Ginger Rogers.

He owns and operates the John Vivyan Answering Service in Los Angeles. Divorced, John lives by himself in the apartment house he owns in West Hollywood. Vivyan is still recognized by a lot of people, who usually call him "Mr. Lucky."

John Vivyan's hair turned snow white when he suffered a serious heart attack several years ago.

Richard Lamparski

Doodles was on the first Kraft Music Hall, which was televised in 1948.

Doodles Weaver

The hayseed comic from early television was born Winstead Sheffield Glendening Dixon Weaver in Los Angeles on May 11, 1914. His father was the wealthy industrialist who founded the All-Year Club that promoted the area's climate and attracted millions to the state in the thirties and forties. His brother is "Pat" Sylvester Weaver, the media executive and former president of NBC.

Because of his freckles and big ears, Winstead's mother began calling him her "doodlebug." Doodles's original goal was to become a school athletic director, but the money he made working in Andy Clyde and Three Stooges shorts hooked him on movies and comedy. He played a farmer in *Topper* (1937), his first feature, and after a few more small parts as a hick he got a reputation as the poor man's Sterling Holloway (single and living in Laguna, California). He was Hannibal Hoops in the early version of *Li'l Abner* (1940) and played a wounded sailor in *The Story of Dr. Wassell* (1944).

Doodles's first real prominence was as "Professor Feedelbaum" with the Spike Jones band for three years, beginning in 1948. He was with Spike's "City Slickers" on their radio show, records, and national tours of presentation houses. He left them when someone at NBC got the idea of starring him in a summer replacement series after seeing his Ajax commercial on the *Colgate Comedy Hour*. In that spot Doodles worked with a live pig.

On the NBC program, which was televised the summer of 1951, Doodles wore crazy costumes, did his bumpkin character, and emitted just about every strange and vulgar sound ever heard. A lot of people found him funny. One who didn't was columnist Jack O'Brian, who over and over rapped the show's mindlessness, including the humor, which he felt was forced.

A local *Day with Doodles* followed the NBC program on New York City's Channel 5 for a short time, and then Weaver returned to Hollywood. For a couple of years in the late fifties his *Doodles Club House* was popular on Channel 2 in Los Angeles. Then he hosted a kiddy program on a San Francisco TV station for one season.

Since his heyday as a TV personality Doodles has been a busy actor, but in his small and frequently serious roles on television and in feature films, he is seldom recognized by the audiences. He was a murderer in *Winchester "73"* (1950) and played the boat owner in a tense scene in Hitchcock's *The Birds* (1963). In the late fifties he had a running part as a hotel owner in the *Lawman* series.

Just mentioning his name on TV can still get a big laugh, but no one will book him as a guest. When, in 1972, he broke the world's record throwing a javelin in the Senior Citizen Olympics, he called all the talk shows about appearing. One producer said he'd never heard of him. Another said, "Oh, yeah. You're Pat Weaver's brother, right?" Someone from the *Tonight* show said to him, "We really like you but we can't figure out what to do with you."

Doodles's marriages have ended in three divorces and one annulment. Two of his wives were twenty-one years old. Two were nineteen. He now lives by himself in a house in Burbank, where he keeps his 1934 LaSalle convertible. Weaver is an arrested alcoholic.

In an interview in 1972 he talked about being out of the limelight: "I don't miss being a star. I don't miss anything because I live in the now."

But in 1981, after four years of illness and a triple-bypass heart operation, he said: "Nothing means anything when you're in pain. I just bought G. David Schine's 1960 Eldorado convertible and I don't feel well enough to drive the damn thing to the market and back. I have a nice house and an income but not a thing to live for."

Sarah Richardson

Doodles Weaver today.

Since he met her in 1979 Doodles has been "enthralled" by TV star Cindy Williams. "She's the reason I can still win gold medals at track and swimming," he says. "I pretend that Cindy's at the finish line."

Grant Williams in 1957, the year in which he starred in the cult film The Incredible Shrinking Man.

Grant Williams

The actor who played "the Incredible Shrinking Man" and then disappeared himself was born John Grant Williams in New York City. His birthday was August 18, 1931. He received his early education in Scotland, his father's birthplace. He is a distant relative of the opera star Mary Garden.

Grant was not quite in his teens when he began acting in summer stock. He studied with Lee Strasberg but was still undecided about pursuing acting as a profession until he became a secretary to Maynard Morris at MCA. It was Morris, an agent with an industrywide reputation for discovering new faces for motion pictures, who told him that he would make a good screen actor.

Williams appeared on Broadway in two plays, *Late Arrival* (1953) and *The Cretan Woman* (1954). Both had very short runs. He acted on many live television dramas that emanated from New York. His performance on one, a *Kraft TV Playhouse,* brought him to the attention of Universal Pictures.

Grant was under contract to Universal Pictures for three years, during which time he made *Red Sundown* (1956), *Four Girls in Town* (1957), and *The Incredible Shrinking Man* (1957). The last, which is the film for which he is most remembered, was quite a success when it was released, and has developed a strong cult following in the years since. Even the poorly received remake with Lily Tomlin has not diminished the interest in the original.

Williams moved from Universal to Warner Brothers, where he stayed for four years. There he did quite a bit of TV work, including a running part on *Hawaiian Eye* for four seasons, and the features *Susan Slade* (1961), *The Couch* (1962), and *PT 109* (1963).

Filmologist Don Miller, like so many who followed Grant's career, finds his story a puzzling one. Says Miller: "He invariably won glowing notices from the reviewers, even in the routine material he appeared in, quite unusual for a young contract player in those days. One waited patiently for the big role that would put him in the top echelon, but something went wrong somewhere. He just gradually faded from view."

Grant's own explanation for why he never

achieved stardom is that he was poorly managed. He denies rumors that he had bitter quarrels with his studios, stating that he never refused a role and was never suspended. He says the only strong disagreement he ever had was with Jack Webb during a *Dragnet* show, his last TV appearance.

The career that once seemed so promising petered out in low-budget exploitation features such as *How's Your Love Life?* (1971) with Leslie Brooks (married to a Los Angeles real estate developer) and Mary Beth Hughes (a beautician in Los Angeles) and *The Creature's Revenge* (1971).

Grant says the reason he doesn't act at all anymore is because "I've outgrown it." He could, however, be persuaded to accept a role if it were outstanding or if he were permitted to write his own part. He is now working on a TV series and a screenplay. "I'll only work with people I respect," he said recently in a voice that still has more than a trace of New Yorkese. "One of my last pictures was edited into a near-porno film. The ads for it suggested that I was playing a character who was gay." Grant Williams says he would never play a homosexual.

He lives by himself in the Miracle Mile area of Los Angeles and keeps several loaded guns in his apartment, which is on grounds that are patroled twenty-four hours a day by private police. He never dates women who are actresses, and has never been married. Williams is a Roman Catholic.

He is also writing a book on acting, to be used in the classes he conducts in West Hollywood. The brochure for his school states: "By popular request, Mr. Williams is interrupting a highly successful career of over twenty-seven years as an actor and writer to present his own concept. . . ."

Michael Knowles

Grant Williams gives classes in acting in West Hollywood.

Lois Wilson left Paramount Pictures in 1927 after almost a decade under contract.

Lois Wilson

The star of silent and early talking pictures was born in Pittsburgh on June 28, 1894, and raised in Birmingham, Alabama. In 1915 shortly after being named the first Miss Alabama she entered a contest to publicize the newly opened Universal City. The winner of the competition suggested Lois for a part in *The Dumb Girl of Portici* (1916), Anna Pavlova's only feature film. After that she made some J. Warren Kerrigan pictures and then worked with Wallace Reid.

Lois was one of the Wampas Baby Stars in 1922, the first year they were picked. Her silents include *What Every Woman Knows* (1921), *Manslaughter* (1922), *Vanishing American* (1925), *The Gingham Girl* (1927) with George K. Arthur (living on Manhattan's Sutton Place). She was with her friend Valentino in *Alimony* (1924) and *Monsieur Beaucaire* (1924). Her favorite film is *Miss Lulu Bett* (1921), which established her as a serious actress. Her most important picture was the silent classic *The Covered Wagon* (1923).

For years Paramount carefully cultivated her image as the soft, marrying kind of woman. When Lois fought for and won the part of Daisy in *The Great Gatsby* (1926) studio head Adolph Zukor was in Europe. When he returned he was furious, but *Photoplay* magazine gave her their Best Performance Award that year and audiences loved her in it.

Her voice, which contains a faint drawl, was perfect for talkies, and she made a graceful transition to more mature parts in *Seed* (1931) with the late Helen Parrish. Some of her others of the era were *Female* (1933) with Phillip Reed (living in Los Angeles), *The Crash* (1932) with the late Paul Cavanaugh, *Bright Eyes* (1934), *The Return of Jimmy Valentine* (1936) with the late Charlotte Henry, and *For Beauty's Sake* (1941) with Marjorie Weaver (living in Los Angeles). Her last movie was *The Girl from Jones Beach* (1949).

Lois Wilson has been on Broadway a number of times, in plays such as *Farewell Summer* (1937), *Chicken Every Sunday* (1944), and *I Never Sang for My Father* (1968). In the late thirties she toured for fifty-seven weeks in *The Women*.

At her peak Lois was an active member of the Hollywood social set. It was in her baby-blue Chandler-Six that John Gilbert met his wife-to-be, Leatrice Joy. Gloria Swanson is one of her oldest friends, and she keeps in touch with Eddie Nugent (living in San Antonio, Texas) and May Allison (living in Chardon, Ohio).

The great love of her life was Richard Dix, but she never married him or anyone else. Lois converted to Roman Catholicism in 1935.

Lois sums herself up this way: "I don't like hippies or long hair on men or nudity. I guess you could call me a square."

From 1937 until recently she lived in Manhattan. When people asked her why, she would respond: "In Hollywood you're only as good as your last picture. In New York you're as welcome as your greatest success."

Lois Wilson shares a home in North Hollywood with her sister. It is filled with fine antiques and mementos of her career. Every Sunday she attends mass with her closest friend, May McAvoy.

Richard Lamparski:

Lois now shares a home in North Hollywood with her sister.

Toby Wing, circa 1934.

Toby Wing

The quintessential chorus girl of early talkies was born Martha Virginia Wing on July 14, 1916, on an estate near Richmond, Virginia.

Toby and her older sister, Pat, lived for a while in the Panama Canal Zone when her father, who was a major in the United States Army, was stationed there. When the family moved to Beverly Hills during the twenties, it was a dream come true for both girls. "We were movie-mad," said Toby recently. "I think all kids were then. All we thought about was breaking into pictures."

Toby played children in the silent vehicles of such stars as Mae Murray and Wanda Hawley, but in those days she, like her sister, was a brunette. It wasn't until Jack Oakie started taking her to parties that Hollywood began to notice her. By that time, Ms. Wing had gone blonde—very blonde.

It was Jack Oakie who introduced Toby to Samuel Goldwyn. She became a Goldwyn Girl along with Paulette Goddard (single and living in Manhattan), the late Anita Louise, and Betty Grable.

Toby was one of the chorus cuties in *The Kid from Spain* (1932), an Eddie Cantor movie that Goldwyn produced. The dance sequences in the picture were directed by the late Busby Berkeley. When Berkeley went to Warner Brothers to choreograph *42nd Street* (1933), he took Toby with him and featured her in the campy production number in which Dick Powell croons to her the song "Young and Healthy."

Paramount put her under contract after *42nd Street.* In the four years she was there, Toby was loaned out almost as much as she was used by her home lot. When they didn't have a film for her, she was sent on personal-appearance tours.

Toby Wing and Jack Oakie never dated seriously, but they were close friends. They remained so until his death in 1978. Her real boyfriends were Tom Brown and Jackie Coogan. Although she considered him a little old at the time, Toby's name was closely linked with Maurice Chevalier's. When the French star returned to his homeland, *Photoplay* magazine ran an article on Ms. Wing entitled "The Girl Chevalier Left Behind." She also went out with Pinky Tomlin and appeared in three of his movies. Their romance, which got a lot of publicity, was, according to Toby, mostly one-sided. "I thought he was a very nice boy," she says, "but I think Pinky had a real crush on me."

Ms. Wing had leads in a few pictures, such

as *Search for Beauty* (1934) and *Silks and Saddles* (1938), but most of her roles were small. Some film buffs insist she holds some kind of record for having appeared in more scenes while speaking less dialogue than anyone else in pictures. Her part in *Murder at the Vanities* (1934) called for little more than giggles, but no one who has seen that picture forgets her in it. Even in walk-ons, Toby was noticed.

Some of her other credits are *Gold Diggers of 1933, Kiss and Make-up* (1934) with Genevieve Tobin (living in Manhattan), *School for Girls* (1935), *Mr. Cinderella* (1936), *Sing While You're Able* (1937), and *True Confessions* (1937).

During the run of *You Never Know* (1938), her only Broadway show, Toby married Dick Merrill, who had become an international celebrity for his air exploits. In 1936 Merrill piloted the late Harry Richman in the first transatlantic round-trip flight. He also flew the plane that made the first commercial trip across the Atlantic, and has logged more flying time than anyone else in history.

Toby's sister, Pat, was under contract for a while to First National Pictures. She is the widow of a doctor and owns a shop that sells handmade pillows in Williamsburg, Virginia.

Toby Wing lives in a large house on De Lido Island in Miami. After marrying and becoming a mother, she lost all interest in her career. For years she received offers from Hollywood and Broadway, but says that she was never tempted to return to work, nor has she ever missed it. "I keep really busy," she said recently in her still noticeable drawl. She gardens, teaches Sunday school at the Episcopal church, and travels. Toby and her husband, who is twenty-one years her senior, have property in Maine and California. They have one son.

Toby Wing and longtime friend Bob Hope.

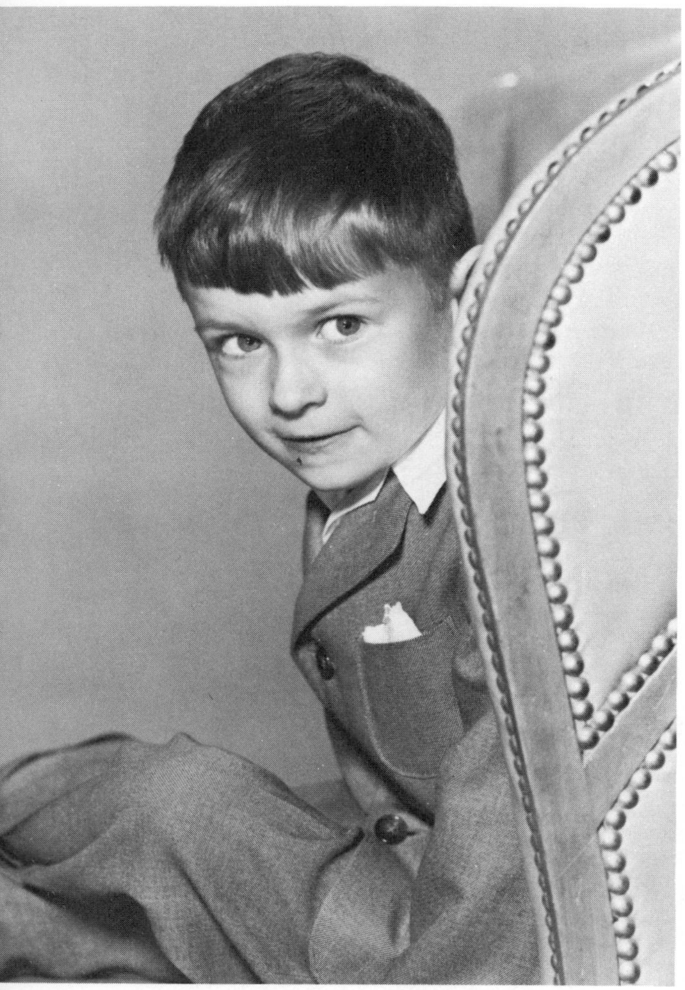

George's voice was only part of his appeal.

George "Foghorn" Winslow

The child actor with the basso profundo voice was born George Wenzlaff on May 3, 1946, in Los Angeles. His first "dada" was uttered in a startlingly deep baritone. He returned home on his first Halloween disappointed because in spite of his mask all the neighbors knew who he was as soon as he spoke.

At the urging of his uncle, George's mother took him to audition for Art Linkletter's show. He came on wearing a trainman's outfit. When Linkletter asked his name he replied: "It's George, but I'd rather be Casey Jones." The audience howled. The program had a strict rule that no child ever appeared more than once. George was brought back about twenty times on Linkletter's radio and TV shows.

Cary Grant caught one of the shows and signed George for his film *Room for One More* (1952) with Betsy Drake (the former Mrs. Grant is now a psychiatric counselor at Mount Sinai Hospital in Los Angeles). Warner's put him under contract, which Twentieth Century–Fox bought in 1953.

He appeared several times on the *Blondie* and *Ozzie and Harriet* TV series and made in all eleven movies. His distinctive voice and delightful attitude made an indelible impression on fans. Along with sounding funny, "Foghorn" had a humor all his own, and he was totally unimpressed by the stars he worked with. When the waspish Clifton Webb made the mistake of being sarcastic with him during the filming of *Mister Scoutmaster* (1953), George topped every one of his lines, to the delight of the crew and other players.

He played Marilyn Monroe's wealthy admirer in *Gentlemen Prefer Blondes* (1953). The scene in which he informs her that she has a "certain animal magnetism" is a classic.

His other pictures include *The Rocket Man* (1954), *Artists and Models* (1955), *Rock, Pretty Baby* (1957), and his last, *Wild Heritage* (1958). His one and only appearance before a camera since then was when he attempted an introduction to the TV premiere of *Mister Scoutmaster* in 1962. He was so awkward that it was never used.

After spending four years in the U.S. Navy, George took a course in photography. The money he'd earned as an actor was used "learning to play pinochle." Many of his friends have no knowledge of his movie career. He never brings up the subject and does not seem comfortable talking about it.

He is most frequently asked about Marilyn Monroe. Says George: "The thing I remember most is working with this beautiful lady from early in the morning until late at night. Then as my folks were getting me dressed to go home she came out of her dressing room without any makeup. If I hadn't recognized her voice I'd never have believed she was the same person."

Today George works for the Sonoma County Council on Aging. One of his responsibilities is to call bingo on Wednesday evenings.

He has used his real name for many years. He now lives in a cabin on the outskirts of Santa Rosa, California. Asked about his future plans, he replies, "Ask again later."

The deep voice that made him famous is completely gone.

Marieka

George now calls himself George Wenzlaff. He lives near Santa Rosa, California, and is single.

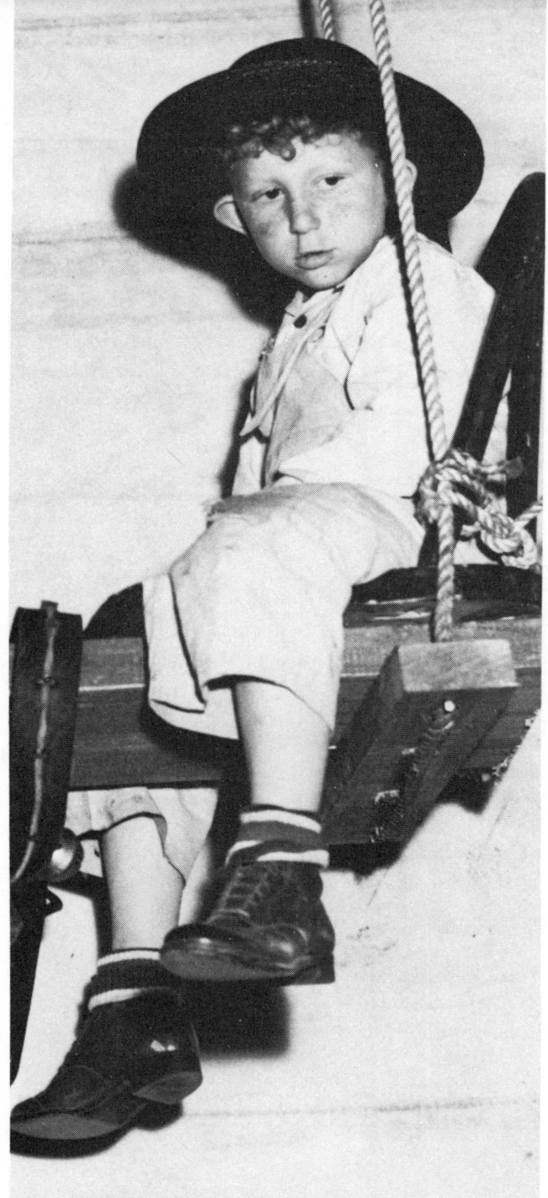

Sidney played "Woim" in twenty-six of the Our Gang shorts in the thirties.

"Woim": Sidney Kilbrick

"Woim" of *Our Gang* was born Sidney Kilbrick in Minneapolis, Minnesota, on July 2, 1928. His father was a scrap metal dealer who brought his family to Los Angeles when Sidney was quite young.

His show business debut was in vaudeville as one of the "Casey Brothers," an act made up of Sidney and his two brothers. For a while they worked with George Jessel.

When a Los Angeles newspaper ran a "Better Babies" contest the Kilbricks entered a picture of brother Leonard, who is four years older than Sidney. He won first prize, which was a screen test at the Hal Roach Studios. Leonard appeared in the *Our Gang* shorts for a year before his kid brother was hired.

In Sidney's first two shorts, *Anniversary Trouble* and *Beginner's Luck* in 1935, the brothers were together. On his own after that, Sidney made *Little Papa* (1935), *Little Sinner* (1935), *Our Gang Follies of 1936* (1935), *Pinch Singer* (1936), *Bored of Education* (1936), *Two Too Young* (1936), *Pay As You Exit* (1936), *Spooky Hooky* (1936), and *Reunion in Rhythm* (1937).

By *Glove Taps* (1937) Sidney was being billed as Sidney "Woim" Kilbrick. In most of the fourteen more *Our Gang* pictures he made he was billed only as "Woim." The character was a quiet but threatening backup for "Butch," the neighborhood bully.

Sidney has only happy memories of making movies. Spanky McFarland, his close friend then, and Sidney had wonderful times playing together on the Roach lot. The only member of the "Gang" Kilbrick wasn't friendly with was Carl "Alfalfa" Switzer. "He was a disagreeable kid," says Sidney.

As he matured, however, he became aware of the limitations a child actor has. "I felt it was confining after I became interested in sports," he recalls. "I had to play close to home always in case a call came in from a casting director."

By the time he played in *Dead End* (1937) and *Boys Town* (1938) Sidney had outgrown the role of "Woim."

While a "Gang" member, Sidney was tutored on the set. Later, when he attended public school he had none of the trouble many child actors had being teased. "My screen image worked very well for me," says Kilbrick. "Nobody wanted any trouble with 'Woim.'"

Some of the money the boys had earned as actors was put in trust for them. The remainder was a great boost to the family income. When the Kilbricks got out of school they joined their father in the scrap metal business for a while but then became contractors. Leonard has done well. Sidney has done extremely well. His offices in Century City are furnished with antiques of museum quality.

Kilbrick's only connection with his *Our Gang* days is his longtime friendships with former child actors Sidney Miller and Gene Reynolds. He is recognized frequently as "Woim," and his son and daughter are ardent *Our Gang* fans.

Sidney Kilbrick is today a millionaire contractor who lives in Los Angeles.

Michael Knowles

Loretta Young's sister, Sally Blane, has said that rejection or disappointment only made her more determined to be a star.

Loretta Young

Gretchen Young was born on January 6, 1912, in Salt Lake City. She was Hollywood's "Steel Butterfly," a title given her by her first husband, actor Grant Withers, for her delicate appearance and awesome resilience. Mrs. Young brought her four children to Los Angeles in 1917 after her husband had deserted them. All of the children worked in silents as extras while their mother ran a boardinghouse.

While still a child Loretta lived for a time with Mae Murray, a superstar of the silent era, whose belief in herself as a superior creature, high and above even her contemporaries, remained with her all of her life. Some believe Ms. Young absorbed much of Mae Murray's attitude.

Energetic and photogenic, Loretta rose from the ranks of the bit players when she answered a call from First National Studios that came for one of her sisters. She got the part and soon caught the eye of the most important star on the lot, Coleen Moore, who changed her first name to Loretta and got her a contract.

Loretta Young survived her family's poverty, the advent of sound, unsuitable roles, and bad personal reviews. By 1939 she had risen to stardom at Twentieth Century–Fox. But she was released that year from her contract, at her own request. By free-lancing, she believed, she could find meatier, more prestigious roles. At that time 3000 theatre owners chose her as their favorite star, yet because she had left one studio the others were reluctant to hire her. Only by taking a whopping salary cut was she able to work again. And her movies after that were usually of poorer quality than those she had done under contract. Still, she seemed to remain as popular as ever with her fans.

Many of her films were programmers, and even among her A pictures there was none that is considered a classic. Among them were *Zoo in Budapest* (1933), *House of Rothschild* (1934), *The Crusades* (1935), *Ramona* (1938), *Suez* (1938), *The Story of Alexander Graham Bell* (1939), *Along Came Jones* (1945), *The Bishop's Wife* (1948), *Rachel and the Stranger* (1948), *Come to the Stable* (her personal favorite and the one that brought her a second Oscar nomination in 1949), and *It Happens Every Thursday* (1953).

It was *The Farmer's Daughter* (1947) that

gave her career the boost she was seeking. In an upset victory she won the Academy Award playing a Swedish immigrant who takes her U.S. citizenship seriously. Yet no part of any real importance followed.

In 1953 she became the first star of her caliber to appear on TV in a series. Her television exposure brought her a wide variety of roles, several Emmys, and huge financial rewards. Some people tuned in just to see what she'd be wearing when she made her famous whirling entrance into tens of millions of homes. She was so admired that the Loretta Young Way, a chain of charm schools, opened nationwide.

Like her career, Loretta Young's personal life is filled with contradictions. She has always maintained a public image of beyond-reproach respectability. "Ethereal" and "otherworldly" are adjectives often used to describe her. Her Catholicism was always featured in her publicity. But the woman who couldn't bring herself to utter the word "divorce" on the screen has been divorced twice—in 1930, after her civil marriage was annulled, and again in 1969, after a bitter parting from her husband-producer. Her second marriage had been "in the church." Between husbands she had intense relationships with Clark Gable and Spencer Tracy, both of whom were married at the time. According to several books, her "adopted" daughter is by Gable, her costar in *Call of the Wild* (1935). Foul language, even vulgarity, was strictly forbidden on the sets of her TV shows. One of her two sons has been convicted of an offense involving the use of teenage boys in porno films.

Although she has not been seen on screens in many years, Loretta is still considered a box-office draw. She does not consider herself retired and readily admits that the right script would bring her back. Her youthful appearance and humor about herself surprise even her most enthusiastic admirers.

Ms. Young has been very generous with her time and money in helping Catholic charities. Her favorites have been an orphanage in Arizona and a home for unwed mothers.

The star drives a Rolls-Royce and lives in a Beverly Hills mansion decorated by her mother, an interior designer. Intimates speak of her jewel collection, which some estimate to be the largest in Hollywood. She is often spotted at the races in a private box, but the surest place for fans to see Loretta Young is at the Church of the Good Shepherd in Beverly Hills, where she attends mass almost every day.

Jon Virzi

Loretta Young says she will never write her memoirs. "My private life is private," says the star.